DAY HIKES AROUND
Big Sur

99 GREAT HIKES

Robert Stone

2nd EDITION

Day Hike Books, Inc.

RED LODGE, MONTANA

Published by Day Hike Books, Inc.
P.O. Box 865 · Red Lodge, Montana 59068
www.dayhikebooks.com

Distributed by The Globe Pequot Press
246 Goose Lane · P.O. Box 480
Guilford, CT 06437-0480
800-243-0495 (direct order) · 800-820-2329 (fax order)
www.globe-pequot.com

Front cover photograph by Robert Stone
Back cover photograph by Joshua Simas
Layout/maps by Paula Doherty

The author has made every attempt to provide accurate information in this book. However, trail routes and features may change—please use common sense and forethought, and be mindful of your own capabilities. Let this book guide you, but be aware that each hiker assumes responsibility for their own safety. The author and publisher do not assume any responsibility for loss, damage, or injury caused through the use of this book.

Copyright © 2014 by Day Hike Books, Inc.
2nd Edition
ISBN: 978-1-57342-068-6

Library of Congress Control Number: 2013933066

Cover photo:
McWay Falls, Hike 48

Back cover photo:
Soberanes Canyon Trail, Hike 11

ALSO BY ROBERT STONE

Day Hikes On the California Central Coast

Day Hikes On the California Southern Coast

Day Hikes Around Sonoma County

Day Hikes Around Napa Valley

Day Hikes Around Big Sur

Day Hikes Around Monterey and Carmel

Day Hikes In San Luis Obispo County, California

Day Hikes Around Santa Barbara

Day Hikes In the Santa Monica Mountains

Day Hikes Around Ventura County

Day Hikes Around Los Angeles

Day Hikes Around Orange County

Day Hikes In Sedona, Arizona

Day Hikes In Yosemite National Park

Day Hikes In Sequoia & Kings Canyon Nat'l. Parks

Day Hikes In Yellowstone National Park

Day Hikes In Grand Teton National Park

Day Hikes In the Beartooth Mountains

Day Hikes Around Bozeman, Montana

Day Hikes Around Missoula, Montana

Table of Contents

THE HIKES

North Big Sur:
Point Lobos to Julia Pfeiffer Burns State Park

Point Lobos State Reserve

Garrapata State Park

Soberanes Point to Molera Point
including Palo Colorado Road and Old Coast Road

Andrew Molera State Park

Pfeiffer Big Sur State Park

Pfeiffer Big Sur State Park
to Julia Pfeiffer Burns State Park

Julia Pfeiffer Burns State Park

Garland Ranch Regional Park

Carmel Valley Road • Tassajara Road
Arroyo Seco Road

South Big Sur:
Lopez Point to Ragged Point

Limekiln State Park

Nacimiento—Fergusson Road
Cone Peak Road (Central Coast Ridge Road)

Pacific Valley

Silver Peak Wilderness Area
to Ragged Point

Hiking Big Sur

Big Sur is an awesome stretch of spectacular coastline where the Santa Lucia Mountains quickly rise over 5,000 feet from the ocean. This magnificent landscape begins near Carmel at Point Lobos State Reserve and extends 75 miles south to Ragged Point in San Luis Obispo County, just south of the Monterey County line. The steep coastal mountain range and rugged shoreline isolate the Big Sur country, which maintains an unspoiled, rustic charm and relaxed, leisurely pace. The coastal side of the mountain range has a Mediterranean-like climate, where conifer forests thrive, while the east side of the range is drier, more typical of open woods and chaparral.

Perched on the western edge of the mountains, Highway 1 snakes along the entire Big Sur coast. The road hugs the edge of the precipitous cliffs and winds its way along the steep headlands. There are endless views of the scalloped coastline and the deep blue Pacific. Awe-inspiring bridges span numerous creeks and deep canyons. Other portions of the road cross flat, grassy marine terraces that gently slope to the eroded shoreline, while wave-worn rock pillars rise offshore.

There is much more to explore than the dramatic coastline, however. Several state parks, two wilderness areas, and five major watersheds lie within the Big Sur area. The Santa Lucia Range runs parallel to the coast in the heart of Big Sur country, from Monterey to San Luis Obispo. The Ventana Wilderness, Silver Peak Wilderness, and Los Padres National Forest all lie within the mountain range. The diverse terrain is a hiker's paradise that has a well-designed trail system of more than 300 miles. The network of trails venture into the beautiful canyons and across the slopes and peaks, offering unparalleled views of the mountains merging with the coastline.

This completely revised and updated edition of *Day Hikes Around Big Sur* includes 99 great day hikes along the coast and throughout the interior mountains. The cross-section of hikes accommodates every level of experience. The trails have been chosen for their scenery, variety, and ability to be hiked within a day. Hikes range from easy beach strolls to strenuous mountain climbs with panoramic vistas.

Highlights along the miles of trails include waterfalls, rivers, valleys, shady canyons, oak-studded meadows, huge stands of redwoods, tidepools, isolated beaches, and stark vertical cliffs with crested ridges. These areas may be enjoyed for a short time or the whole day.

Use the hikes' statistics and summaries, located at the beginning of each hike, to find a hike that is appropriate to your ability and intentions. The hikes are roughly divided into the northern end of Big Sur—Hikes 1—75, and the southern end of Big Sur—Hikes 76—99. The map on page 14 identifies the overall locations of the hikes, major access roads, and the area's larger parks. (The majority of hikes are accessed from either Highway 1 or Carmel Valley Road.) Many additional overall maps, as well as a map for each hike, provide closer details. Times are calculated for continuous hiking. Allow extra time for exploration.

The selection of hikes begins at the north end of the Big Sur coastline—just south of Monterey and Carmel—at a rugged peninsula known as Point Lobos State Reserve. The incredible reserve is the crown jewel among California's state parks. The 1,276-acre tract of land has bold headlands, ragged cliffs, sculpted coves, eroded inlets with tidepools, isolated beaches, craggy islets, marine terraces, large stands of Monterey cypress, rolling meadows, and miles of hiking trails. Hikes 1—10 are found around Point Lobos.

Hikes 11—15 explore the region between Point Lobos and Rocky Point around Garrapata State Park. At Rocky Point, Palo Colorado Road heads inland to a remote area of the Ventana Wilderness (Hikes 16—21).

Hikes 22—24 are found along the Old Coast Road, used before the 714-foot Bixby Creek Bridge was built. The bridge is one of the most impressive canyon crossings along Highway 1. Point Sur, jutting outward from the coast, is home to a historic lightstation (Hike 25).

The awesome coastline continues southward, a meeting of mountains and sea. Some of California's better-known state parks lie interspersed along the coast, including Andrew Molera State Park, Pfeiffer Big Sur State Park, and Julia Pfeiffer Burns State Park. These parks include a crenelated coastline of coves, hidden beaches, rocky points, and pounding surf. Scenic meadows, canyons, rivers, waterfalls, and peaks lie inland and upward along the ascending mountains. Hikes 26–50 are located along this amazing stretch of coastline.

Opposite the coastline, on the east side of the Santa Lucia Range, is Carmel Valley. The Carmel River flows down this verdant valley from the upper reaches of the Ventana Wilderness, joining the coast between Point Lobos and Carmel. Garland Ranch (Hikes 51–62) rises from the willow-lined banks of the river. The area crosses meadows and woodlands to the peaks of the Santa Lucia Mountains, with panoramic coastal, mountain, and valley views. Continuing southeast through Carmel Valley leads to Tassajara Road, which accesses trails along a ridge at the northeast end of the Ventana Wilderness (Hikes 63–75). The headwaters of several waterways, including the Carmel River, drain from either side of Tassajara Road. The remote trails along the ridge offer expansive views to the Pacific, while canyon hikes offer forested solitude.

The southern Big Sur coastal area can be discovered in Hikes 76–99. The area is characterized by towering redwoods, forests, narrow canyons, waterfalls and cascades, marine terraces, and steep ocean cliffs. Limekiln State Park (Hikes 76–78) is home to redwoods, waterfalls, and massive kilns from the 1880s. Several hikes are around Cone Peak (Hikes 79–85), the second highest peak in the Santa Lucia Range. The peak rises nearly a mile from the ocean in just over three miles. The Vicente Flat Trail, on the coastal side of Cone Peak, is one of the most scenic and diverse trails in Big Sur. The Silver Peak Wilderness offers access from the coast into the canyons and rivers emerging from the Santa Lucia Mountains. The Big Sur coast is framed on its south end by Ragged Point, where a trail leads out to a peninsula overlooking the coast and mountain peaks (Hike 99).

When hiking, bring the basic necessities to help ensure an optimum outing. Wear supportive, comfortable hiking shoes, and layered clothing. Take along hats, sunscreen, sunglasses, water, snacks, and appropriate outerwear. Be aware that ticks and poison oak may be present. Use good judgement about your capabilities, and allow extra time to enjoy this beautiful area of California.

From a leisurely walk to a vertical climb, you will experience Big Sur to its fullest by exploring on foot. Enjoy the trails!

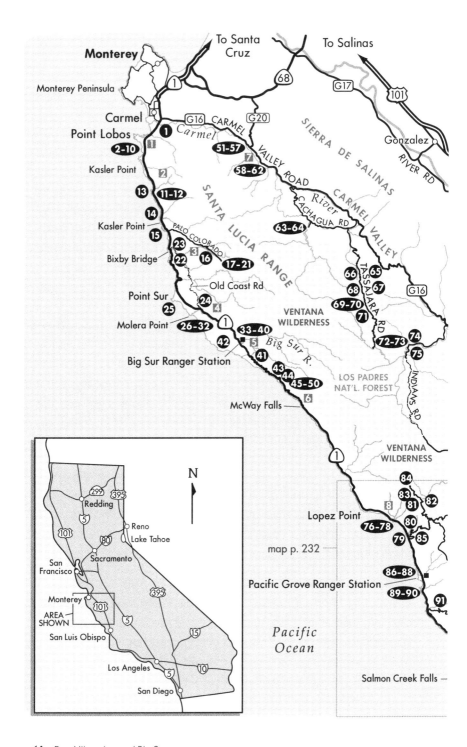

Monterey

To Santa Cruz

To Salinas

Monterey Peninsula

Carmel
Point Lobos
2-10
Kasler Point
13
11-12
14
Kasler Point
15
23
Bixby Bridge
22
16
17-21
Point Sur
24
25
Molera Point
26-32
Big Sur Ranger Station
42
33-40
41
43
44
45-50
McWay Falls

Carmel
51-57
7
58-62

CARMEL

G16

G20

SIERRA DE SALINAS

Gonzalez

RIVER RD

SANTA LUCIA RANGE

PALO COLORADO

Old Coast Rd

CACHAGUA RD

River

CARMEL VALLEY

63-64

66
65
68
67
69-70
71
72-73
74
75

VENTANA WILDERNESS

Big Sur R.

LOS PADRES NAT'L. FOREST

INDIANS RD

VENTANA WILDERNESS

Lopez Point
76-78
79
85
map p. 232
Pacific Grove Ranger Station
86-88
89-90
91

84
83
82
8
81
80

Salmon Creek Falls

Pacific Ocean

N

299
395
Redding
5
Reno
Lake Tahoe
101
80
Sacramento
San Francisco
395
Monterey
101
AREA SHOWN
5
San Luis Obispo
15
Los Angeles
5
10
San Diego

Map of the Hikes

BIG SUR COASTLINE
Point Lobos to Ragged Point

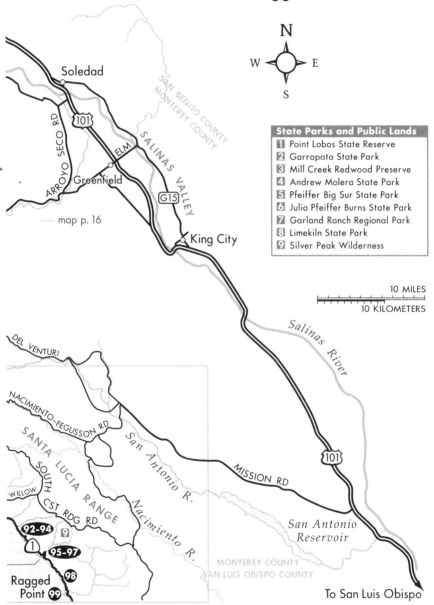

State Parks and Public Lands
1. Point Lobos State Reserve
2. Garrapata State Park
3. Mill Creek Redwood Preserve
4. Andrew Molera State Park
5. Pfeiffer Big Sur State Park
6. Julia Pfeiffer Burns State Park
7. Garland Ranch Regional Park
8. Limekiln State Park
9. Silver Peak Wilderness

Soledad

101

ARROYO SECO RD

ELM

Greenfield

map p. 16

SAN BENITO COUNTY
MONTEREY COUNTY

SALINAS VALLEY

G15

King City

N
W E
S

10 MILES
10 KILOMETERS

Salinas River

DEL VENTURI

NACIMIENTO-FEGUSSON RD

SANTA LUCIA RANGE

SOUTH

WILLOW

CST RDG RD

San Antonio R.

Nacimiento R.

92-94
9
1
95-97
98

Ragged
Point 99

MISSION RD

101

San Antonio
Reservoir

MONTEREY COUNTY
SAN LUIS OBISPO COUNTY

To San Luis Obispo

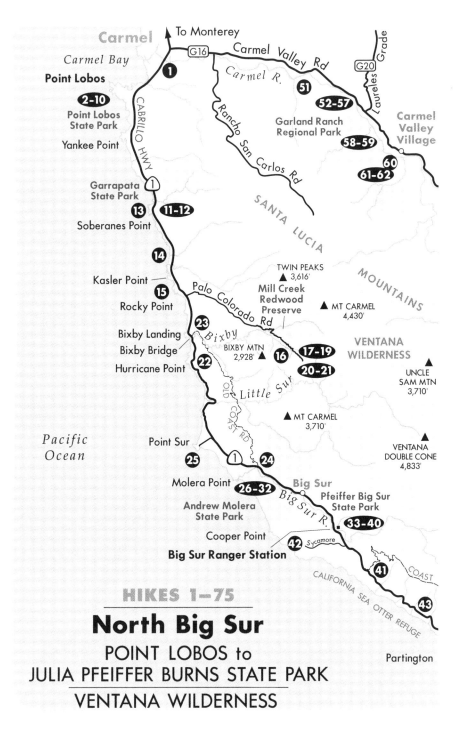

Carmel

To Monterey

Carmel Bay

Point Lobos

2-10

Point Lobos
State Park

Yankee Point

Carmel Valley Rd

G16

Carmel R.

51

52-57

Garland Ranch
Regional Park

58-59

G20

Laureles Grade

Carmel
Valley
Village

60

61-62

CABRILLO HWY

Rancho San Carlos Rd

SANTA LUCIA MOUNTAINS

Garrapata
State Park

1

13

11-12

Soberanes Point

14

Kasler Point

15

Rocky Point

Palo Colorado Rd

TWIN PEAKS
▲ 3,616'

Mill Creek
Redwood
Preserve

▲ MT CARMEL
4,430'

23

Bixby

Bixby Landing

Bixby Bridge

22

Hurricane Point

BIXBY MTN
2,928' ▲

16

17-19

20-21

VENTANA
WILDERNESS

▲
UNCLE
SAM MTN
3,710'

OLD COAST RD

Little Sur

▲ MT CARMEL
3,710'

▲
VENTANA
DOUBLE CONE
4,833'

Pacific
Ocean

Point Sur

25

1

24

Molera Point

26-32

Andrew Molera
State Park

Cooper Point

Big Sur Ranger Station

Big Sur R.

Big Sur

Pfeiffer Big Sur
State Park

33-40

42

Sycamore

41

CALIFORNIA SEA OTTER REFUGE

COAST

43

Partington

HIKES 1-75

North Big Sur
POINT LOBOS to
JULIA PFEIFFER BURNS STATE PARK
VENTANA WILDERNESS

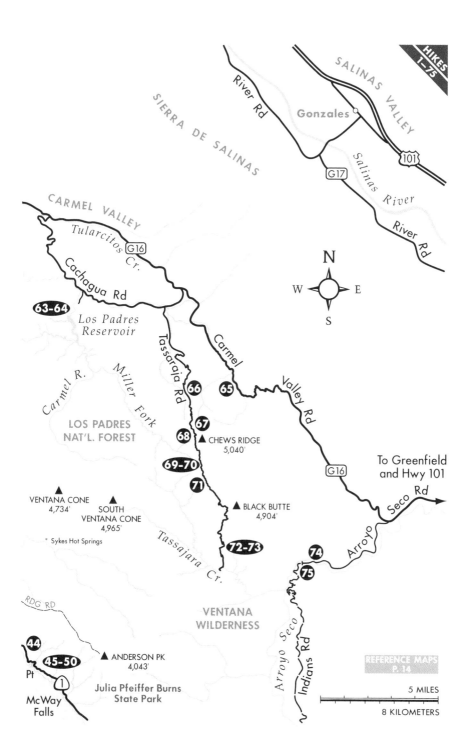

SALINAS VALLEY

River Rd

Gonzales

101

G17

Salinas River

River Rd

SIERRA DE SALINAS

CARMEL VALLEY

Tularcitos Cr.

G16

Cachagua Rd

N
W   E
S

63-64

Los Padres Reservoir

Carmel R.

Miller Fork

Tassaraja Rd

Carmel

Valley Rd

LOS PADRES NAT'L. FOREST

66   65

67

68

CHEWS RIDGE
5,040'

69-70

G16

To Greenfield
and Hwy 101

Seco Rd

71

VENTANA CONE
4,734'

SOUTH
VENTANA CONE
4,965'

* Sykes Hot Springs

BLACK BUTTE
4,904'

Tassajara Cr.

72-73

74

75

Arroyo

RDG RD

44

45-50

Pt

1

McWay
Falls

ANDERSON PK
4,043'

Julia Pfeiffer Burns
State Park

VENTANA
WILDERNESS

Arroyo Seco

Indians Rd

REFERENCE MAPS
P. 14

5 MILES

8 KILOMETERS

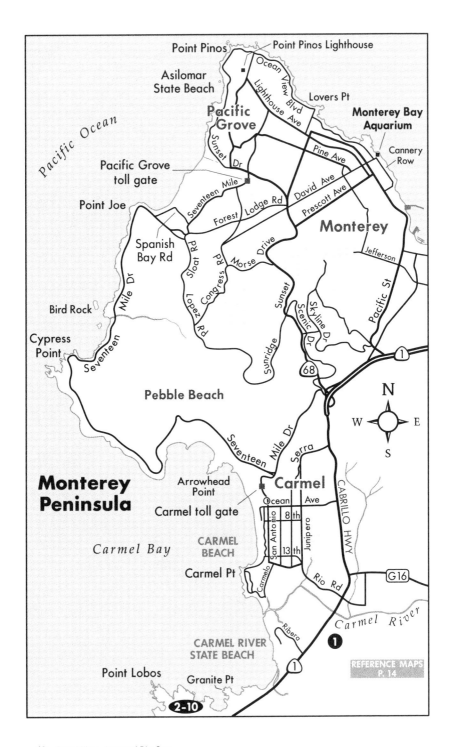

1. Palo Corona Regional Park

A free access permit is required to hike the trail
www.mprpd.org · 831-659-4488, then select option 5

Hiking distance: 5 miles round trip
Hiking time: 2.5 hours
Configuration: out-and-back with a central loop
Elevation gain: 800 feet
Difficulty: easy to moderate
Exposure: exposed meadows and shaded forest
Dogs: not allowed
Maps: U.S.G.S. Monterey · Palo Corona Regional Park Trail Map

**map
page 21**

Palo Corona Regional Park sits at the northwest corner of the Santa Lucia Range, south of Carmel and above Monastery Beach and Point Lobos State Park. The 10,000-acre Palo Corona Ranch, stretching over 7 miles in length, was acquired by a collaboration between public agencies and conservation groups in 2004. The sprawling open-space park contains the headwaters to thirteen watersheds. It is a crucial wildlife corridor, protecting a diverse and endangered plant and animal species. The park's significant wildlife habitats include streamside riparian forests, redwood and madrone forests, coast live oak woodlands, a coastal terrace prairie, grasslands, native buckwheat, and vernal wetlands.

The 680-acre "Front Ranch" portion of the park, managed by the Monterey Peninsula Regional Park District, is open to the public. The park, bordered by the Carmel River to the north and Highway 1 to the west, has a trail system that crosses the grassy terrace and riparian corridor to Inspiration Point, an overlook on an oceanfront saddle. From the viewpoint is a bird's-eye view of the Carmel Coast, Point Lobos, Carmel, and Pebble Beach. The trail continues to Animas Pond, a secluded, reed-filled wetland.

Access is by permit only due to limited parking. Contact information is included above.

To the trailhead

From Highway 1 and Rio Road in Carmel, drive 0.6 miles south on Highway 1 to the signed Palo Corona Regional Park entrance on the left. It is located just after crossing the bridge over the

Carmel River. Park on the east (inland) side of the shoulder of Highway 1, just north of the trailhead gate.

The hike

Pass through the entrance gate and sign in. Walk east on the unpaved road, passing an old barn on the right. Continue on the Palo Corona Trail, or walk parallel to the trail on the dirt road. Pass the corrals and go through a cattle gate to a Y-fork near the base of the mountain. The right fork is the direct route to Inspiration Point, one mile ahead.

For this hike, go to the left on the Vista Lobos Trail. Walk 75 yards to a trail split. Veer right on the Laguna Vista Loop and head up the gentle slope. Curve around the south side of the knoll, where a side path leads 50 yards up to a bench atop the knoll by an oak grove. Descend and rejoin the Vista Lobos Trail. Go to the right a short distance, and veer left on the posted Oak Knoll Loop. As the name implies, the path loops through a gorgeous oak grove and rejoins the Vista Lobos Trail. Bear left (east) to a cattle gate and the Talus Trail on the right. Detour through the gate, straight ahead. Stay on the Vista Lobos Trail under the shade of the oaks. Drop down to the riparian corridor of the Carmel River among sycamores, willows, and cottonwoods. Stroll among the dense foliage, parallel to the south side of the river to the east gate. The Southbank Trail continues outside the gate on an old farm road. After the gate, the level, dog-friendly path leads 1.5 miles, parallel to the Carmel River, to Rancho San Carlos Road.

Return to the Talus Trail junction at the gate and take it to the left. Head south towards the vertical mountain wall to a T-junction back with the Palo Corona Trail. For an easy return, go to the right, completing the loop. To head to Inspiration Point and Animas Pond, bear left and traverse the north-facing slope. Steadily climb, slowly looping to the right. With every step, expanding views emerge of the Carmel River corridor and Carmel Valley. At the top is a grassland meadow surrounded by pines and a junction. Veer right and walk 250 yards to Inspiration Point. The point is located on a bluff overlooking the Carmel River, including the lagoon at the ocean, Carmel by the Sea, and Pebble Beach. After savoring the views, continue south on the Palo Corona Trail. Pass a second overlook on the right, and gently descend through open meadows to Animas Creek, the north fork of San Jose Creek. Cross a footbridge over the creek to Animas Pond on the left. As of this writing, public access beyond the point is prohibited. Return by retracing your steps. ▦

To Rancho
San Carlos
Road

SOUTHBANK
TR

VISTA LOBOS TR

Inspiration
Point

TALUS TR

PALO CORONA TR

Animas Pond

Animas Creek

VISTA LOBOS

OAK KNOLL
LOOP

LAGUNA
VISTA LOOP

PALO CORONA TR

Carmel River

corrals

To
Carmel

PALO CORONA TR

barn

E

N ◈ S

W

1

To Big Sur

1.

Palo Corona Regional Park

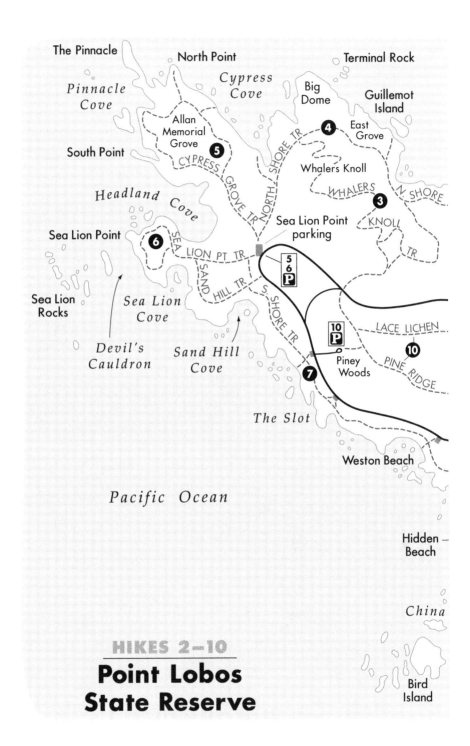

The Pinnacle

North Point

Terminal Rock

Pinnacle Cove

Cypress Cove

Big Dome

Guillemot Island

Allan Memorial Grove **5**

East Grove **4**

South Point

CYPRESS

Whalers Knoll

Headland *Cove*

GROVE TR

NORTH SHORE TR

WHALERS

N SHORE

Sea Lion Point

6

SEA

Sea Lion Point parking

KNOLL **3**

TR

LION PT TR

5 6 P

Sea Lion Rocks

Sea Lion Cove

SAND HILL TR

S SHORE TR

10 P

LACE LICHEN

10

Devil's Cauldron

Sand Hill Cove

Piney Woods

PINE RIDGE

7

The Slot

Weston Beach

Pacific Ocean

Hidden — Beach

China

Point Lobos State Reserve

Bird Island

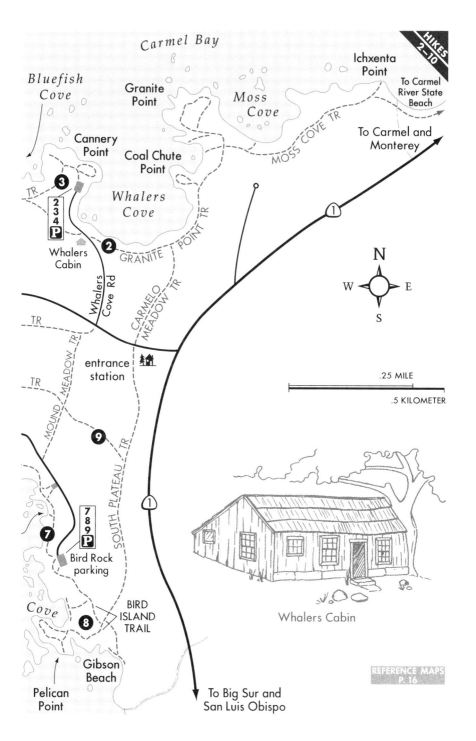

Carmel Bay

Bluefish
Cove

Granite
Point

Moss
Cove

Ichxenta
Point

To Carmel
River State
Beach

Cannery
Point

Coal Chute
Point

MOSS COVE TR

To Carmel and
Monterey

3

Whalers
Cove

2
3
4
P

Whalers
Cabin

2

GRANITE POINT TR

TR

1

N

W   E

S

Whalers Cove Rd

CARMELO MEADOW TR

TR

entrance
station

.25 MILE

.5 KILOMETER

TR

MOUND MEADOW TR

9

SOUTH PLATEAU TR

1

7

7
8
9
P

Bird Rock
parking

Cove

8

BIRD
ISLAND
TRAIL

Whalers Cabin

Gibson
Beach

Pelican
Point

To Big Sur and
San Luis Obispo

2. Granite Point
Whalers Cove to Ichxenta Point
POINT LOBOS STATE RESERVE

Hiking distance: 2 miles round trip
Hiking time: 1 hour
Configuration: out-and-back
Elevation gain: near level
Difficulty: east
Exposure: open coastal bluffs and open fields
Dogs: not allowed
Maps: U.S.G.S. Monterey · Point Lobos State Reserve map

Point Lobos State Reserve is the crown jewel among California's state parks. It is located along the north end of the Big Sur coastline just south of Monterey and Carmel. The incredible 1,276-acre reserve has bold headlands, ragged cliffs, sculpted coves, large stands of Monterey cypress, rolling meadows, and many miles of hiking trails. The eroded inlets are home to tidepools, isolated beaches, craggy islets, and marine terraces. It is a great area to view oceanside wildlife.

The Granite Point Trail begins from Whalers Cabin, a historic cabin built by Chinese fishermen in the 1850s that is currently a history museum. The trail curves around Whalers Cove to coastal overlooks on Coal Chute Point and Granite Point. Views extend across Carmel Bay and its sandy beaches to the golf courses at Pebble Beach. The hike continues on the Moss Cove Trail across open fields to Ichxenta Point, a low granite headland overlooking Monastery Beach.

To the trailhead

CARMEL. From Highway 1 and Rio Road in Carmel, drive 2.2 miles south on Highway 1 to the signed Point Lobos State Reserve entrance. Turn right (west) to the entrance station. Continue 0.1 mile to the Whalers Cove turnoff. Turn right and drive 0.3 miles to the parking area at the end of the road. An entrance fee is required.

BIG SUR RANGER STATION. From the ranger station, drive 24 miles north on Highway 1 to the state park entrance and turn left.

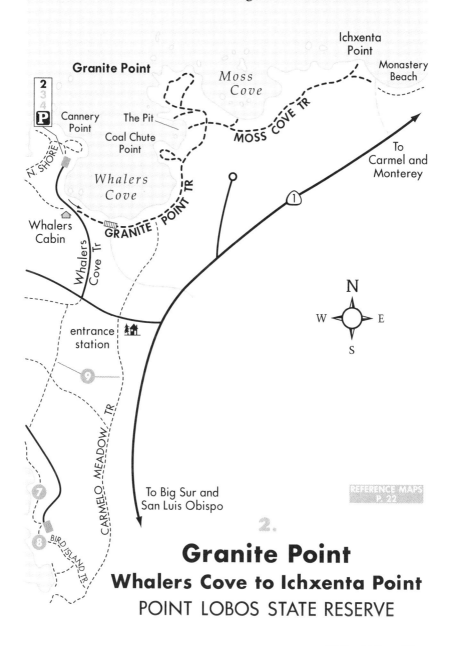

Carmel Bay

Granite Point

Ichxenta
Point

Monastery
Beach

Moss
Cove

2
3
4
P

Cannery
Point

The Pit

Coal Chute
Point

MOSS COVE TR

To
Carmel and
Monterey

N. SHORE

Whalers
Cove

GRANITE POINT TR

Whalers
Cabin

GRANITE POINT TR

Whalers Cove Tr

N

W — E

S

entrance
station

9

CARMELO MEADOW TR

7

8

BIRD ISLAND TR.

To Big Sur and
San Luis Obispo

2.

Granite Point
Whalers Cove to Ichxenta Point
POINT LOBOS STATE RESERVE

The hike

Walk back up the park road 0.1 mile to Whalers Cabin on the right. Across the road is the posted Granite Point Trail. Take the footpath left (east) and follow the crescent-shaped Whalers Cove. Carmel and Pebble Beach are beautifully framed between Cannery Point and Coal Chute Point. Cross a bridge over a seasonal stream, passing a junction with the Carmelo Meadow Trail. At the east end of the cove, enter a forest of Monterey pines, curving left to an unsigned trail fork. Detour to the left and loop around Coal Chute Point through wind-sculpted Monterey pines and cypress. The trail overlooks Whalers Cove and The Pit, a small sandy beach in a sculpted cove with natural rock arches. Return to the Granite Point Trail, and head north above The Pit. Drop over a small knoll to views of Moss Cove, Escobar Rocks, and Monastery Beach.

Descend steps to the Moss Cove Trail at a 4-way junction. The sharp left fork leads down a draw to The Pit. The middle fork climbs steps to a loop around Granite Point. The right fork continues east on the Moss Cove Trail and crosses Hudson Meadow, a flat, grassy marine terrace overlooking Moss Cove. Escobar Rocks forms a natural barrier to the beach cove. Carmelite Monastery can be seen peering out above the trees on the inland hillside. The trail ends at the northeast park boundary above Monastery Beach. Just before reaching the fenced boundary, a short path on the left ascends up to the rocky Ichxenta Point. ▨

3. Whalers Knoll Trail
POINT LOBOS STATE RESERVE

Hiking distance: 2 miles round trip
Hiking time: 1 hour
Configuration: out-and-back with large loop
Elevation gain: 180 feet
Difficulty: easy
Exposure: a mix of open and shaded forest
Dogs: not allowed
Maps: U.S.G.S. Monterey · Point Lobos State Reserve map

**map
page 28**

Whalers Knoll was an historic lookout for spotting whales. The trail twists 200 feet up the hillside through an open Monterey pine forest draped with lace lichen to the exposed knob. At the summit is a bench and panoramic views of Big Dome, Carmel Bay, and the coastline to Pebble Beach. This hike begins from Whalers Cove and connects with Whalers Knoll via the North Shore Trail (Hike 4). The hike returns back down to Whalers Cabin, built by Chinese fishermen in the 1850s. The cabin now houses a museum.

To the trailhead

CARMEL. From Highway 1 and Rio Road in Carmel, drive 2.2 miles south on Highway 1 to the signed Point Lobos State Reserve entrance. Turn right (west) to the entrance station. Continue 0.1 mile to the Whalers Cove turnoff. Turn right and drive 0.3 miles to the parking area at the end of the road. An entrance fee is required.

BIG SUR RANGER STATION. From the ranger station, drive 24 miles north on Highway 1 to the state park entrance and turn left.

The hike

From the far north end of the parking area, take the signed North Shore Trail. Climb rock steps to an overlook of Cannery Point, Granite Point, Coal Chute Point, Whalers Cove, Carmel, Pebble Beach, Carmel Bay, and the Santa Lucia Mountains. Stay left up a long flight of wooden steps to a trail split. The right fork leads to an overlook of Bluefish Cove. Bear left on the North Shore Trail towards Whalers Knoll. The serpentine path curves around Bluefish Cove, passing the first junction with Whalers Knoll Trail, the return route.

Begin the loop to the right, staying on the coastal path along the jagged cliffs. Pass a side trail on the right that overlooks Guillemot Island. Cross the inland side of Big Dome to the posted Whalers Knoll Trail on the left. Climb up the hillside on the Whalers Knoll Trail, zigzagging through the Monterey pines to views of Sea Lion Point. Curve left, steadily climbing to the summit and a bench on the knoll. Savor the commanding views of Big Dome and Carmel Bay. Continue across the knoll and descend past two junctions with the Pine Ridge Trail on the right. Complete the loop back at Bluefish Cove on the North Shore Trail. Bear right to a signed junction on the right to the Whalers Cabin Trail, and descend through a native Monterey pine forest to the cabin at the park road. Take the park road 0.1 mile back to the left. ■

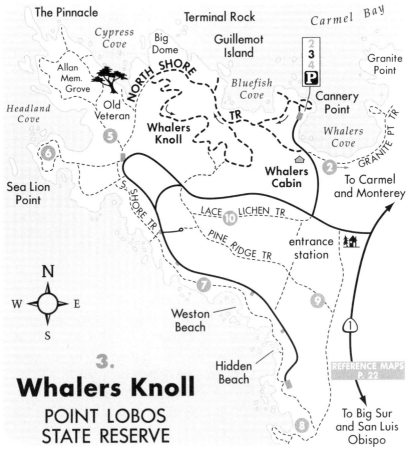

The Pinnacle   Terminal Rock   Carmel Bay

Cypress Cove   Big Dome   Guillemot Island

NORTH SHORE

Allan Mem. Grove

Granite Point

Bluefish Cove

Headland Cove

Old Veteran

Whalers Knoll

TR

Cannery Point

Whalers Cove

GRANITE PT TR

Sea Lion Point

Whalers Cabin

To Carmel and Monterey

LACE LICHEN TR

S. SHORE TR

PINE RIDGE TR

entrance station

N
W   E
S

Weston Beach

Hidden Beach

REFERENCE MAPS P. 22

To Big Sur and San Luis Obispo

3.
Whalers Knoll
POINT LOBOS STATE RESERVE

4. North Shore Trail
POINT LOBOS STATE RESERVE

Hiking distance: 2.8–3.2 miles round trip
Hiking time: 1.5–2 hours
Configuration: out-and-back
Elevation gain: 250 feet
Difficulty: easy
Exposure: shaded forest and open hillside
Dogs: not allowed
Maps: U.S.G.S. Monterey · Point Lobos State Reserve map

map
page 31

The North Shore Trail parallels the northern headlands of Point Lobos State Reserve at the southern end of Carmel Bay. The beautiful trail follows the exposed and rugged coast past sheer granite cliffs and coves. A spur trail leads to an overlook of Guillemot Island, a rocky offshore nesting site for seabirds. A second spur trail leads to Cypress Cove and Old Veteran, a windswept, gnarled Monterey cypress clinging to the cliffs of the cove. The main trail, perched above the rocky cliffs, winds through a canopy of Monterey pines and cypress draped with veils of lichen.

Additional side trips lead to vistas atop Whalers Knoll and to Whalers Cabin, an old cabin that now houses a museum.

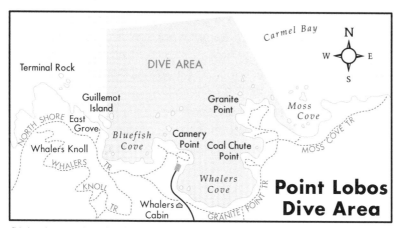

Diving is permitted only at Whalers Cove and Bluefish Cove. Proof of certification is required. Permission to dive is given when entering the reserve. Reservations are recommended and a must for weekends and holidays.

To the trailhead

CARMEL. From Highway 1 and Rio Road in Carmel, drive 2.2 miles south on Highway 1 to the signed Point Lobos State Reserve entrance. Turn right (west) to the entrance station. Continue 0.1 mile to the Whalers Cove turnoff. Turn right and drive 0.3 miles to the parking area at the end of the road. An entrance fee is required.

BIG SUR RANGER STATION. From the ranger station, drive 24 miles north on Highway 1 to the state park entrance and turn left.

The hike

Walk up the rock steps at the north end of the parking lot to a junction. The right fork loops around Cannery Point at the west end of Whalers Cove. Back at the first junction, ascend a long set of steps, and enter the forest to another junction. The short fork on the right leads to an overlook of Bluefish Cove. On the North Shore Trail, curve around the cove to a junction with the Whalers Knoll Trail on the left. Continue weaving along the coastal cliffs around Bluefish Cove to a short spur trail leading to the Guillemot Island overlook. Back on the main trail, continue northwest past a native grove of Monterey cypress in East Grove. Cross a saddle past Big Dome to a second junction with the Whalers Knoll Trail. At Cypress Cove, detour on the Old Veteran Trail to view the twisted Monterey cypress and the cove. The North Shore Trail ends in the coastal scrub at the Cypress Grove trailhead by the Sea Lion Point parking area. Return along the same trail.

The North Shore Trail curves around the north side of Whalers Knoll, a historic lookout for spotting whales. For a side trip, take the twisting Whalers Knoll Trail 200 feet up the hillside. At the summit is a bench and panoramic views.

Whalers Cabin is located on the park road 0.1 mile before the parking area. The cabin was built by fishermen in the 1850s. ■

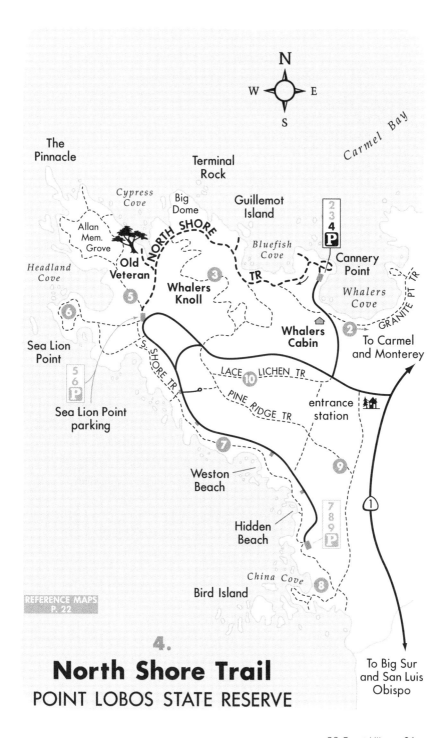

N
W · E
S

The Pinnacle

Terminal Rock

Cypress Cove

Big Dome

Guillemot Island

Allan Mem. Grove

Carmel Bay

2 3 **4** P

Bluefish Cove

Old Veteran

NORTH SHORE

Cannery Point

Headland Cove

Whalers Knoll

③

TR

Whalers Cove

⑤

②

GRANITE PT. TR

⑥

Whalers Cabin

To Carmel and Monterey

Sea Lion Point

S. SHORE TR.

LACE ⑩ LICHEN TR

5 6 P

PINE RIDGE TR

entrance station

Sea Lion Point parking

⑦

⑨

Weston Beach

7 8 9 P

①

Hidden Beach

China Cove

⑧

REFERENCE MAPS P. 22

Bird Island

4.
North Shore Trail
POINT LOBOS STATE RESERVE

To Big Sur and San Luis Obispo

5. Allan Memorial Grove
Cypress Grove Trail
POINT LOBOS STATE RESERVE

Hiking distance: 0.8-mile loop
Hiking time: 30 minutes
Configuration: small loop with spur trails to coast
Elevation gain: 100 feet
Difficulty: east
Exposure: open coastal bluffs and shaded forest
Dogs: not allowed
Maps: U.S.G.S. Monterey · Point Lobos State Reserve map

The Cypress Grove Trail is a clifftop loop trail around Allan Memorial Grove in Point Lobos State Reserve. The trail passes through one of only two natural stands of Monterey cypress in the world. (The other occurs at Cypress Point on the west side of the Monterey Peninsula.) The hike loops around rugged, weathered cliffs with stunning views of Cypress Cove, Pinnacle Cove, South Point, Headland Cove, and The Pinnacle, a narrow peninsula at the northernmost point in the reserve.

To the trailhead

CARMEL. From Highway 1 and Rio Road in Carmel, drive 2.2 miles south on Highway 1 to the signed Point Lobos State Reserve entrance. Turn right (west) to the entrance station. Continue 0.7 miles to the Sea Lion Point parking area on the right side of the road. An entrance fee is required.

BIG SUR RANGER STATION. From the ranger station, drive 24 miles north on Highway 1 to the state park entrance and turn left.

The hike

Two well-marked trails begin on the north end of the parking lot. To the right is the North Shore Trail (Hike 4). Take the Cypress Grove Trail to the left through coastal scrub 0.2 miles to a trail split. Begin the loop around Allan Memorial Grove to the right. Follow the edge of Cypress Cove to a short spur trail on the right, leading to an overlook of Cypress Cove and Carmel Bay. Back on the loop, pass through an indigenous Monterey cypress grove. A spur trail at the north end of the loop leads to the North Point over-look and views of The Pinnacle. Back on the main trail, granite steps lead up to Pinnacle Cove on a rocky promontory, where there are stunning views of South Point and Headland Cove. Continue past South Point and Headland Cove, completing the loop. ■

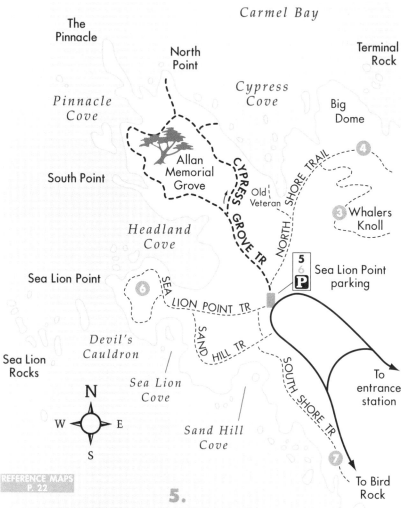

5.
Allan Memorial Grove
Cypress Grove Trail
POINT LOBOS STATE RESERVE

6. Sea Lion Point Trail
POINT LOBOS STATE RESERVE

Hiking distance: 0.7-mile double loop
Hiking time: 30 minutes
Configuration: two connected loops
Elevation gain: 50 feet
Difficulty: easy
Exposure: open coastal bluffs
Dogs: not allowed
Maps: U.S.G.S. Monterey · Point Lobos State Reserve map

The Sea Lion Point Trail leads to a spectacular, surreal landscape on the coastal bluff above Headland Cove in Point Lobos State Reserve. From the bluffs are vistas of Sea Lion Cove, Sea Lion Rocks, the churning whitewater at Devil's Cauldron, wave-pounded inlets, and sloping layers of rock. The offshore sea stacks and rocky coves are often abundant with sea otters, harbor seals, and barking California sea lions. The return route follows the eroded cliffs between Sea Lion Cove and Sand Hill Cove.

To the trailhead

CARMEL. From Highway 1 and Rio Road in Carmel, drive 2.2 miles south on Highway 1 to the signed Point Lobos State Reserve entrance. Turn right (west) to the entrance station. Continue 0.7 miles to the Sea Lion Point parking area on the right side of the road. An entrance fee is required.

BIG SUR RANGER STATION. From the ranger station, drive 24 miles north on Highway 1 to the state park entrance and turn left.

The hike

From the far west end of the parking area, take the signed Sea Lion Point Trail. The path crosses through coastal scrub to a trail split. Stay to the right, heading toward the point. At the crest of the rocky bluffs is a trail junction and an incredible vista point. The views include South Point, The Pinnacle, Sea Lion Cove, Devil's Cauldron, and Sea Lion Rocks. On the right, descend the natural staircase of weathered rock to the headland. From the lower level, circle the point around Headland Cove to close up views of Devil's Cauldron and Sea Lion Rocks. Loop back around by the sandy beach at Sea Lion Cove. Return up the steps to the overlook. Proceed south on Sand Hill Trail, following the cliffs above Sea Lion Cove and Sand Hill Cove. Pass the South Shore Trail on the right (Hike 7), and complete the loop at the parking area. ▪

6.
Sea Lion Point
POINT LOBOS STATE RESERVE

7. South Shore Trail
POINT LOBOS STATE RESERVE

Hiking distance: 2 miles round trip
Hiking time: 1 hour
Configuration: out-and-back
Elevation gain: 30 feet
Difficulty: easy
Exposure: open coastal bluffs
Dogs: not allowed
Maps: U.S.G.S. Monterey · Point Lobos State Reserve map

The South Shore Trail explores the eroded sandstone terrain along the jagged southern ridges and troughs of Point Lobos State Reserve. The trail begins near Bird Island and ends by Sea Lion Point, weaving past tidepools and rocky beach coves tucked between the cliffs. The beach coves include rock-enclosed Hidden Beach and Weston Beach, covered with multi-colored pebbles and flat rock slabs. The trail continues past The Slot (a narrow channel bound by rock) and the 100-foot cliffs at Sand Hill Cove.

To the trailhead

CARMEL. From Highway 1 and Rio Road in Carmel, drive 2.2 miles south on Highway 1 to the signed Point Lobos State Reserve entrance. Turn right (west) to the entrance kiosk. Continue 1.6 miles to the Bird Rock parking area at the end of the road. An entrance fee is required.

BIG SUR RANGER STATION. From the ranger station, drive 24 miles north on Highway 1 to the state park entrance and turn left.

The hike

The signed South Shore Trail begins at the north end of the parking area overlooking China Cove. Head north (right), walking along the edge of the cliffs to a junction with the path to Hidden Beach on the left. Stone steps descend to the oval beach cove. Return to the main trail and follow the contours of the jagged coastline past numerous coves, tidepools, and rock islands. A few connector trails on the right lead to parking areas along the park road. At Sand Hill Cove, steps lead up to a T-junction with the

Sand Hill Trail—Hike 6. This is the turn-around spot. Return along the same trail. ▓

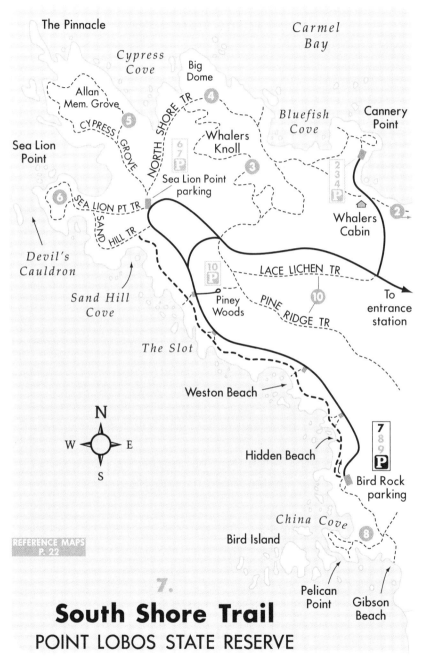

The Pinnacle

Carmel Bay

Cypress Cove

Big Dome

Allan Mem. Grove

Bluefish Cove

Cannery Point

CYPRESS GROVE

NORTH SHORE TR

④

Whalers Knoll

Sea Lion Point

⑤

6 7 P

③

2 3 4 P

Sea Lion Point parking

SEA LION PT TR

⑥

SAND HILL TR

Whalers Cabin

②

Devil's Cauldron

LACE LICHEN TR

To entrance station

Sand Hill Cove

10 P

Piney Woods

PINE RIDGE TR

⑩

The Slot

N

W ✛ E

S

Weston Beach

Hidden Beach

7 8 9 P

Bird Rock parking

China Cove

Bird Island

⑧

Pelican Point

Gibson Beach

REFERENCE MAPS P. 22

7.

South Shore Trail
POINT LOBOS STATE RESERVE

8. Bird Island Trail

China Cove—Pelican Point—Gibson Beach

POINT LOBOS STATE RESERVE

Hiking distance: 0.8 miles round trip
Hiking time: 30 minutes
Configuration: out-and-back with small loop
Elevation gain: 20 feet
Difficulty: easy
Exposure: open coastal bluffs
Dogs: not allowed
Maps: U.S.G.S. Monterey · Point Lobos State Reserve map

The Bird Island Trail follows the rocky coastline through a Monterey pine forest along the cliff tops overlooking the sea. The trail passes chasms, arches, sea caves, and the beautiful white sand beaches of China Cove and Gibson Beach. Both beach coves are surrounded by granite cliffs with staircase accesses. The hike then loops around Pelican Point, where off-shore Bird Island can be viewed. The island is inhabited by nesting colonies of cormorants and brown pelicans.

To the trailhead

CARMEL. From Highway 1 and Rio Road in Carmel, drive 2.2 miles south on Highway 1 to the signed Point Lobos State Reserve entrance. Turn right (west) to the entrance kiosk. Continue 1.6 miles to the Bird Rock parking area at the end of the road. An entrance fee is required.

BIG SUR RANGER STATION. From the ranger station, drive 24 miles north on Highway 1 to the state park entrance and turn left.

The hike

Ascend the steps at the south end of the parking lot, and head through a Monterey pine forest to an overlook of China Cove and Bird Island. Follow the cliffside path as it curves around the head of China Cove to a signed junction. A long set of stairs to the right descends the cliffs to the sandy beach and cave in China Cove.

After exploring the beach, return to the Bird Island Trail. Continue along the cliffs to a posted T-junction and overlook of

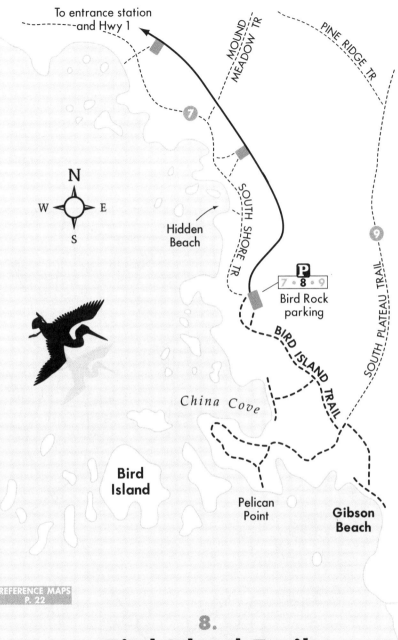

To entrance station
and Hwy 1

MOUND MEADOW TR

PINE RIDGE TR

N
W E
S

Hidden Beach

SOUTH SHORE TR

SOUTH PLATEAU TRAIL

P 7 • **8** • 9
Bird Rock parking

BIRD ISLAND TRAIL

China Cove

Bird Island

Pelican Point

Gibson Beach

REFERENCE MAPS P. 22

8.
Bird Island Trail
POINT LOBOS STATE RESERVE

the crescent-shaped Gibson Beach below the Carmel Highlands. For a short detour to Gibson Beach, bear left on the South Plateau Trail a few yards to the posted beach access on the right. Descend a long flight of steps to the sandy beach at the base of the cliffs.

Returning to the T-junction, head west towards Pelican Point through coastal scrub to a trail split. The paths loop around the flat bench, overlooking Bird Island, the magnificent offshore rock outcroppings, chasms, sea caves, and China Cove. Complete the loop and return along the same route. ▓

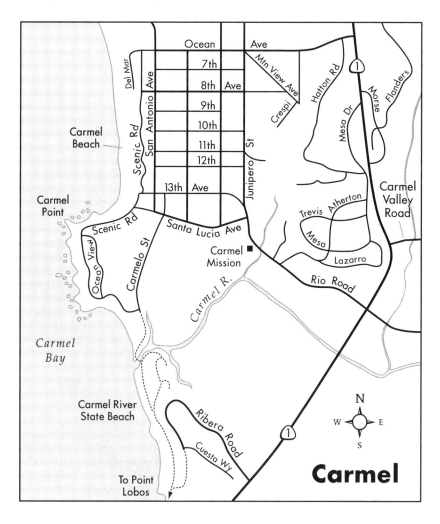

9. South Plateau— Mound Meadow Loop

POINT LOBOS STATE RESERVE

Hiking distance: 1.6-mile loop
Hiking time: 1 hour
Configuration: loop
Elevation gain: 100 feet
Difficulty: easy
Exposure: mix of shaded and open forest and exposed marine terrace
Dogs: not allowed
Maps: U.S.G.S. Monterey · Point Lobos State Reserve map
Big Sur and Ventana Wilderness map

map
page 43

The South Plateau Trail, an interpretive trail, connects the white sands of China Cove and Gibson Beach with the entrance station to Point Lobos State Reserve. The nature trail crosses Vierra's Knoll as it winds through a forest of Monterey pine and coastal live oak. Along the trail are 12 stations with information about the region's plants and animals. (An interpretive pamphlet is available at the entrance station.) The hike returns on the Mound Meadow Trail across an ancient marine terrace. Along the coastal section of the loop, the hike offers access to China Cove, Gibson Beach, and Hidden Beach (a pocket beach surrounded by rocks).

To the trailhead

CARMEL. From Highway 1 and Rio Road in Carmel, drive 2.2 miles south on Highway 1 to the signed Point Lobos State Reserve entrance. Turn right (west) to the entrance kiosk. Continue 1.6 miles to the Bird Rock parking area at the end of the road. An entrance fee is required.

BIG SUR RANGER STATION. From the ranger station, drive 24 miles north on Highway 1 to the state park entrance and turn left.

The hike

Take the posted Bird Island Trail at the south (far) end of the parking lot to begin hiking the loop counter-clockwise. Climb a long set of steps and curve along the cliffs that overlook China Cove and Bird Island. A stair access leads to the gorgeous pocket beach. Loop around China Cove towards Gibson Beach and a T-junction. The Bird Island Trail (Hike 8) goes right. Take the left fork on the South Plateau Trail a short distance to the Gibson Beach access on the right. For a detour to Gibson Beach, bear right and descend a long flight of steps to the sandy crescent beach.

Return to the South Plateau Trail. Head inland and wind through chaparral to Vierra's Knoll, entering a Monterey pine forest. Gently descend from the knoll into a forest of twisted live oaks draped with lace lichen. Wind through the dense forest, passing the Pine Ridge Trail on the left. Continue straight, parallel to Highway 1, through large patches of poison oak, wood mint, and blackberries. The South Plateau Trail ends by the park entrance.

Go to the left and follow the park entrance road 0.1 mile to the paved service road on the left (across from Whalers Cove Road). Walk ten yards to the left, and pick up the signed trail at a Y-junction. The Lace Lichen Trail (Hike 10) forks right. Take the Mound Meadow Trail to the left, and meander through the pine forest, passing a 4-way junction with the intersection of the Pine Ridge Trail. Continue south towards the ocean, which can be seen through the trees. Emerge from the forest at the park road. Cross the road to the South Shore Trail at a small, rocky beach cove. Bear left and follow the coastline south for 0.2 miles—passing numerous ocean inlets and the Hidden Beach access—back to the parking lot. ■

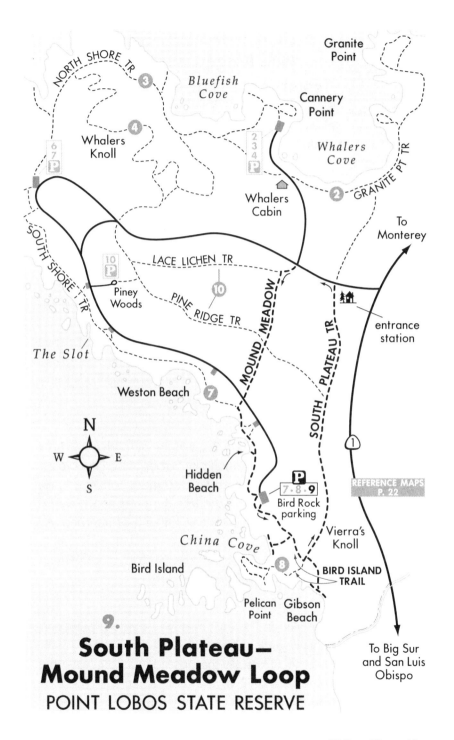

NORTH SHORE TR

Granite Point

Bluefish Cove

3

Cannery Point

Whalers Cove

4

Whalers Knoll

2·3·4 P

GRANITE PT TR

6·7 P

Whalers Cabin

2

To Monterey

SOUTH SHORE TR

10 P

LACE LICHEN TR

Piney Woods

10

PINE RIDGE TR

MOUND MEADOW

SOUTH PLATEAU TR

entrance station

The Slot

Weston Beach

7

N

W E

S

Hidden Beach

P **7·8·9** Bird Rock parking

REFERENCE MAPS P. 22

1

China Cove

Vierra's Knoll

Bird Island

8

BIRD ISLAND TRAIL

Pelican Point

Gibson Beach

To Big Sur and San Luis Obispo

9.
South Plateau–
Mound Meadow Loop
POINT LOBOS STATE RESERVE

10. Lace Lichen—Mound Meadow— Pine Ridge Loop

POINT LOBOS STATE RESERVE

Hiking distance: 1.2-mile loop
Hiking time: 30 minutes
Configuration: loop
Elevation gain: level
Difficulty: easy
Exposure: mix of shaded and open forest and exposed marine terrace
Dogs: not allowed
Maps: U.S.G.S. Monterey · Point Lobos State Reserve map
Big Sur and Ventana Wilderness map

Lace lichen is a combination of fungus and algae that looks like a stringy beard hanging from the tree branches. This short, easy loop parallels the park road through a cool, humid pine and oak forest draped with lace lichen. The trail loops across an ancient marine terrace and winds through open forests of native Monterey pine and coastal live oak, with views of Bird Island and the ocean. Where the pine forest and a meadow meet is a foraging ground for deer.

To the trailhead

CARMEL. From Highway 1 and Rio Road in Carmel, drive 2.2 miles south on Highway 1 to the signed Point Lobos State Reserve entrance. Turn right (west) to the entrance station. Continue 1 mile to the Piney Woods turnoff on the left. Turn left and drive 0.1 mile to the Piney Woods Picnic Area at the end of the road. An entrance fee is required.

BIG SUR RANGER STATION. From the ranger station, drive 24 miles north to the state park entrance and turn left.

The hike

Take the signed Pine Ridge Trail east through a shaded forest canopy to a T-junction. Begin the loop to the left through a predominantly Monterey pine forest. At the posted junction, leave the Pine Ridge Trail, and bear right on the Lace Lichen Trail. The level path weaves through the forest of Monterey pine and coastal live oak that is heavily draped in lace lichen. Continue to a signed trail fork near the park entrance road by Whalers Cove Road.

Bear right on Mound Meadow Trail, and meander through the open forest to a posted 4-way junction with the Pine Ridge Trail. The Mound Meadow Trail continues south to the coastline near Hidden Beach. Take the Pine Ridge Trail to the right, and follow the ridge through the forest to a vista point with a bench. The views extend south to Mound Meadow, Weston Beach, Bird Island, Pelican Point, and Yankee Point by the Carmel Highlands. Complete the loop a short distance ahead. ■

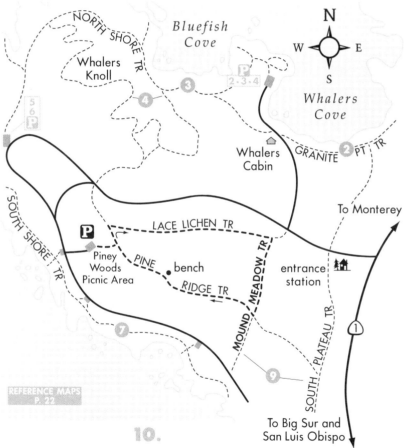

10.
Lace Lichen–Pine Ridge Loop
POINT LOBOS STATE RESERVE

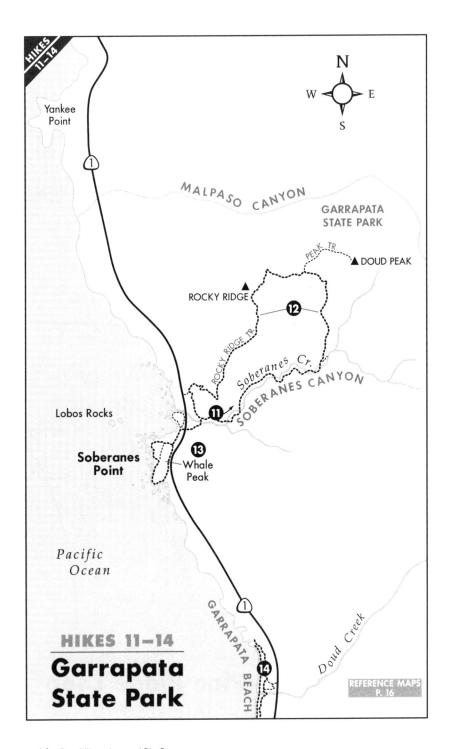

N
W · E
S

Yankee
Point

1

MALPASO CANYON

GARRAPATA
STATE PARK

PEAK TR
▲ DOUD PEAK

ROCKY RIDGE ▲

12

ROCKY RIDGE TR

Soberanes Cr.

SOBERANES CANYON

Lobos Rocks

11

**Soberanes
Point**

13
Whale
Peak

Pacific
Ocean

GARRAPATA BEACH

1

14

Doud Creek

HIKES 11–14
Garrapata
State Park

REFERENCE MAPS
P. 16

11. Soberanes Canyon Trail
GARRAPATA STATE PARK

Hiking distance: 3 miles round trip
Hiking time: 1.5 hours
Configuration: out-and-back
Elevation gain: 900 feet
Difficulty: moderate
Exposure: shaded canyon
Dogs: not allowed
Maps: U.S.G.S. Soberanes Point · Garrapata State Park map
      Big Sur and Ventana Wilderness map

**map
page 49**

Just south of Point Lobos, the undeveloped Garrapata State Park stretches along four miles of scenic coastline and into the inland mountains. Soberanes Creek flows through the south end of the park and empties into the Pacific by the rocky headlands of Soberanes Point. The Soberanes Canyon Trail follows the creek up a wet, narrow canyon through magnificent stands of huge redwoods (back cover photo). The trail crosses the creek seven times before climbing up to the head of the canyon. At the top, the trail emerges onto the dry, chaparral-covered hillside with panoramic views.

If you wish to make the hike into a loop, it is recommended to start on the Rocky Ridge Trail—Hike 12—to avoid the steep climb from Soberanes Creek up to the ridge.

To the trailhead

CARMEL. From Highway 1 and Rio Road in Carmel, drive 6.8 miles south on Highway 1 to the unsigned parking turnouts on either side of the road. The turnouts are located by a tin roof barn behind a grove of cypress trees on the inland side of the highway.

BIG SUR RANGER STATION. From the ranger station, drive 19.4 miles north on Highway 1 to the parking turnouts.

The hike

From the inland side of the highway, walk past the trailhead gate, following the old ranch road through a cypress grove. Curve left around the barn and down to Soberanes Creek. Cross the bridge to a signed junction. The left fork leads to Rocky Ridge, the rounded 1,435-foot peak to the north—Hike 12.

Take the right fork and head up the canyon along the north side of the creek. Cross another footbridge and curve left, staying in Soberanes Canyon. Recross the creek on a third footbridge and head steadily uphill. Rock-hop over the creek, entering a beautiful redwood forest. Follow the watercourse through the redwoods to a lush grotto. The trail crosses the creek three consecutive times, then climbs a long series of steps. Traverse the canyon wall on a cliff ledge that climbs high above the creek. Switchbacks descend back to the creek. Climb up more steps to the head of the canyon. The lush canyon gives way to the dry sage-covered hills and an unsigned trail split, the turn-around point. Return down canyon along the same trail.

If you feel up for the climb, take the left fork up the steep slope towards Rocky Ridge and Doud Peak. The trail follows the dry, exposed hillside. The hike is strenuous, but the views of the ocean, coastline, and mountains are fantastic. Taking this return loop does not make the hike any longer, but it adds an additional 1,000 feet in elevation. ▪

12. Rocky Ridge— Soberanes Canyon Loop
GARRAPATA STATE PARK

Hiking distance: 6-mile loop
Hiking time: 3 hours
Configuration: loop
Elevation gain: 1,600 feet
Difficulty: very strenuous
Exposure: open hillside and shaded canyon
Dogs: not allowed
Maps: U.S.G.S. Soberanes Point · Garrapata State Park map
       Big Sur and Ventana Wilderness map

map
page 51

Rocky Ridge is a 1,435-foot rounded grassy peak between Soberanes Canyon and Malpaso Canyon in Garrapata State Park. The steep trail up to Rocky Ridge follows a dry, exposed hillside.

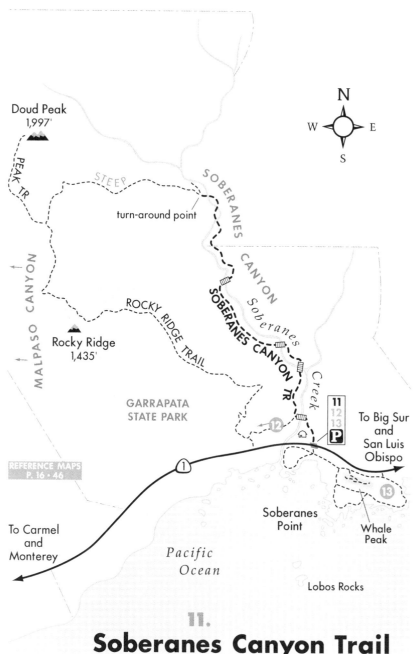

11.
Soberanes Canyon Trail
GARRAPATA STATE PARK

The rewards are sweeping views of the ocean, coastline and mountains, then a return hike down a cool, stream-fed canyon. This hike is strenuous and only recommended for serious hikers.

To the trailhead

CARMEL. From Highway 1 and Rio Road in Carmel, drive 6.8 miles south on Highway 1 to the unsigned parking pullouts on both sides of the road. The pullouts are located by a tin roof barn behind a grove of cypress trees on the inland side of the highway.

BIG SUR RANGER STATION. From the Big Sur Ranger Station, drive 19.4 miles north on Highway 1 to the parking pullouts.

The hike

From the inland side of the highway, walk past the trailhead gate, following the old ranch road through a cypress grove. Curve left around the barn down to Soberanes Creek. The rounded mountain peak straight ahead is Rocky Ridge. Cross the bridge to a signed junction. The right fork heads up Soberanes Canyon (Hike 11), the return route.

Bear left (north), parallel to the highway, on the lower grassy slopes of Rocky Ridge. Cross a couple of gullies to a trail split. The left fork returns to the highway. Take the right fork, which curves right and ascends the rugged, sage-covered slope to a ridge. Begin a much steeper ascent, reaching a knoll. After resting, cross a saddle, finally reaching Rocky Ridge at 1,435 feet. Continue uphill and around the ridge, overlooking the Malpaso Creek drainage to a junction with the Peak Trail (North Ridge Trail) at 3.3 miles. The 0.7-mile spur trail bears left, gaining 300 feet to Doud Peak, the highest point in the state park at 1,977 feet.

Continue the loop on the right fork towards Soberanes Canyon. Descend down the south-facing ridge on the very steep and rocky trail, losing 1,000 feet in less than a mile. At the head of Soberanes Canyon, follow the north canyon wall down to Soberanes Creek along the cool, shaded canyon floor. The lush path follows the watercourse through a redwood forest with six creek crossings. ▨

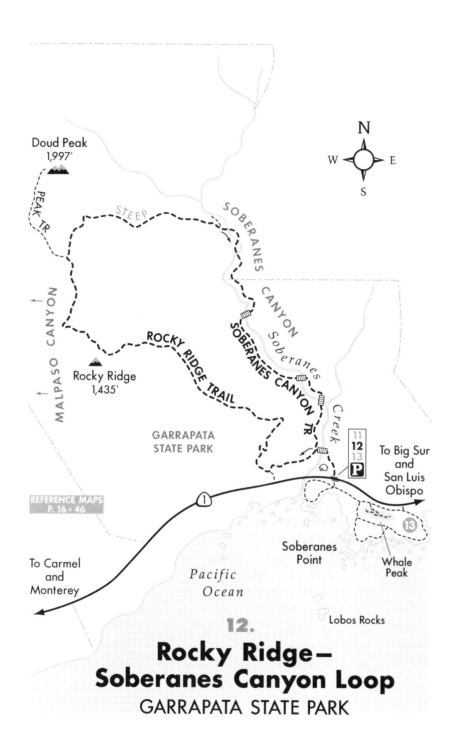

Doud Peak
1,997'

PEAK TR

STEEP

SOBERANES CANYON

MALPASO CANYON

ROCKY RIDGE TRAIL

Rocky Ridge
1,435'

SOBERANES CANYON TR

Soberanes Creek

GARRAPATA
STATE PARK

N
W · E
S

REFERENCE MAPS
P. 16 · 46

11
12
13
P

To Big Sur
and
San Luis
Obispo

13

1

To Carmel
and
Monterey

Soberanes
Point

Whale
Peak

*Pacific
Ocean*

Lobos Rocks

12.
Rocky Ridge–
Soberanes Canyon Loop
GARRAPATA STATE PARK

13. Soberanes Point Trails
GARRAPATA STATE PARK

Hiking distance: 1.8 miles round trip
Hiking time: 1 hour
Configuration: loop
Elevation gain: 200 feet
Difficulty: easy
Exposure: open coastal bluffs
Dogs: allowed
Maps: U.S.G.S. Soberanes Point · Garrapata State Park map
  Big Sur and Ventana Wilderness map

Soberanes Point is a popular whale-watching spot in Garrapata State Park. The serrated headland is backed by Whale Peak, a 280-foot cone-shaped hill overlooking the Pacific. These coastal bluff trails along the point lead to a myriad of crenelated coves, hidden beaches, and rocky points. The trail circles the headland, overlooking sea caves, offshore stacks, and narrow inlets, then climbs Whale Peak. From the summit of the peak are 360-degree panoramic views, from Yankee Point in the north to Point Sur in the south.

To the trailhead

CARMEL. From Highway 1 and Rio Road in Carmel, drive 6.8 miles south on Highway 1 to the unsigned parking turnouts on both sides of the road. The turnouts are located by a tin roof barn on the inland side of the highway.

BIG SUR RANGER STATION. From the ranger station, drive 19.4 miles north on Highway 1 to the parking turnouts.

The hike

Walk through the trailhead gate on the ocean side of the highway, bearing left through a grove of cypress trees. Continue south towards Soberanes Point and Whale Peak, curving around the north side of the peak to an unsigned junction. The left fork circles the base of the hill. Take the right fork west along the coastal terrace to the northwest end of Soberanes Point. Follow the ocean cliffs to the southern point. From the south end, the trail returns toward Highway 1 by a gate. Stay on the footpath to the left, following the hillside trail to an unsigned junction. The left fork climbs a quarter mile up to the grassy ridge of Whale Peak. A trail follows the crest to the two summits. From the overlooks are coastal views north to Yankee Point and south to Point Sur. Return to the base of the hill, and continue to the north to complete the loop. ▪

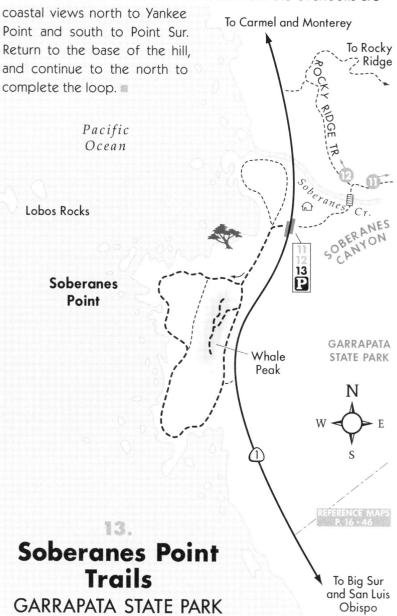

Pacific
Ocean

To Carmel and Monterey

To Rocky
Ridge

ROCKY RIDGE TR.

Soberanes Cr.

SOBERANES
CANYON

Lobos Rocks

Soberanes
Point

Whale
Peak

GARRAPATA
STATE PARK

N
W — E
S

REFERENCE MAPS
P. 16 · 46

13.
Soberanes Point
Trails
GARRAPATA STATE PARK

To Big Sur
and San Luis
Obispo

14. Garrapata Beach and Bluff Trail
GARRAPATA STATE PARK

Hiking distance: 1—2.5 miles round trip
Hiking time: 1—1.5 hours
Configuration: out-and-back trail along the bluffs
Elevation gain: 50 feet
Difficulty: easy
Exposure: open coastal bluffs and beach
Dogs: allowed
Maps: U.S.G.S. Soberanes Point · Garrapata State Park map
  Big Sur and Ventana Wilderness map

Garrapata Beach lies to the south of Soberanes Point along the coastal end of the 2,879-acre Garrapata State Park. The pristine beach is a half-mile crescent of white sand with rocky tide-pools. At the south end, Garrapata Creek empties into the Pacific through a granite gorge. A trail follows the bluffs through an ice plant meadow above the beach. Stairways access the beach for a walk along the water. The beautiful sandy strand is an unofficial clothing-optional beach.

To the trailhead

CARMEL. From Highway 1 and Rio Road in Carmel, drive 9.6 miles south on Highway 1 to the unsigned parking turnouts on both sides of the highway. The turnouts are located between two historic bridges—1.2 miles south of the Granite Creek Bridge and 0.2 miles north of the Garrapata Creek Bridge.

BIG SUR RANGER STATION. From the ranger station, drive 16.6 miles north on Highway 1 to the turnouts.

The hike

Walk through gate 19 and descend a few steps. Follow the path to the edge of the oceanfront cliffs and a trail split. To the left, steps lead down the cliffs to the sandy beach. From the beach, head south (left) a short distance to Garrapata Creek and the jagged rocks at the point. Return north and beachcomb for a half mile along the base of the cliffs to the north point.

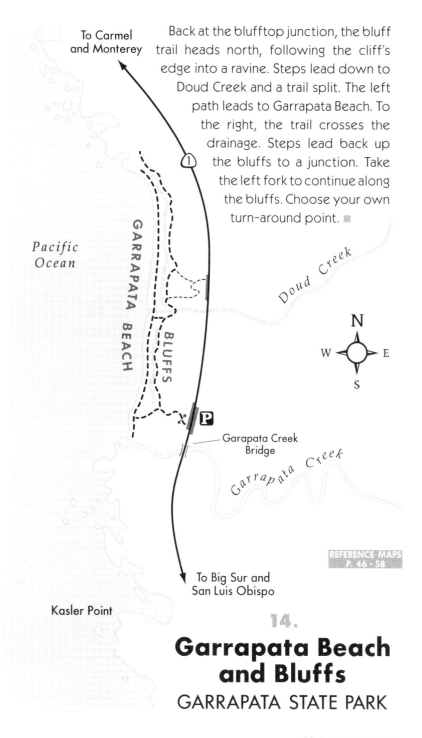

To Carmel
and Monterey

Back at the blufftop junction, the bluff trail heads north, following the cliff's edge into a ravine. Steps lead down to Doud Creek and a trail split. The left path leads to Garrapata Beach. To the right, the trail crosses the drainage. Steps lead back up the bluffs to a junction. Take the left fork to continue along the bluffs. Choose your own turn-around point. ■

Pacific
Ocean

GARRAPATA BEACH

BLUFFS

Doud Creek

N
W ◆ E
S

P
Garapata Creek
Bridge

Garrapata Creek

REFERENCE MAPS
P. 46 • 58

To Big Sur and
San Luis Obispo

Kasler Point

14.

Garrapata Beach and Bluffs
GARRAPATA STATE PARK

15. Rocky Point

Hiking distance: 1.3 miles round trip
Hiking time: 30 minutes
Configuration: out-and-back with shoreline exploration
Elevation gain: 100 feet
Difficulty: physically easy but moderately technical
Exposure: open coastal bluffs
Dogs: allowed
Maps: U.S.G.S. Soberanes Point

Rocky Point is a dramatic rock formation jutting out to sea with powerful waves crashing against the rocks. The point is located just south of Kasler Point and is accessed directly from Highway 1. The point has a series of summits and overlooks with amazing coastal views that include Rocky Creek Bridge, spanning 500 feet and hovering 150 feet above the creek; the Point Sur Lightstation, jutting out to sea a few miles to the south; and the scalloped coastline and offshore rocks. This area can be hazardous due to large, sporadic waves and jagged rocky ledges. Step carefully and use extreme caution.

Parking is available at the trailhead for patrons of the Rocky Point Restaurant, cutting 0.8 miles off the round trip mileage.

To the trailhead

CARMEL. From Highway 1 and Rio Road in Carmel, drive 10.7 miles south on Highway 1 to the signed Rocky Point Restaurant entrance. Park in the large turnout on the right side of the highway, 0.2 miles south of the entrance. There is also a small turnout on the left (inland) side of the highway directly across from the entrance.

BIG SUR RANGER STATION. From the ranger station, drive 16 miles north on Highway 1 to Rocky Point, located 0.4 miles north of Palo Colorado Road.

The hike

Follow Highway 1 northbound 0.2 miles to Rocky Point Road. Follow the road west towards the ocean and the Rocky Point Restaurant. Curve left to the south end of the parking lot by the "Hazardous Waves" sign and a footpath at 0.4 miles. Walk towards the point and the first summit. Views open up to the numerous rock formations and crevices. Vistas of Rocky Creek Bridge and the jagged coastline continue to the south. Skirt around the right side of the summit to a trail split. Detour on the left fork to a point overlooking rock caves and crashing whitewater. Return to the junction and descend on the right fork down a grassy saddle to an overlook of the jagged rock fingers, water inlets, and a natural arch. Ascend to the west, climbing out of the saddle to the perch on the summit of Rocky Point. ▣

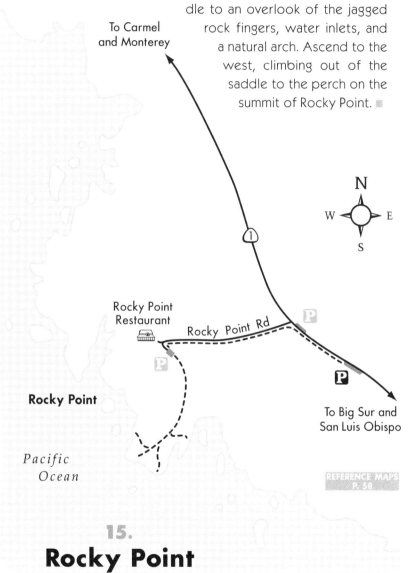

To Carmel
and Monterey

N

W ◈ E

S

Rocky Point
Restaurant

Rocky Point Rd

P

P

Rocky Point

P

To Big Sur and
San Luis Obispo

*Pacific
Ocean*

REFERENCE MAPS
P. 58

15.
Rocky Point

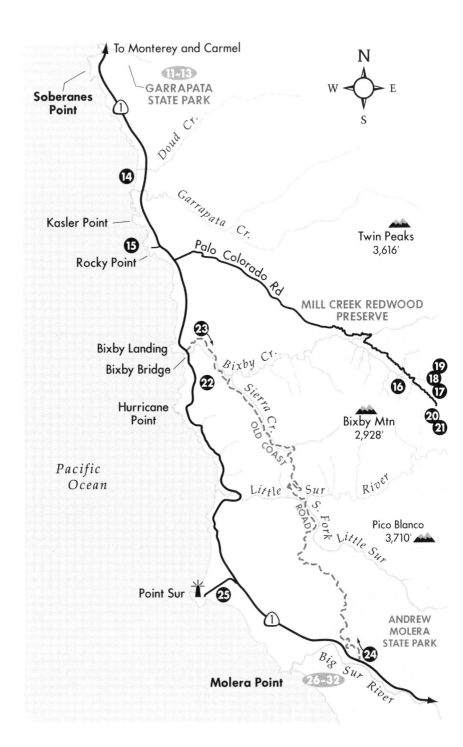

To Monterey and Carmel

Soberanes Point

1

11-13
GARRAPATA STATE PARK

Doud Cr.

14

Kasler Point

15

Rocky Point

Palo Colorado Rd

Garrapata Cr.

N
W   E
S

Twin Peaks
3,616'

MILL CREEK REDWOOD PRESERVE

23

Bixby Landing

Bixby Bridge

22

Hurricane Point

Bixby Cr.

Sierra Cr.

OLD COAST

16

19
18
17

20
21

Bixby Mtn
2,928'

Pacific Ocean

Little Sur River

S. Fork Little Sur

ROAD

Pico Blanco
3,710'

Point Sur

25

1

Molera Point

Big Sur River

26-32

ANDREW MOLERA STATE PARK

24

Soberanes Point to Molera Point

PALO COLORADO ROAD
OLD COAST ROAD

Carmel River

Los Padres Reservoir 62 61

▲▲
Mt Carmel
4,430'

Danish Cr.

VENTANA
WILDERNESS

▲▲
Uncle Sam Mtn
4,781'

Little Sur River

REFERENCE MAPS
P. 16

3 MILES

5 KILOMETERS

SANTA LUCIA RANGE

▲▲
Ventana Double Cone
4,833'

▲▲
Ventana Cone
4,734'

To San Luis
Obispo

Mount Manuel
▲▲ 3,379'

16. Mill Creek Redwood Preserve

A free access permit is required to hike the trail
www.mprpd.org · (831) 659-4488 then select option 5

Hiking distance: 5.5 miles round trip
Hiking time: 3 hours
Configuration: out-and-back
Elevation gain: 230 feet
Difficulty: easy to slightly moderate
Exposure: shaded forest
Dogs: allowed
Maps: U.S.G.S. Big Sur · Mill Creek Redwood Preserve Trail map

The Mill Creek Redwood Preserve encompasses 1,534 acres in a richly atmospheric forest along the upper reaches of Palo Colorado Road, just shy of Bottchers Gap. The preserve sits in the shade of dense second-growth redwoods, sycamores, tanbark oaks, and maples on the northern slope of Bixby Mountain. Mill Creek flows through the forest and down the canyon, where it joins with Bixby Creek.

The area has a rich and storied logging history that dates from the 1800s through the 1980s. Homesteader Charles Bixby ran a timber logging business and sawmill along Mill Creek in the late 1800s. The area was later used for mining limestone. Remnants of the old logging operation and logging road are still evident. Holes in the trunks of redwoods, where planks were inserted for loggers to stand on while cutting the trees, can be spotted. The regional park was purchased in 1989 through the combined efforts of the Big Sur Land Trust and the Regional Park District.

A near-level trail through the length of the preserve was completed in 2007. The trail took eight years to build and was constructed by hand. The beautifully terraced path winds through the canyon, following the curvature of the steep mountain slope. The trail ends on a panoramic coastal overlook atop a 1,986-foot exposed knoll, where there are views into the surrounding canyons and the ocean. En route, the serpentine footpath crosses several bridges and passes a waterfall, rock formations, and tree

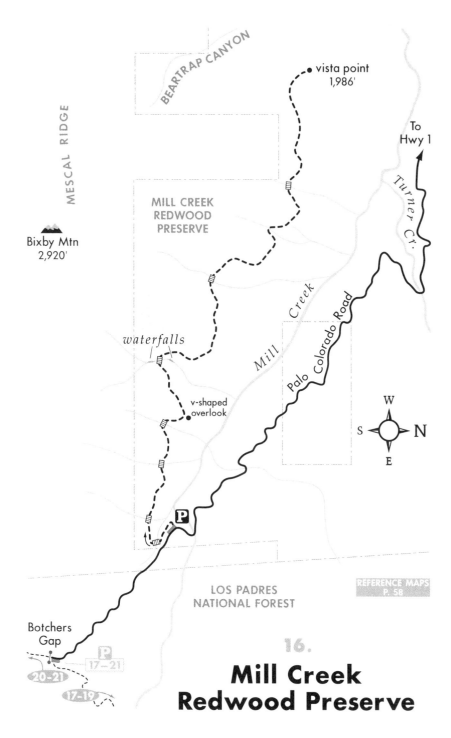

BEARTRAP CANYON

MESCAL RIDGE

Bixby Mtn
2,920'

MILL CREEK
REDWOOD
PRESERVE

waterfalls

v-shaped
overlook

vista point
1,986'

To
Hwy 1

Turner Cr.

Mill Creek

Palo Colorado Road

W
S ✦ N
E

P

LOS PADRES
NATIONAL FOREST

REFERENCE MAPS
P. 58

Botchers
Gap

P
17–21

20–21

17–19

16.

Mill Creek
Redwood Preserve

trunks blanketed in lichen. The path then ends with a wide open vista of the rugged Big Sur coastline and deep mountain canyons of the Santa Lucia Range.

Access is by a free permit, due to limited parking.

To the trailhead

CARMEL. From Highway 1 and Rio Road in Carmel, drive 11.1 miles south on Highway 1 to Palo Colorado Canyon Road, located 0.4 miles south of Rocky Point. Turn inland and drive 6.8 miles up the narrow, winding mountain road to the pullout on the right by the signed trailhead. The pullout is located 0.1 miles after crossing the bridge over Mill Creek.

BIG SUR RANGER STATION. From the ranger station, drive 15.1 miles north on Highway 1 to Palo Colorado Road.

The hike

Walk down the slope into the dense, shaded forest among tan-bark oaks and redwoods. The old logging road can be spotted on the right by the massive redwoods. Cross a bridge over a seasonal tributary of Mill Creek. Traverse the hillside on the north-facing slope of Mill Creek Canyon. Cross a series of three more bridges over feeder streams among madrones and maples to a V-shaped view of the ocean. Cross a bridge over a stream by a small waterfall and pools. One hundred yards ahead is a view of a 50-foot waterfall below the trail. Continue westbound, passing limestone formations at a mostly level grade with a few minor dips and rises. Weave in and out of a redwood-filled drainage with a lush understory of ferns, crossing another footbridge. The trail breaks out of the trees and follows an open ridge, with Palo Colorado Canyon on the right and Beartrap Canyon (a box canyon) on the left. The trail ends on an overlook knoll with four benches at the end of the trail. From the 1,986-foot vista point are spectacular coastal panoramas and views into the surrounding canyons. ▨

17. Skinner Ridge Trail to Skinner Ridge Overlook

Hiking distance: 4.5 miles round trip
Hiking time: 2.5 hours
Configuration: out-and-back
Elevation gain: 1,400 feet
Difficulty: moderate to somewhat strenuous
Exposure: shaded forest and open meadows
Dogs: allowed
Maps: U.S.G.S. Big Sur and Mt. Carmel · Ventana Wilderness Map

**map
page 65**

Skinner Ridge Trail begins from Bottchers Gap at the end of Palo Colorado Road, 2,000 feet above sea level. The trail follows the upper reaches of Mill Creek through the shade of oaks and madrones, reaching the crest of Skinner Ridge at the Ventana Wilderness boundary. From the 3,400-foot ridge are spectacular vistas southwest of the Little Sur watershed, Pico Blanco's white marble cone, the folded layers and ridges of the coast range, and the Pacific Ocean. The trail continues strenuously up to Devil's Peak and Mount Carmel (Hike 18).

To the trailhead

CARMEL. From Highway 1 and Rio Road in Carmel, drive 11.1 miles south on Highway 1 to the signed Palo Colorado Road, located 0.4 miles south of Rocky Point. Turn inland and drive 7.6 miles up the winding mountain road to the Bottchers Gap parking lot at the end of the paved road. A parking fee is required.

BIG SUR RANGER STATION. From the ranger station, drive 15.1 miles north on Highway 1 to Palo Colorado Road.

The hike

From the upper end of the parking lot, take the posted Skinner Ridge Trail into the forest, skirting the campground sites on the left. Pass through oak groves and chaparral. The northwest views extend into the Mill Creek drainage and across several ridges to the ocean. For a short distance, the trail parallels Mill Creek, then drops down to the creek. Ascend the hillside and wind through the woods, crossing a stream in a fern-lined gully. Cross two additional tributary streams, reaching Skinner Ridge on a sloping meadow at 2.2 miles. Curve left and head north up the grassy meadow to a knoll and a magnificent overlook. After savoring the views, return along the same trail.

To hike up to Mount Carmel, continue with the next hike. ▪

18. Skinner Ridge Trail to Mount Carmel

Hiking distance: 9.6 miles round trip
Hiking time: 5 hours
Configuration: out-and-back
Elevation gain: 2,500 feet
Difficulty: very strenuous
Exposure: shaded forest and open ridge
Dogs: allowed
Maps: U.S.G.S. Big Sur and Mt. Carmel · Ventana Wilderness Map

**map
page 67**

Mount Carmel, at 4,417 feet, is the highest peak in the northwest reaches of the Ventana Wilderness. From the summit are endless vistas across the rugged mountainous interior to the Pacific Ocean, including prominent Pico Blanco, Ventana Double Cone, the Little Sur watershed, and Monterey Bay. This is a strenuous trail that climbs up to Skinner Ridge, skirts the twin summits of Devil's Peak, and continues the ascent up to Mount Carmel.

To the trailhead

CARMEL. From Highway 1 and Rio Road in Carmel, drive 11.1 miles south on Highway 1 to the signed Palo Colorado Road, located 0.4 miles south of Rocky Point. Turn inland and drive 7.6 miles up the winding mountain road to the Bottchers Gap parking lot at the end of the paved road. A parking fee is required.

BIG SUR RANGER STATION. From the ranger station, drive 15.1 miles north on Highway 1 to Palo Colorado Road.

Mount Carmel
4,417'

Turner Creek
Camp

TURNER CREEK TR

To Palo Colorado
Road and Long Ridge

Turner Creek

To Mount Carmel

VENTANA
WILDERNESS

waterfall

Apple Tree
Camp

19

18

N
W E
S

SKINNER

Skinner Ridge
Overlook

RIDGE

SKINNER RIDGE TRAIL

Mill Creek

To Hwy 1

Palo Colorado Road

LOS PADRES
NATIONAL FOREST

REFERENCE MAPS
P. 58

P
17–21

Bottchers
Gap

PICO BLANCO RD

20-21

17.

Skinner Ridge Trail
to Skinner Ridge
Overlook

To Little
Sur River

The hike

From the upper end of the parking lot, take the posted Skinner Ridge Trail into the forest, skirting the campground sites on the left. Pass through oak groves and chaparral. The northwest views extend into the Mill Creek drainage and across several ridges to the ocean. For a short distance, the trail parallels Mill Creek, then drops down to the creek. Ascend the hillside and wind through the woods, crossing a stream in a fern-lined gully. Cross two additional tributary streams, reaching Skinner Ridge on a sloping meadow at 2.2 miles. Curve left and head north up the grassy meadow to a knoll and the magnificent Skinner Ridge Overlook.

After enjoying the views and a rest, walk along the ridge past oaks and madrones for 0.2 miles. Leave the ridge and descend along the path to a saddle and posted junction with the Turner Creek Trail on the left—Hike 19. (The trail leads to Turner Creek Camp and eventually back to Palo Colorado Road.) Continue straight ahead and ascend the hillside through thick brush and spectacular vistas. Over the next mile, steadily climb up the steeper grade. Pass through oak, manzanita, and madrone groves to a sandy ridge near Devil's Peak. Follow the ridge to the left, viewing Mount Carmel to the north and Pico Blanco to the south. Curve around the right side of the second summit of Devil's Peak to a trail split. The right fork (straight ahead) leads to Comings Camp and Big Pines. Curve left 30 yards to a second fork. Curve to the left again and descend to a grassy saddle. Cross the saddle and follow the ridge through oak groves and dense oak scrub that crowd the trail. The path ends at the summit of Mount Carmel, crowned by a 10-foot granite rock outcropping and an old climbing pole. A survey pin in the rock marks the summit. Make one last climb up the rock for a 360-degree panorama. After enjoying the views, return along the same trail. ▨

N
W E
S

Mount Carmel
4,417'

Turner Creek
Camp

TURNER CREEK TR

Turner Creek

To Palo Colorado
Road and Long Ridge

Devil's Peak
4,158'

To Comings
Camp and
Big Pines

VENTANA
WILDERNESS

waterfall

Apple Tree
Camp

19

SKINNER

Skinner Ridge
Overlook
(end Hike 17)

SKINNER RIDGE TRAIL

RIDGE

Mill Creek

To Hwy 1

Palo Colorado Road

P
17–21

Bottchers
Gap

LOS PADRES
NATIONAL FOREST

REFERENCE MAPS
P. 58

PICO BLANCO RD

20–21

To Little
Sur River

18.

Skinner Ridge Trail to Mount Carmel

19. Skinner Ridge Trail and Turner Creek Trail

APPLE TREE CAMP • TURNER CREEK CAMP

Hiking distance: 8.3 miles round trip
Hiking time: 4 hours
Configuration: out and back
Elevation gain: 1,450 feet
Difficulty: moderate to strenuous
Exposure: shaded forest and open ridge
Dogs: allowed
Maps: U.S.G.S. Big Sur and Mount Carmel
Big Sur and Ventana Wilderness map

This hike from the end of Palo Colorado Road leads to two gorgeous creekside campsites—Apple Tree Camp and Turner Creek Camp. The hike begins at Bottchers Gap, 2,000 feet above sea level, then vigorously climbs over the crest of Skinner Ridge. From the ridge, the trail drops down a forested draw to the headwaters of Turner Creek. The path follows the creek downstream under a cool, shady canopy of trees, passing a small waterfall at Apple Tree Camp.

To the trailhead

CARMEL. From Highway 1 and Rio Road in Carmel, drive 11.1 miles south on Highway 1 to the signed Palo Colorado Road, located 0.4 miles south of Rocky Point. Turn inland and drive 7.6 miles up the winding mountain road to the Bottchers Gap parking lot at the end of the paved road. A parking fee is required.

BIG SUR RANGER STATION. From the ranger station, drive 15.1 miles north on Highway 1 to Palo Colorado Road.

The hike

From the upper end of the parking lot, take the posted Skinner Ridge Trail into the forest, skirting the campground sites on the left. Pass through oak groves and chaparral. The northwest views extend into the Mill Creek drainage and across several ridges to the ocean. For a short distance, the trail parallels Mill Creek, then drops down to the creek. Ascend the hillside and wind through

Turner Creek Camp

Mount Carmel
4,417'

To Palo Colorado
Road and Long Ridge

Turner Creek

TURNER CREEK TRAIL

To Mount Carmel

VENTANA
WILDERNESS

waterfall

Apple Tree
Camp

18

N
W E
S

SKINNER

Skinner Ridge Overlook
(end Hike 17)

RIDGE

Mill Creek

SKINNER RIDGE TRAIL

To Hwy 1

Palo Colorado Road

LOS PADRES
NATIONAL FOREST

P
17–21

Bottchers
Gap

REFERENCE MAPS
P. 58

PICO BLANCO RD

20–21

19.

Skinner Ridge Trail
Turner Creek Trail
APPLE TREE CAMP
TURNER CREEK CAMP

To Little
Sur River

the woods, crossing a stream in a fern-lined gully. Cross two additional tributary streams, reaching Skinner Ridge on a sloping meadow at 2.2 miles. Curve left and head north up the grassy meadow to a knoll and the magnificent Skinner Ridge Overlook.

After enjoying the views and a rest, walk along the ridge past oaks and madrones for 0.2 miles. Leave the ridge and descend along the path to a saddle and posted junction with the Turner Creek Trail on the left. The main trail continues to Mount Carmel (Hike 18).

Bear left and drop down into the draw under the shady canopy of madrones, reaching the headwaters of Turner Creek at a quarter mile. Follow the creek down to its confluence with a tributary stream at Apple Tree Camp. The upper camp is on the right, before crossing the stream. Follow a side path to the right—30 yards upstream—to the base of a 25-foot waterfall. Return to the main trail. Cross the stream and bear left to the lower camp on the banks of Turner Creek under towering bay trees. Turn around here for a 6.5-mile round-trip hike.

To continue hiking to Turner Creek Camp, the trail crosses the creek below Apple Tree Camp and heads 0.9 miles downhill. The large camp has mature alder trees and a grassy meadow. Turner Creek Trail continues west along Long Ridge to Palo Colorado Road. To return back to the Bottchers Gap trailhead, retrace your footsteps over Skinner Ridge. ▨

20. Little Sur River Camp from Pico Blanco Road

Hiking distance: 5.6 miles round trip
Hiking time: 3 hours
Configuration: out and back
Elevation gain: 1,200 feet
Difficulty: moderate to somewhat strenuous
Exposure: mostly shaded forest
Dogs: allowed
Maps: U.S.G.S. Big Sur · Big Sur and Ventana Wilderness map

**map
page 72**

Little Sur River Camp sits on a scenic riverside flat amidst tanbark oak trees and towering redwoods under the shadow of Pico Blanco. The hike begins from the end of Palo Colorado Road on a mountain saddle at Bottchers Gap. The route follows a vehicle-restricted road as it winds down the canyon into the Little Sur watershed. En route are magnificent views of Pico Blanco's north face. A series of campsites with fire pits and benches stretch along the cascading river.

To the trailhead

CARMEL. From Highway 1 and Rio Road in Carmel, drive 11.1 miles south on Highway 1 to the signed Palo Colorado Road, located 0.4 miles south of Rocky Point. Turn inland and drive 7.6 miles up the winding mountain road to the Bottchers Gap parking lot at the end of the paved road. A parking fee is required.

BIG SUR RANGER STATION. From the ranger station, drive 15.1 miles north on Highway 1 to Palo Colorado Road.

The hike

Take the posted Pico Blanco Road at the lower end of the parking lot. Walk around the locked vehicle gate, and descend on the unpaved road. At the first left horseshoe bend is a great close-up view of Pico Blanco and Dani Ridge, which extends to the Pacific Ocean. Continue winding downhill to the second left horseshoe bend and posted junction at 1.8 miles. The road continues downhill to the Pico Blanco Boy Scout Camp (Hike 21).

Leave the road and take the Little Sur River Camp Trail to the right. The narrow footpath winds down the hillside past mossy tree trunks under the shade of oaks and fir. The trail gradually descends one mile by way of eight switchbacks, ending at the streamside and Little Sur River Camp. Campsites line the creekside, while the sylvan river tumbles over boulders under a canopy of redwoods. After strolling up and down the riverbank, return along the same route. ▨

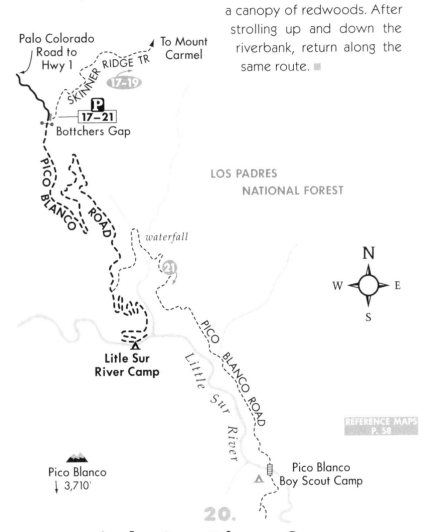

Little Sur River Camp
from PICO BLANCO ROAD

21. Pico Blanco Road
Bottchers Gap to Little Sur River

Hiking distance: 7.2 miles round trip
Hiking time: 3.5 hours
Configuration: out-and-back
Elevation gain: 1,200 feet
Difficulty: moderate to strenuous
Exposure: mostly shaded forest
Dogs: allowed
Maps: U.S.G.S. Big Sur · Ventana Wilderness Map

map
page 75

Pico Blanco Road is an unpaved, vehicle-restricted road that winds through the mountains under the shadow of Pico Blanco. The road parallels and descends to the Little Sur River. En route are magnificent views of Pico Blanco's north face. The road is on private land with a right-of-way for hikers.

The hike begins on a mountain saddle at Bottchers Gap at an elevation of 2,050 feet. The road/trail descends 1,100 feet to a bridge crossing the river at Pico Blanco Boy Scout Camp. The camp was donated to the boy scouts by William Randolph Hearst in 1948. Redwoods planted between 1910 and 1921 surround the camp.

An optional two-mile side trip leads from the road to the picturesque Little Sur River Camp about half way into the hike—Hike 20.

To the trailhead

CARMEL. From Highway 1 and Rio Road in Carmel, drive 11.1 miles south on Highway 1 to the signed Palo Colorado Road, located 0.4 miles south of Rocky Point. Turn inland and drive 7.6 miles up the winding mountain road to the Bottchers Gap parking lot at the end of the paved road. A parking fee is required.

BIG SUR RANGER STATION. From the ranger station, drive 15.1 miles north on Highway 1 to Palo Colorado Road.

The hike

From the lower end of the parking lot, pass the locked gate and head down the unpaved Pico Blanco Road. Descend down the winding mountain road past several magnificent close-up views of Pico Blanco, Dani Ridge, and the Pacific Ocean. At 1.8 miles, on a left horseshoe bend, is the posted junction with the Little Sur River Camp Trail on the right. For a side trip to the camp, the narrow footpath descends one mile down eight switchbacks to the camp at the river, sitting amidst tanbark oak trees and towering redwoods (Hike 20).

On the main road, continue downhill through a redwood forest. Pass a tributary stream with a 15-foot waterfall dropping off a vertical rock ledge. After the stream, the road enters the boy scout property. Stay on the road and continue parallel to the creek, passing a couple of cabins. Pass another group of cabins by the main lodge. At the river, cross the long wooden footbridge, and follow the trail signs to the posted Pico Blanco Trail at the camp crossroads. The Pico Blanco Trail leads up the hill to a trail fork with the Little Sur River Trail. This is the turn-around spot.

To extend the hike, the left fork leads 0.7 miles to Jackson Camp on the south bank of the Little Sur River, where the trail ends. The right fork climbs Pico Blanco and connects with the Mount Manuel Trail from Pfeiffer Big Sur State Park (Hike 39). ▦

Palo Colorado
Road to
Hwy 1

To Mount Carmel

SKINNER RIDGE TR
17-19

P
17-21
Bottchers Gap

LOS PADRES
NATIONAL FOREST

waterfall

20

PICO BLANCO ROAD

Litle Sur
River Camp

Little Sur River

N
W E
S

REFERENCE MAPS
P. 58

Pico Blanco
Boy Scout Camp

Jackson
Camp

PICO BLANCO TR

LITTLE SUR

RIVER TRAIL

DANI RIDGE

To Pico Blanco
and Mount
Manuel

Pico Blanco
3,710'

21.

Pico Blanco Road
BOTTCHERS GAP to LITTLE SUR RIVER

22. Brazil Ranch

Hiking distance: 4.2 miles round trip
Hiking time: 2.5 hours
Configuration: out-and-back
Elevation gain: 1,100 feet
Difficulty: moderate
Exposure: exposed hillside and ridge
Dogs: allowed
Maps: U.S.G.S. Point Sur
Big Sur and Ventana Wilderness map · Brazil Ranch map

Brazil Ranch stretches across 1,255 oceanfront acres along the Big Sur coast. The rocky shoreline includes the dramatic scalloped promontory of Hurricane Point. The old ranchland encompasses Sierra Hill, the 1,545-foot mountain that spans between Bixby Bridge to the north and the Little Sur River on the south. Tony and Margaret Brazil operated the ranch for nearly a century. In 1977 it was purchased by Allen Funt, creator of the television show *Candid Camera*. Funt developed the land and raised quarter horses and cattle. The U.S. Forest Service acquired the ranch in 2002.

This hike follows an old ranch road straight up the ridge of Sierra Hill to a series of flats with spectacular coastal and mountain vistas. The path follows the rolling grassy ridge to the summit.

To the trailhead

CARMEL. From Highway 1 and Rio Road in Carmel, drive 14.9 miles south on Highway 1 to the long, narrow pullout on the right, directly across the road from the gated, paved ranch road. The pullout is located 2.7 miles south of Palo Colorado Canyon Road and a half mile south of Bixby Bridge.

BIG SUR RANGER STATION. From the ranger station, drive 13 miles north on Highway 1 to the pullout on the left.

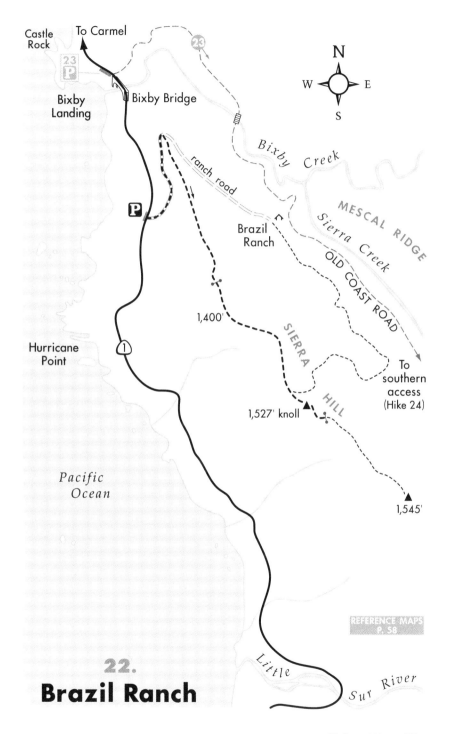

Castle
Rock

To Carmel

23
P

Bixby
Landing

Bixby Bridge

23

Bixby Creek

N

W ⊕ E

S

Sierra Creek

MESCAL RIDGE

P

ranch road

Brazil
Ranch

OLD COAST ROAD

1,400'

SIERRA

HILL

To
southern
access
(Hike 24)

Hurricane
Point

1

1,527' knoll

*Pacific
Ocean*

▲
1,545'

REFERENCE MAPS
P. 58

22.
Brazil Ranch

Little

Sur River

The hike

Pass through the trail gate and head up the old paved ranch road. Traverse the oceanfront slope overlooking Hurricane Point. At 0.45 miles is a U-shaped right bend. Round the bend into the interior mountains above Sierra Creek Canyon, with a view of the Brazil Ranch, Mescal Ridge, and the Old Coast Road. At the far end of the bend is a signed trail.

Bear right and take the grassy footpath up the spine of Sierra Hill. Steadily climb the ridge, with a few steep sections and past several false summits. With every step, the far-reaching coastal and mountain vistas expand. Pass through a trail gate, and climb to a 1,400-foot grassy flat. The coastal views include the mouth of the Little Sur River, the Point Sur Lighthouse, Hurricane Point, and mountain views into Sierra Creek Canyon and the surrounding ridges. Walk to a posted fork and take the designated trail to the right. Gently climb and cross over the rounded grassy knoll at 1,527 feet. Follow the rolling ridge to a gated fence at the end of the public access. Beyond the fence, the grassy road continues a half mile to the 1,545-foot summit of Sierra Hill. Return along the same route. ▨

23. Old Coast Road
NORTHERN ACCESS

Hiking distance: 11.5 miles round trip (or 10.2-mile shuttle)
Hiking time: 5.5 hours
Configuration: out-and-back; optional shuttle with Hike 24
Elevation gain: 2,000 feet
Difficulty: strenuous
Exposure: shaded forest and open grassland
Dogs: allowed
Maps: U.S.G.S. Point Sur and Big Sur
       Big Sur and Ventana Wilderness map

**map
page 82**

The Old Coast Road was the original coastal route connecting Carmel with Big Sur before the Bixby Bridge was completed in 1932. The hike begins at the frequently photographed Bixby Bridge—at the north end of the Old Coast Road—and follows the twisting, unpaved back road through a shaded canyon dense with coastal redwoods and lush ferns. The trail parallels vBixby Creek and Sierra Creek and crosses two bridges over the Little Sur River. The road is open to the public but is bordered by private property. The hike may be combined with Hike 24 for a one-way, 10.2-mile shuttle hike with the road's southern access.

To the trailhead

CARMEL. From Highway 1 and Rio Road in Carmel, drive 12.7 miles south on Highway 1 to the Bixby Bridge. The parking pullout is at the north end of the bridge on the ocean side of the highway.

BIG SUR RANGER STATION. From the ranger station, drive 13.5 miles north on Highway 1 to the parking pullouts on the left, just after crossing Bixby Bridge.

The hike

From the north end of Bixby Bridge, take the signed Coast Road inland along the north side of Bixby Creek. At 0.3 miles, as the road curves right, is a great view down canyon of Bixby Bridge and the offshore rocks. Curve south and descend to the canyon floor. Cross a bridge over Bixby Creek. Gently ascend the lower reaches of Sierra Hill along the west wall of the canyon, passing homes tucked into the trees and numerous cliffside tributary streams. As the old road wends south through a lush redwood forest, Bixby Creek curves away to the east. The road continues parallel to Sierra Creek, a tributary of Bixby Creek. The road crosses the creek five consecutive times. At the sixth crossing, leave Sierra Creek on a hairpin right bend. Climb out of the shaded canyon to open rolling hillsides on the summit of the Sierra Grade. Descend 1,000 feet along the contours of the mountains on the chaparral slopes of the Sierra Grade. Pico Blanco, rising 3,710 feet, dominates the views to the southeast. At the bottom of the grade, walk through a stand of bishop pines to the Little Sur River. Two consecutive metal bridges cross the South Fork and Main Fork of the Little Sur River, just above their confluence.

Return along the same trail, or continue southward with the next hike for a one-way shuttle hike. ▪

24. Old Coast Road
SOUTHERN ACCESS

Hiking distance: 9 miles round trip (or 10.2-mile shuttle)
Hiking time: 4.5 hours
Configuration: out-and-back; optional shuttle with Hike 23
Elevation gain: 1,650 feet
Difficulty: strenuous
Exposure: shaded forest and open grassland
Dogs: allowed
Maps: U.S.G.S. Big Sur
      Big Sur and Ventana Wilderness map

map
page 83

The Old Coast Road was the primary route of travel along this mountainous coastal stretch prior to 1932, when the 260-foot-high Bixby Bridge was opened. This hike begins at the Big Sur Valley in Andrew Molera State Park near the mouth of the Big Sur River—at the south end of the Old Coast Highway. The winding, breathtaking route curves along hillsides, offering panoramic vistas of the coastline and interior mountains. The road slowly descends into a shaded canyon to the Little Sur River, rich with lush ferns and coastal redwoods. The road is open to the public, but the adjacent land is privately owned. The hike may be combined with Hike 23 for a one-way, 10.2-mile shuttle hike with the road's northern access.

To the trailhead

CARMEL. From Highway 1 and Rio Road in Carmel, drive 21.4 miles south on Highway 1 to the signed Andrew Molera State Park entrance. Turn right and drive down to the entrance kiosk and parking lot. A parking fee is required.

BIG SUR RANGER STATION. From the ranger station, drive 4.8 miles north on Highway 1 to the Andrew Molera State Park entrance and turn left.

The hike

Walk back up to Highway 1, and cross the highway to the signed Coast Road. Head up the winding, unpaved road on a northern course to steadily improving coastal views. At 1.5 miles, weave through groves of oaks, sycamores, and redwoods, reaching a 942-foot summit. Views extend to the coastal marine terrace, Andrew Molera State Park, inland to the South Fork Canyon, and across Dani Ridge to the towering 3,710-foot Pico Blanco in the east. Slowly descend, passing a ranch on the left, and enter a lush redwood forest. Skirt around the west edge of Dani Ridge. Parallel the South Fork Little Sur River down the narrow, shaded canyon through oaks, maples, pines, redwoods, and an understory of ferns. At the canyon floor, two consecutive metal bridges cross the South Fork and Main Fork of the Little Sur River just above their confluence.

Return along the same trail or continue northward with Hike 23 for a one-way shuttle hike. ▪

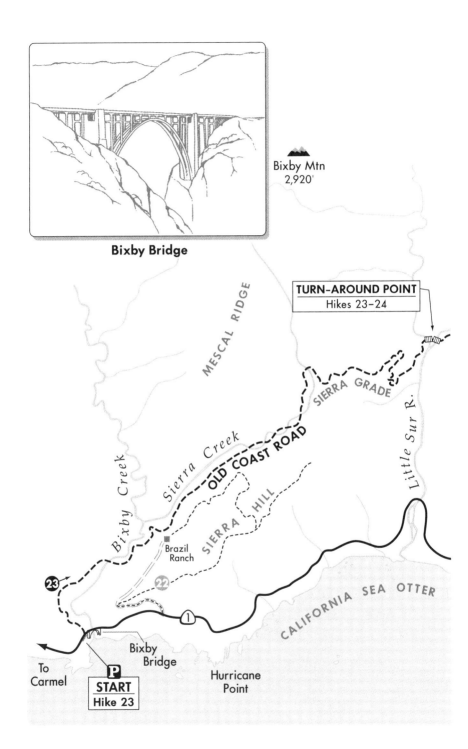

Bixby Mtn
2,920'

Bixby Bridge

TURN-AROUND POINT
Hikes 23-24

MESCAL RIDGE

SIERRA GRADE

Sierra Creek

OLD COAST ROAD

Little Sur R.

Bixby Creek

SIERRA HILL

Brazil
Ranch

23

22

CALIFORNIA SEA OTTER

1

Bixby
Bridge

To
Carmel

P
START
Hike 23

Hurricane
Point

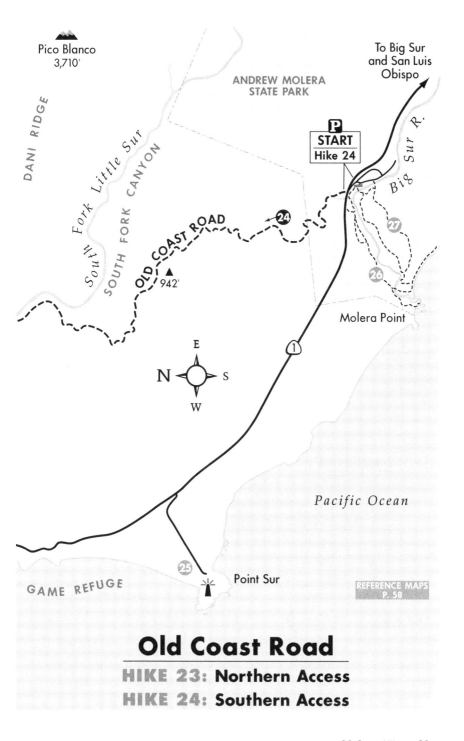

Old Coast Road

HIKE 23: Northern Access
HIKE 24: Southern Access

25. Point Sur Lightstation State Historic Park

Docent led hike: call for scheduled tour times (831) 625-4419

Hiking distance: 1 mile round trip
Hiking time: 3 hours (docent-led hike)
Configuration: out-and-back with small loop
Elevation gain: 360 feet
Difficulty: easy
Exposure: exposed headland
Dogs: not allowed
Maps: U.S.G.S. Point Sur · Big Sur and Ventana Wilderness map

Point Sur is a 361-foot offshore metamorphic rock that is connected to the mainland by a sand bar called a tombolo. The El Sur Ranch owns the surrounding land except for the 34-acre volcanic rock. The Point Sur Lightstation atop the basaltic rock was built in 1889. This docent-led hike follows an old horse and buggy route used in the 1800s. The trail overlooks massive offshore rocks and crashing surf. The tour climbs the spiral staircase to the lamp tower at the top of the 38-foot stone lightstation, where there are magnificent views of the ocean and mountains from 270 feet above the water. Atop the point are intact sandstone buildings, restored historic barns, and a visitor center.

To the trailhead

CARMEL. From Highway 1 and Rio Road in Carmel, drive 18.6 miles south on Highway 1 to the signed Point Sur Lightstation entrance. Park in the pullout along the right side of the highway. A docent will lead a car caravan into the gated property. The base of Point Sur is 0.7 miles ahead. A tour fee is required.

BIG SUR RANGER STATION. From the ranger station, drive 7.6 miles north on Highway 1 to the Point Sur Lightstation entrance.

The hike

Ascend the hill on the paved lighthouse road, following the tour guide. The road steadily climbs and curves, overlooking the jagged coastline. Dramatic rocks with crashing whitewater are just offshore. Part of the trail follows an old railway route along the steep cliff. At the lightstation, a spiral staircase leads to the lamp and catwalk. A long set of wooden steps heads up to a ridge and an overlook of the light beacon. The old road leads past a blacksmith and carpenter shop, restored barn, two-foot-thick sandstone buildings (once home to lighthouse keepers), and a visitor center at the top of Point Sur. ■

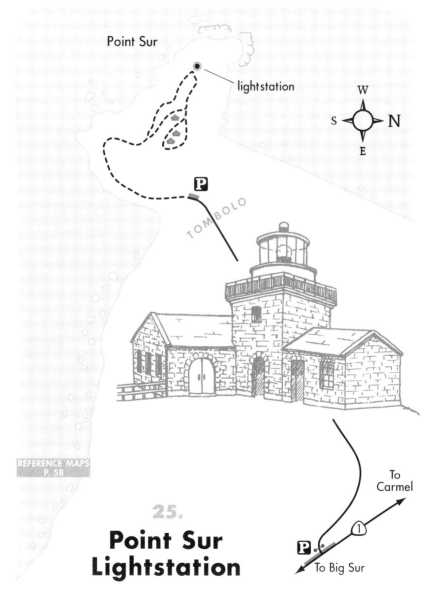

Point Sur

lightstation

W
S — N
E

TOMBOLO

To
Carmel

To Big Sur

REFERENCE MAPS
P. 58

25.

Point Sur
Lightstation

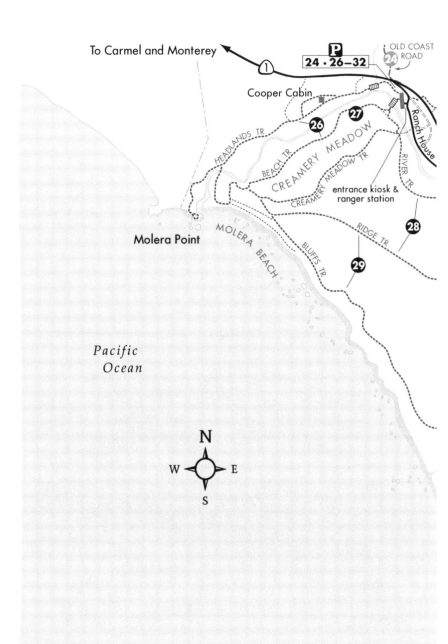

To Carmel and Monterey

1

P
24 · 26–32

OLD COAST ROAD

Cooper Cabin

HEADLANDS TR

BEACH TR

CREAMERY MEADOW

CREAMERY MEADOW TR

Ranch House

RIVER TR

entrance kiosk & ranger station

Molera Point

MOLERA BEACH

BLUFFS TR

RIDGE TR

26

27

28

29

Pacific
Ocean

N
W   E
S

HIKES 26–32
Andrew Molera State Park

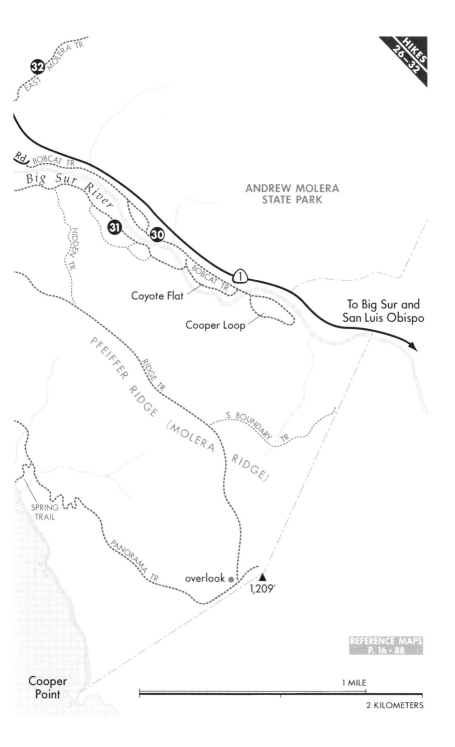

EAST MOLERA TR

32

Rd. BOBCAT TR

Big Sur River

HIDDEN TR

31 **30**

ANDREW MOLERA STATE PARK

1

Coyote Flat

BOBCAT TR

Cooper Loop

To Big Sur and San Luis Obispo

PFEIFFER RIDGE (MOLERA RIDGE)

RIDGE TR

S. BOUNDARY TR

SPRING TRAIL

PANORAMA TR

overlook ●

▲ 1,209'

REFERENCE MAPS P. 16 • 88

Cooper Point

1 MILE

2 KILOMETERS

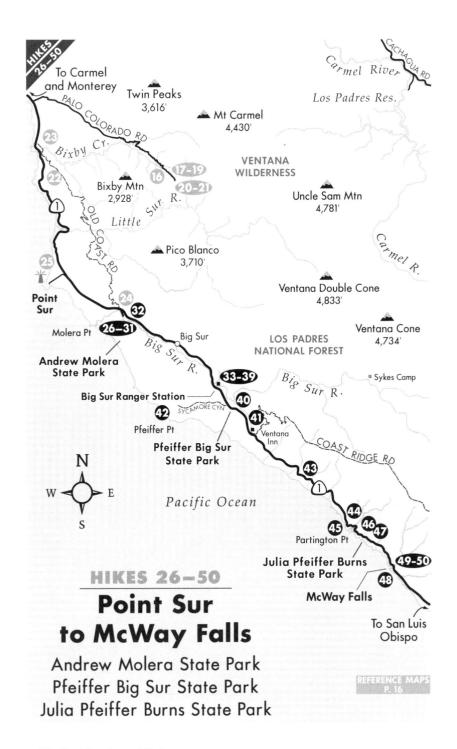

To Carmel
and Monterey

CACHAGUA RD

Carmel River

PALO COLORADO RD

Twin Peaks
3,616'

Mt Carmel
4,430'

Los Padres Res.

Bixby Cr.

VENTANA
WILDERNESS

23

22

17-19

16

20-21

1

Bixby Mtn
2,928'

Little

Sur

R.

OLD COAST RD

Uncle Sam Mtn
4,781'

Carmel R.

Pico Blanco
3,710'

25

Point
Sur

24

Ventana Double Cone
4,833'

32

Molera Pt

26-31

Big Sur R.

Big Sur

LOS PADRES
NATIONAL FOREST

Ventana Cone
4,734'

Sykes Camp

Andrew Molera
State Park

Big Sur R.

33-39

Big Sur Ranger Station

42

40

SYCAMORE CYN

Pfeiffer Pt

41

Ventana
Inn

COAST RIDGE RD

Pfeiffer Big Sur
State Park

N

W   E

S

Pacific Ocean

43

1

44

45

46 47

Partington Pt

49-50

Julia Pfeiffer Burns
State Park

48

McWay Falls

HIKES 26–50

Point Sur
to McWay Falls

To San Luis
Obispo

Andrew Molera State Park
Pfeiffer Big Sur State Park
Julia Pfeiffer Burns State Park

REFERENCE MAPS
P. 16

26. Molera Point and Molera Beach
ANDREW MOLERA STATE PARK

Hiking distance: 2.5 miles round trip
Hiking time: 1.5 hours
Configuration: loop
Elevation gain: 70 feet
Difficulty: easy
Exposure: open marine terrace
Dogs: not allowed
Maps: U.S.G.S. Big Sur · Andrew Molera State Park map
      Big Sur and Ventana Wilderness map

**map
page 91**

Andrew Molera State Park, the largest state park on the Big Sur coast, encompasses 4,800 acres and extends along both sides of Highway 1. The park has mountains, meadows, a 2.5-mile strand of beach, and over 15 miles of hiking trails. The Big Sur River flows through the park to the Pacific Ocean.

This hike parallels the Big Sur River along ocean bluffs to Molera Point and Molera Beach at the coastline. From the ridge are views of this diverse park, its numerous hiking trails, Molera Beach, the Point Sur Lighthouse, and Cooper Point at the south end of the bay. A side trip leads to Cooper Cabin. Built with redwood logs in 1861, the cabin is the oldest surviving ranch structure in Big Sur. The return trail meanders through a grassy meadow lined with sycamores.

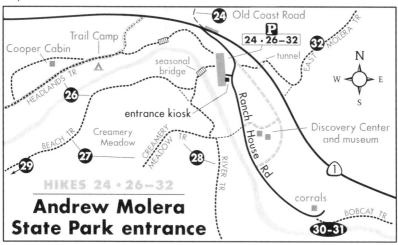

To the trailhead

CARMEL. From Highway 1 and Rio Road in Carmel, drive 21.4 miles south on Highway 1 to the signed Andrew Molera State Park entrance. Turn right and drive down to the entrance kiosk and parking lot on the coast side of the highway. A parking fee is required.

BIG SUR RANGER STATION. From the ranger station, drive 4.8 miles north on Highway 1 to the state park entrance and turn left (towards the coast).

The hike

The signed trail is at the far northwest end of the parking lot. Walk past the Trail Camp sign and up into a shady grove. Cross a footbridge over a tributary stream, and parallel the Big Sur River. At 0.3 miles, the trail merges with an old ranch road. Bear left, entering Trail Camp, and walk through the campground past large oaks and sycamores. Cooper Cabin is to the south in a eucalyptus grove. After viewing the historic cabin, continue southwest on the ranch road, following the river to a signed junction and map at one mile. The left fork leads to a seasonal bridge crossing the Big Sur River to Molera Beach—the return route. First, continue on the right fork on the Headlands Trail, taking the wooden steps up to the ridge. Walk out to sea on the headlands, circling the point.

Return to the seasonal bridge, and head down to Molera Beach at the mouth of the Big Sur River. The beach extends south for two miles, but the tide often makes further access impossible. After exploring the beach, head to the back of the beach to the Beach Trail. Pass the Bluffs Trail and the Creamery Meadow Trail, both on the right. Stay left on the Beach Trail, and follow the river upstream a short distance. Soon the river veers left, and the footpath curves through the grassy meadow dotted with sycamore and cottonwood trees. The trail is separated from the river by dense willow thickets. Meander through Creamery Meadow to a junction with the River Trail and another seasonal bridge over the Big Sur River. Head left over the bridge, back to the parking lot. ▪

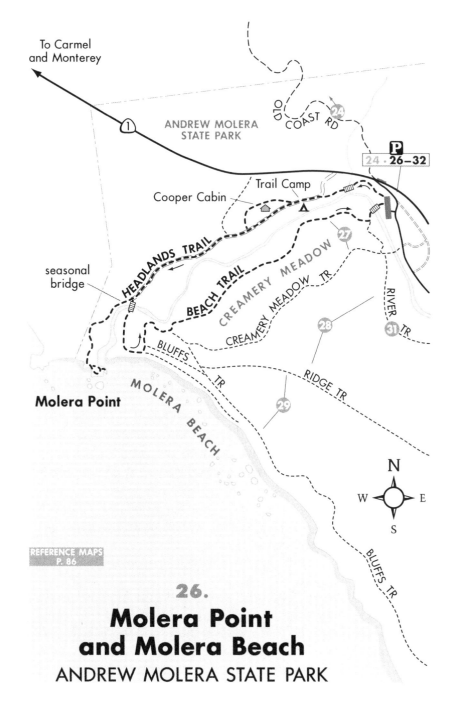

To Carmel
and Monterey

ANDREW MOLERA
STATE PARK

(1)

OLD COAST RD

(24)

P
24 · 26–32

Trail Camp

Cooper Cabin

HEADLANDS TRAIL

seasonal
bridge

BEACH TRAIL

CREAMERY MEADOW

(27)

CREAMERY MEADOW TR

RIVER TR

(28)

(31)

BLUFFS TR

Molera Point

MOLERA BEACH

RIDGE TR

(29)

N
W · E
S

BLUFFS TR

REFERENCE MAPS
P. 86

26.
Molera Point
and Molera Beach
ANDREW MOLERA STATE PARK

27. Creamery Meadow— Molera Beach Loop

ANDREW MOLERA STATE PARK

Hiking distance: 2-mile loop
Hiking time: 1 hour
Configuration: loop
Elevation gain: level
Difficulty: easy
Exposure: mostly open meadows
Dogs: not allowed
Maps: U.S.G.S. Big Sur · Andrew Molera State Park map
        Big Sur and Ventana Wilderness map

This is an easy, level hike to Molera Beach in Andrew Molera State Park. The loop hike meanders through grassy Creamery Meadow, lined with sycamore, willow, alder, and cottonwood trees, to Molera Beach. The coastal beach sits below Molera Point and the rocky headlands, where the Big Sur River empties into the ocean. The beach extends south for two miles, although the tide often makes further access impossible. The return trail runs parallel to the river through riparian vegetation.

To the trailhead

CARMEL. From Highway 1 and Rio Road in Carmel, drive 21.4 miles south on Highway 1 to the signed Andrew Molera State Park entrance. Turn right and drive down to the entrance kiosk and parking lot on the coast side of the highway. A parking fee is required.

BIG SUR RANGER STATION. From the ranger station, drive 4.8 miles north on Highway 1 to the state park entrance and turn left (towards the coast).

The hike

Cross the seasonal footbridge over the Big Sur River (or wade across if removed) to a trail split. The Beach Trail—the return route—bears right. Begin the loop to the left on the River Trail to a second junction 50 yards ahead. Again bear left, staying on the River Trail to a third junction. Take the Creamery Meadow Trail to the right, following the base of the hillside along the edge of the meadow. As the trail nears the coast, pass the Ridge Trail on the left to a junction with the Beach Trail at 0.9 miles. To the right is the return route.

First, bear left on the Beach Trail along the Big Sur River to the back of the sand beach. The Bluffs Trail (Hike 29) heads uphill to

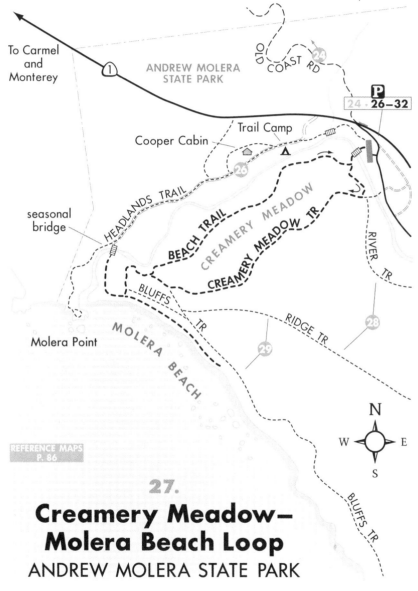

27.
Creamery Meadow– Molera Beach Loop
ANDREW MOLERA STATE PARK

the left. Continue straight to the sandy shoreline. To the north-west, the beach ends at the mouth of the Big Sur River along the base of Molera Point and the Headland Bluffs (Hike 26). After exploring the beach, return to the junction with the Creamery Meadow Trail. Stay left on the Beach Trail and follow the river upstream a short distance. Soon the river veers left, and the footpath curves through the grassy meadow dotted with syca-more and cottonwood trees. The trail is separated from the river by dense willow thickets. Meander through Creamery Meadow, completing the loop near the river. Return to the left. ▣

28. Pfeiffer Ridge (short loop)
Ridge Trail—Hidden Trail—River Trail
ANDREW MOLERA STATE PARK

Hiking distance: 3.6-mile loop
Hiking time: 2 hours
Configuration: loop
Elevation gain: 700 feet
Difficulty: easy to slightly moderate
Exposure: shaded forest and open grassy slopes
Dogs: not allowed
Maps: U.S.G.S. Big Sur · Andrew Molera State Park map
      Big Sur and Ventana Wilderness map

This relatively easy hike loops through the heart of Andrew Molera State Park, from the Big Sur River to a ridge with wonder-ful views of the coastline. The trail climbs 570 feet, winding in and out of shady live oak glens and grassy coyote brush slopes, to Pfeiffer Ridge (Molera Ridge). From the ridge are 360-degree panoramic views of the crenelated coastline, Point Sur, the Big Sur River canyon, Mount Manuel, and Pico Blanco. The path fol-lows the ridge, the backbone of Andrew Molera State Park, then returns back through Creamery Meadow.

To the trailhead

CARMEL. From Highway 1 and Rio Road in Carmel, drive 21.4 miles south on Highway 1 to the signed Andrew Molera State Park

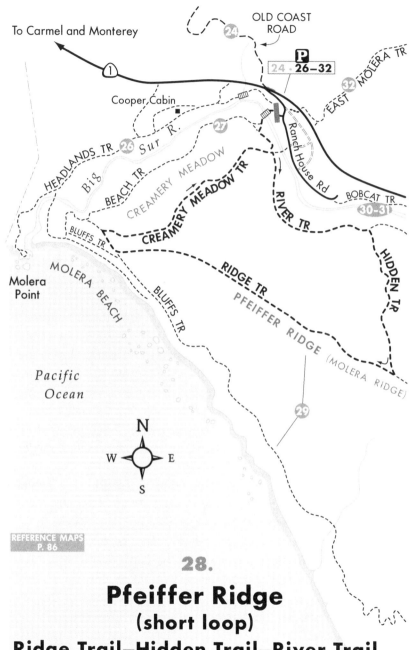

To Carmel and Monterey

OLD COAST ROAD

1

24

P
24 · 26–32

32 EAST MOLERA TR

Cooper Cabin

HEADLANDS TR 26

Big Sur R.

27

BEACH TR

CREAMERY MEADOW

CREAMERY MEADOW TR

Ranch House Rd

RIVER TR

BOBCAT TR
30–31

BLUFFS TR

RIDGE TR

PFEIFFER RIDGE (MOLERA RIDGE)

HIDDEN TR

MOLERA BEACH

BLUFFS TR

Molera Point

Pacific Ocean

29

N
W · E
S

REFERENCE MAPS
P. 86

28.
Pfeiffer Ridge
(short loop)
Ridge Trail–Hidden Trail–River Trail
ANDREW MOLERA STATE PARK

entrance. Turn right and drive down to the entrance kiosk and parking lot on the coast side of the highway. A parking fee is required.

BIG SUR RANGER STATION. From the ranger station, drive 4.8 miles north on Highway 1 to the state park entrance and turn left (towards the coast).

The hike

Take the posted Beach Trail across the Big Sur River to a trail split. (Wade across if the seasonal footbridge has been removed.) Follow the River Trail, bearing left at two consecutive junctions, to the foot of the hill and a trail split. The Creamery Meadow Trail goes to the right (Hike 27). Stay on the River Trail to the left. Curve right around the base of the hillside, following the Big Sur River upstream. Skirt the west edge of the meadow along the foot of the hill. The path gains elevation through an oak canopy to the posted junction on the right.

Take the Hidden Trail to the right and ascend the hill, alternating between oak groves and small open meadows. Cross a two-plank bridge over a small gulch to the open chaparral. Along the Big Sur River below are distinct groves of redwoods that tower above the oaks and pines. Continuing up the trail, wooden steps help curb erosion and aid in stable footing. The 0.7-mile Hidden Trail ends at a posted T-junction with the Ridge Trail. The left fork follows Pfeiffer Ridge to the 1,050-foot summit along a longer loop—Hike 29.

Take the right fork, following the ridge up a short hill to a level flat at 703 feet. There are grand coastal vistas of Molera Point and the Point Sur Lightstation. Descend along the seaward ridge, overlooking the state park, to a 3-way junction on a flat at the ridge bottom. The left fork follows the Bluffs Trail south. Take the right fork, dropping into Creamery Meadow. Bear right along the south edge of the meadow, contouring the base of the hillside and completing the loop back at the River Trail. Retrace your steps to the left. ▦

29. Pfeiffer Ridge—Bluff Loop
(long loop)
Bluffs Trail—Panorama Trail—Ridge Trail
ANDREW MOLERA STATE PARK

Hiking distance: 9-mile loop
Hiking time: 4.5 hours
Configuration: loop
Elevation gain: 1,100 feet
Difficulty: moderate to strenuous
Exposure: open bluffs and meadows, shaded forest
Dogs: not allowed
Maps: U.S.G.S. Big Sur · Andrew Molera State Park map
Big Sur and Ventana Wilderness map

map
page 99

This long loop hike circles the western side of Andrew Molera State Park through a diverse cross-section of landscapes that include coastal bluffs, isolated beach coves, forested stream canyons, redwood forests, overlooks, meadows, and a river crossing. The trail travels across the flat marine terrace for two miles, then climbs up Pfeiffer Ridge at the south park boundary to sweeping views of the coast and mountains. The trail descends along the ridge through oak forests, massive redwood groves, and open grasslands. Throughout the hike are vistas of the Big Sur coastline.

To the trailhead

CARMEL. From Highway 1 and Rio Road in Carmel, drive 21.4 miles south on Highway 1 to the signed Andrew Molera State Park entrance. Turn right and drive down to the entrance kiosk and parking lot on the coast side of the highway. A parking fee is required.

BIG SUR RANGER STATION. From the ranger station, drive 4.8 miles north on Highway 1 to the state park entrance and turn left (towards the coast).

The hike

At the signed Beach Trail near the middle of the parking lot, cross the Big Sur River on the seasonal footbridge (or wade across if removed) to a trail fork. Stay to the left on the River Trail. Bear left again fifty yards ahead, staying on the River Trail to a posted junction at the base of the hillside. The River Trail curves left. Take the Creamery Meadow Trail to the right, and contour along the base of the hill southwest, skirting the edge of the meadow. At 0.8 miles is a junction with the Ridge Trail on the left. Take the Ridge Trail and leave the meadow, heading up the ridge to an open flat and a trail fork a short distance ahead.

Begin the loop to the right on the Bluffs Trail. Cross the wide marine terrace between the jagged coastal cliffs and the inland hills. Pass several side paths that lead to the edge of the cliffs. Curve around a pair of eroding, spring-fed gullies. Dip in and out of another gulch to the end of the Bluffs Trail at a posted trail junction. The Spring Trail bears right and zigzags a short distance down a draw to a small pocket beach.

Continue on the Panorama Trail, dropping into a drainage. Climb out and steadily wind up the hillside to the park's south boundary and views of Pacific Valley and the Big Sur coast. Curve along the fenced boundary to the end of the Panorama Trail on the summit at 4.6 miles. A bench, set among the cypress trees, offers a respite with sweeping coastal views.

Take the posted Ridge Trail north, descending towards the towering redwoods ahead. The spongy, needle-covered path levels out and meanders through a shady grove of massive redwoods and twisted oaks draped with lace lichen. Pass the South Boundary Trail on the right, and follow Pfeiffer (Molera) Ridge across the exposed grass and chaparral. Cross two long, sweeping saddles to a junction with Hidden Trail. Continue down the seaward Ridge Trail, completing the loop at the base of the ridge at the Bluffs Trail. Retrace your steps along the Creamery Meadow Trail back to the parking lot. ■

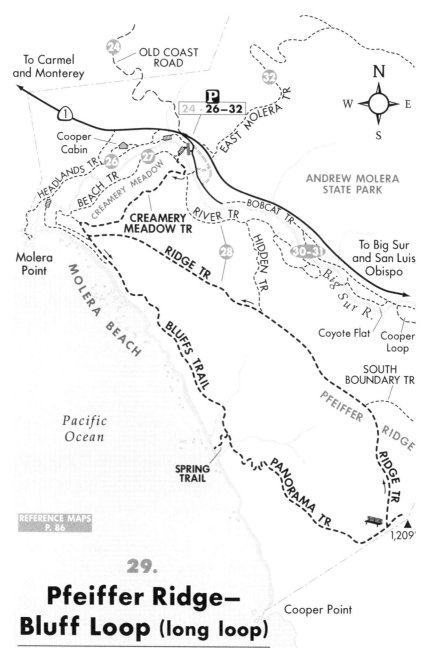

29.
Pfeiffer Ridge–
Bluff Loop (long loop)
Bluffs Trail–Panorama Trail–Ridge Trail
ANDREW MOLERA STATE PARK

30. Bobcat Trail to Coyote Flat
ANDREW MOLERA STATE PARK

Hiking distance: 4.5 miles round trip
Hiking time: 2 hours
Configuration: out-and-back
Elevation gain: level
Difficulty: easy
Exposure: shaded forest and open meadows
Dogs: not allowed
Maps: U.S.G.S. Big Sur · Andrew Molera State Park map
        Big Sur and Ventana Wilderness map

The Big Sur River flows through Andrew Molera State Park and empties into the Pacific at Molera Beach. This near-level hike parallels the east bank of the Big Sur River along the Bobcat Trail, meandering through redwood groves and lush carpets of ferns. The trail crosses small seasonal streams and loops through two meadows.

To the trailhead

CARMEL. From Highway 1 and Rio Road in Carmel, drive 21.4 miles south on Highway 1 to the signed Andrew Molera State Park entrance. Turn right and drive down to the entrance kiosk and parking lot on the coast side of the highway. A parking fee is required.

BIG SUR RANGER STATION. From the ranger station, drive 4.8 miles north on Highway 1 to the state park entrance and turn left (towards the coast).

The hike

Walk back to the entrance of the parking lot. Ten yards past the kiosk, take the unpaved Ranch House road to the right. Follow the road southeast through oak and maple groves, passing a river crossing on the right and barns on the left. At the far (south) end of the corrals, the road ends at the posted Bobcat Trail on the right.

Take the footpath through a shady grove lush with ferns, poison oak and towering redwoods. Weave through the forest between the Big Sur River and Highway 1, passing a trail access from

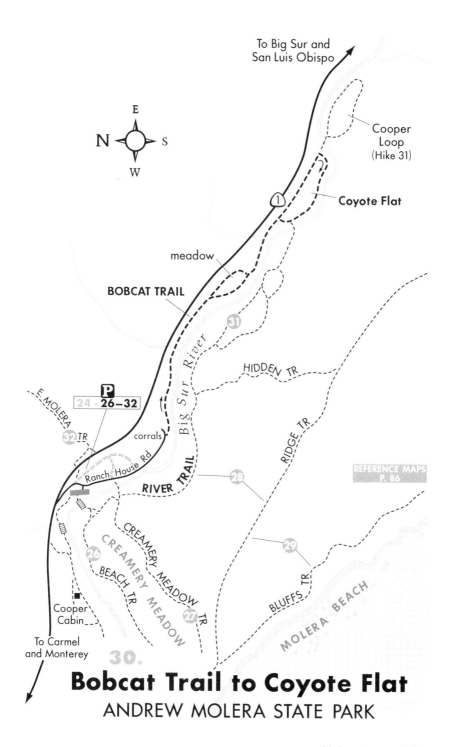

Bobcat Trail to Coyote Flat
ANDREW MOLERA STATE PARK

Highway 1. Curve away from the highway to an open meadow. A path loops around the perimeter of the meadow. Take the right fork along the west edge of the meadow. Beyond the meadow, the trail descends to a small sandy beach by a rock cliff on the banks of the Big Sur River. Across the river is River Trail (the return route for Hike 31). Continue following the watercourse upstream. Cross a tributary stream, and wind through a redwood grove to a Y-fork. Curve right and descend into Coyote Flat and a trail split. Again a trail circles the large meadow. Take the right fork along the southwest border of the meadow. A side path on the right leads to a large pool in the river. At the far end of Coyote Flat, the loop trail connects at a Y-junction. To the right is a wide river crossing. Across the river is the Cooper Loop Trail at the far end of Hike 31. If you prefer to keep your feet dry, this is the turn-around point. Return along the same route, completing the two meadow loops along the way. ▦

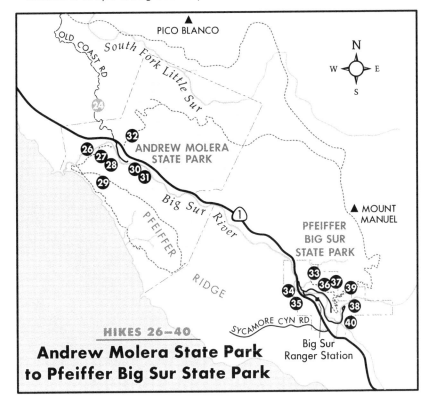

HIKES 26–40
Andrew Molera State Park to Pfeiffer Big Sur State Park

31. Bobcat Trail—River Trail Loop along the Big Sur River

ANDREW MOLERA STATE PARK

Hiking distance: 5 miles round trip
Hiking time: 2.5 hours
Configuration: inter-connecting loops
Elevation gain: 50 feet
Difficulty: easy to slightly moderate
Exposure: shaded forest and open meadows
Dogs: not allowed
Maps: U.S.G.S. Big Sur · Andrew Molera State Park map
      Big Sur and Ventana Wilderness map

map
page 105

The Bobcat Trail and River Trail make a long loop around both sides of the Big Sur River in Andrew Molera State Park. The route crosses four meadows, winds through numerous redwood groves and pockets of mature hardwood trees, passes a few swimming holes, and crosses the Big Sur River four times.

To the trailhead

CARMEL. From Highway 1 and Rio Road in Carmel, drive 21.4 miles south on Highway 1 to the signed Andrew Molera State Park entrance. Turn right and drive down to the entrance kiosk and parking lot on the coast side of the highway. A parking fee is required. The trail is also accessible from several gates along Highway 1, which may involve wading through the Big Sur River.

BIG SUR RANGER STATION. From the ranger station, drive 4.8 miles north on Highway 1 to the state park entrance and turn left (towards the coast).

The hike

Walk back to the entrance of the parking lot. Ten yards past the kiosk, take the unpaved Ranch House Road to the right. Follow the road southeast through oak and maple groves, passing a river crossing on the right and barns on the left. At the far (south) end of the corrals, the road ends at the posted Bobcat Trail on the right.

Take the footpath through a shady grove lush with ferns, poison oak, and towering redwoods. Weave through the forest between the Big Sur River and Highway 1, passing a trail access from Highway 1. Curve away from the highway to an open meadow. A path loops around the perimeter of the meadow. Take the right fork along the west edge. Beyond the meadow, the trail descends to a small, sandy beach by a rock cliff on the banks of the Big Sur River. Across the river is the River Trail—the return route. Continue following the watercourse upstream. Cross a tributary stream, and wind through a redwood grove to a Y-fork. Curve right and descend into Coyote Flat and a trail split. Again a trail circles the large meadow. Take the right fork along the southwest border of the meadow. A side path on the right leads to a large pool in the river. At the far end of Coyote Flat, the loop trail connects at a Y-junction. To the right is a wide river crossing.

Wade across the river to a trail fork at the beginning of the Cooper Loop. The Cooper Loop may be hiked in either direction. This route begins on the left fork, hiking clockwise. Wind through the thick forest to the banks of the river. Follow the river upstream to the far end of the loop. Curve right, leaving the river, and enter a dense redwood grove with lush ferns and mosses. Complete the 0.7-mile loop, and cross back over the river.

Return through Coyote Flat, now taking the right fork around the east end of the meadow. Pass a highway access trail on the right. Beyond Coyote Flat, descend through redwoods, crossing a tributary stream to a small pocket beach at the river by rock cliffs. Wade across the river to the west bank, and pick up the unsigned River Trail. Stay to the right on the route closest to the river, passing open meadows dotted with trees and views of the surrounding mountains. Skirt the west side of the meadow along the base of the cliffs. Curve left up a small rise, passing a junction with the Hidden Trail on the left. Gradually descend back to the meadow, and follow the hillside to the north end of the hill and a junction. Bear left 20 yards to the Creamery Meadow Trail. Curve right, staying on the River Trail to the signed parking lot junction. Cross the Big Sur River back to the parking lot. ▩

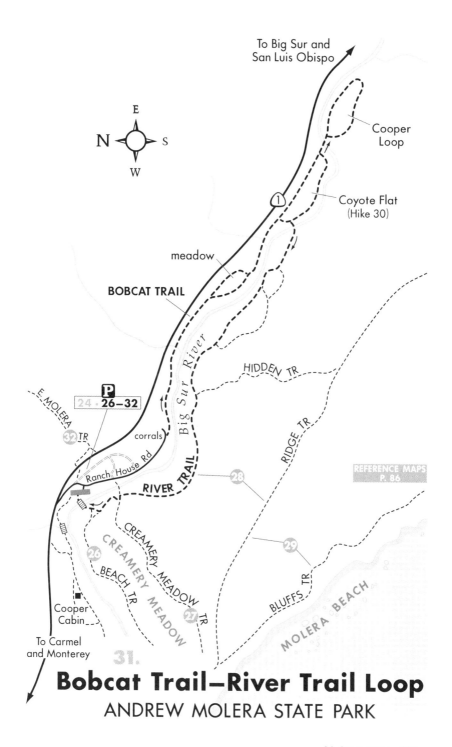

To Big Sur and
San Luis Obispo

Cooper
Loop

Coyote Flat
(Hike 30)

1

meadow

BOBCAT TRAIL

HIDDEN TR

Big Sur River

E. MOLERA

P
24 · **26–32**

32 TR

corrals

RIDGE TR

Ranch House Rd

RIVER TRAIL

28

REFERENCE MAPS
P. 86

CREAMERY MEADOW

26

CREAMERY MEADOW

BEACH TR

29

27

BLUFFS TR

MOLERA BEACH

Cooper
Cabin

To Carmel
and Monterey

31.

Bobcat Trail–River Trail Loop
ANDREW MOLERA STATE PARK

32. East Molera Trail
ANDREW MOLERA STATE PARK

Hiking distance: 4 miles round trip
Hiking time: 2 hours
Configuration: out-and-back
Elevation gain: 1,500 feet
Difficulty: moderate to strenuous
Exposure: open hillside
Dogs: not allowed
Maps: U.S.G.S. Big Sur · Andrew Molera State Park map
Big Sur and Ventana Wilderness map

Andrew Molera State Park encompasses 4,800 acres along both sides of Highway 1, with the majority of the acreage east of the highway. The East Molera Trail climbs up the coastal slope of the Santa Lucia Mountains to amazing vistas of the entire state park and up the coastline to the Point Sur Lightstation. The path crosses an old pasture to a ridge, where there is a beautiful grove of stately redwoods backed by towering Pico Blanco. The views include Molera Beach, Molera Point, Creamery Meadow, the Big Sur River, Trail Camp, Pfeiffer Ridge, and the expansive coastline.

To the trailhead

CARMEL. From Highway 1 and Rio Road in Carmel, drive 21.4 miles south on Highway 1 to the signed Andrew Molera State Park entrance. Turn right and drive down to the entrance kiosk and parking lot on the coast side of the highway. A parking fee is required.

BIG SUR RANGER STATION. From the ranger station, drive 4.8 miles north on Highway 1 to the park entrance and turn left.

The hike

Walk past the entrance kiosk and up the road to the left bend. Bear right on the unpaved road, marked "Authorized Personnel Only." Walk a short distance to the signed East Molera Trail on the left. Take the footpath uphill and through the tunnel under Highway 1. At 0.2 miles is a signed junction. To the right is an access trail to Highway 1. Bear left uphill through a shady oak grove to an old ranch road. Follow the forested road to the left, passing a water tank on the right. The trail emerges from the forest canopy to the open, sloping grassland. Cross the slopes to the southern edge of the ridge. Veer left and traverse the west face of the mountain. Continue up two long, sweeping switchbacks. Wind around the south side of the mountain to the head of the canyon and a beautiful stand of redwoods on the ridge. Across the inland canyon is pyramid-shaped Pico Blanco and the South Fork Little Sur River canyon. A path follows the ridge in both directions. To the right are stately oaks and views up the Big Sur Valley. To the left is the summit and awesome coastal views. After marveling at the vistas, return along the same route. ▩

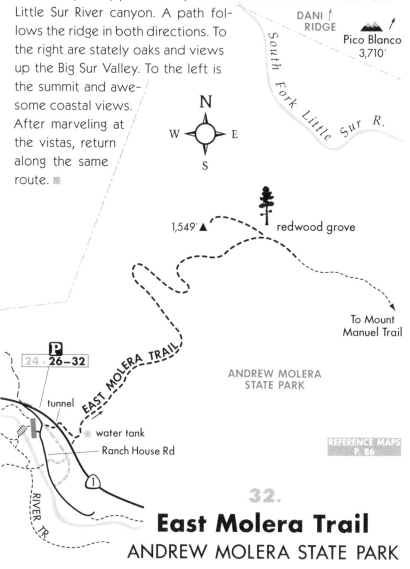

DANI RIDGE

Pico Blanco
3,710'

South Fork Little Sur R.

N
W E
S

1,549' ▲   redwood grove

To Mount
Manuel Trail

P
24 · 26–32

EAST MOLERA TRAIL

ANDREW MOLERA
STATE PARK

tunnel

water tank

Ranch House Rd

REFERENCE MAPS
P. 86

RIVER TR.

32.

East Molera Trail
ANDREW MOLERA STATE PARK

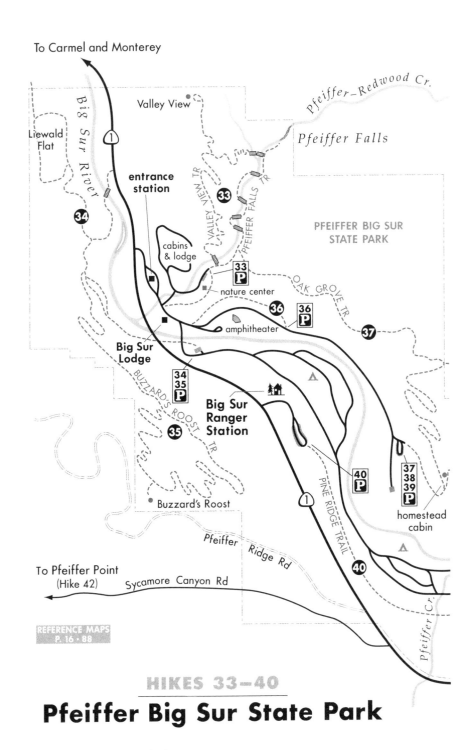

To Carmel and Monterey

Valley View

Big Sur River

Liewald Flat

1

entrance station

34

cabins & lodge

VALLEY VIEW TR

Pfeiffer–Redwood Cr.

Pfeiffer Falls

33

PFEIFFER FALLS TR

33 P

nature center

PEIFFER BIG SUR STATE PARK

OAK GROVE TR

36

36 P

37

amphitheater

Big Sur Lodge

34 35 P

BUZZARD'S ROOST TR

Big Sur Ranger Station

35

Buzzard's Roost

40 P

PINE RIDGE TRAIL

37 38 39 P

homestead cabin

1

40

Pfeiffer Ridge Rd

To Pfeiffer Point (Hike 42)

Sycamore Canyon Rd

Pfeiffer Cr.

REFERENCE MAPS
P. 16 • 88

HIKES 33–40

Pfeiffer Big Sur State Park

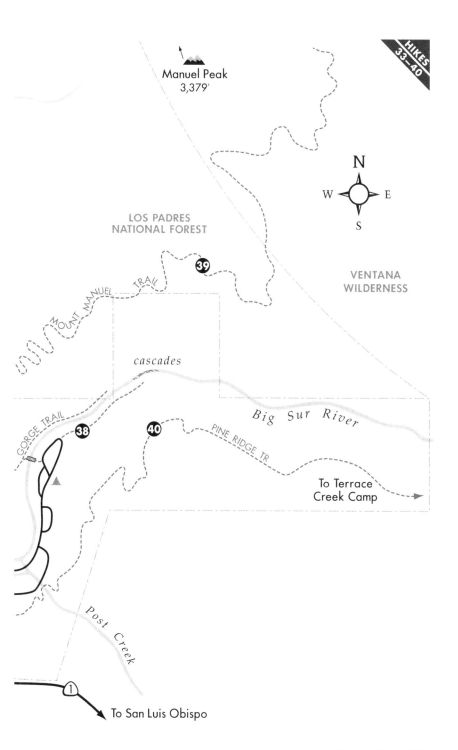

Manuel Peak
3,379'

N
W   E
S

LOS PADRES
NATIONAL FOREST

VENTANA
WILDERNESS

39

MOUNT MANUEL TRAIL

cascades

Big Sur River

GORGE TRAIL

38

40

PINE RIDGE TR

To Terrace
Creek Camp

Post Creek

1

To San Luis Obispo

33. Pfeiffer Falls
Valley View Overlook
PFEIFFER BIG SUR STATE PARK

Hiking distance: 2.2-mile loop
Hiking time: 1 hour
Configuration: loop with short spur trail to overlook
Elevation gain: 500 feet
Difficulty: easy
Exposure: shaded forest
Dogs: not allowed
Maps: U.S.G.S. Big Sur · Pfeiffer Big Sur State Park map
Big Sur and Ventana Wilderness map

Pfeiffer Big Sur State Park is home to lush forests and open meadows surrounding the Big Sur River along Highway 1. This hike follows a moist, fern-lined trail along Pfeiffer-Redwood Creek up a steep-walled canyon through a redwood forest to the base of

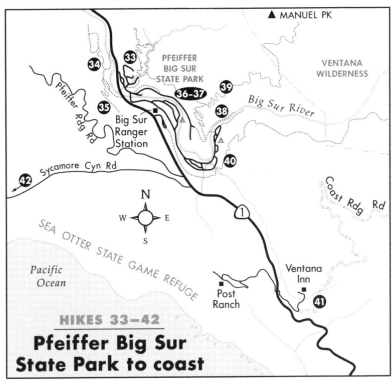

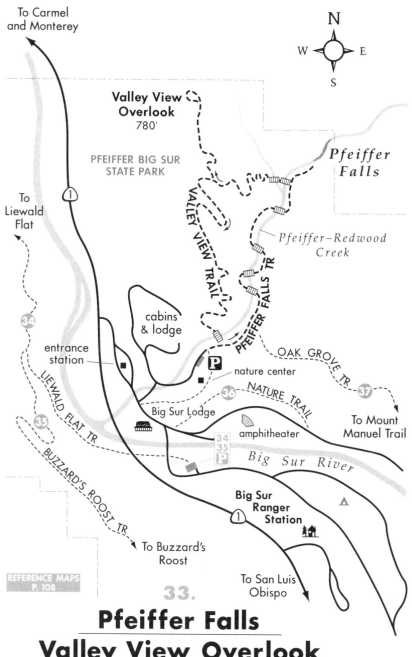

To Carmel
and Monterey

N
W   E
S

**Valley View
Overlook**
780'

**PFEIFFER BIG SUR
STATE PARK**

*Pfeiffer
Falls*

To
Liewald
Flat

1

VALLEY VIEW TRAIL

*Pfeiffer–Redwood
Creek*

PFEIFFER FALLS TR

cabins
& lodge

34

entrance
station

LIEWALD FLAT TR

35

BUZZARD'S ROOST TR

P

nature center

OAK GROVE TR

37

36

NATURE TRAIL

To Mount
Manuel Trail

Big Sur Lodge

amphitheater

34
35
P

Big Sur River

To Buzzard's
Roost

**Big Sur
Ranger
Station**

1

To San Luis
Obispo

REFERENCE MAPS
P. 108

33.

Pfeiffer Falls
Valley View Overlook
PFEIFFER BIG SUR STATE PARK

Pfeiffer Falls. The waterfall spills 60 feet over granite rock in a small fern grotto with a pool. On the return, the Valley View Trail climbs out of the canyon into an oak and chaparral woodland. A spur trail to a 780-foot overlook offers sweeping views of the Santa Lucia Range, the Big Sur Valley, Point Sur, and the blue Pacific Ocean.

To the trailhead

From the Big Sur Ranger Station, located 27 miles south of Carmel, drive 0.5 miles north on Highway 1 to the signed Pfeiffer Big Sur State Park entrance. Turn right (inland) to the entrance station. Continue to a stop sign. Turn left and a quick right, following the trail signs 0.2 miles to the signed trailhead parking area on the right. An entrance fee is required.

The hike

Take the trail at the far northeast end of the parking area. Head gradually uphill through the redwood forest. Parallel Pfeiffer-Redwood Creek to the signed Valley View Trail on the left. Begin the loop to the right on the Pfeiffer Falls Trail. Ascend a long series of steps to a signed junction with the Oak Grove Trail on the right (Hike 37). Continue up the canyon towards Pfeiffer Falls as the path zigzags upstream over four wooden footbridges. After the fourth crossing is the second junction with the Valley View Trail on the left—the return route. Stay to the right to see Pfeiffer Falls, climbing two sets of stairs to a platform in front of the falls.

Return to the junction and take the Valley View Trail, crossing a bridge over the creek and another bridge over a tributary stream. Switchbacks lead up the south-facing slope to a signed junction. Bear right towards the Valley View Overlook. Ascend the ridge 0.3 miles to a short loop at the overlook. Return back downhill to the junction, and bear right to the canyon floor on the Valley View Trail. Cross the bridge over the creek, completing the loop on the Pfeiffer Falls Trail. Return to the trailhead on the right. ▪

34. Liewald Flat
PFEIFFER BIG SUR STATE PARK

Hiking distance: 1.6 miles round trip
Hiking time: 1 hour
Configuration: out and back with loop
Elevation gain: 200 feet
Difficulty: easy
Exposure: shaded forest
Dogs: not allowed
Maps: U.S.G.S. Big Sur · Pfeiffer Big Sur State Park map
Big Sur and Ventana Wilderness map

map
page 115

Liewald Flat is an oval-shaped meadow dotted with oak trees and rimmed with pines in Pfeiffer Big Sur State Park. The trail to the flat follows an old road parallel to the Big Sur River. The meandering path winds through a quiet pastoral forest with large old growth redwood trees, oaks, and bay laurels.

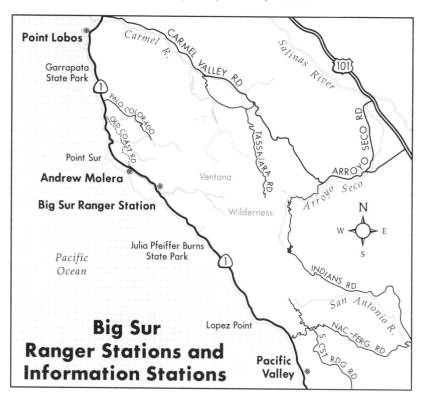

To the trailhead

From the Big Sur Ranger Station, located 27 miles south of Carmel, drive 0.5 miles north on Highway 1 to the signed Pfeiffer Big Sur State Park entrance. Turn right (inland) past the entrance station to the stop sign at the intersection. Continue straight and turn right after passing the Big Sur Lodge on the right. Drive 0.1 mile, crossing a bridge over the Big Sur River and curving left to the trailhead parking area on the left. An entrance fee is required.

The hike

Take the signed trail, crossing under the bridge that spans the Big Sur River. Follow the river downstream and under Highway 1. Gradually ascend the hillside past redwoods in the shade of the forest to a trail split. The left fork gently ascends the hillside. The right fork stays close to the river and climbs steps, where the two forks rejoin. A short distance ahead is the signed Buzzard's Roost Trail on the left, which leads up the 1,050-foot ridge (Hike 35).

Go straight on the main trail, high above the Big Sur River, to a T-junction at the group campground. The right fork leads through the campground. Take the left fork on the old road above the campground. The trail emerges from the dense forest into Liewald Flat, an open meadow with oak groves. Begin the loop around the meadow to the right. At the far (north) end of the meadow, an unsigned footpath veers to the right into the forest. Stay on the main path and continue above the meadow, completing the loop. Return along the same route. ▨

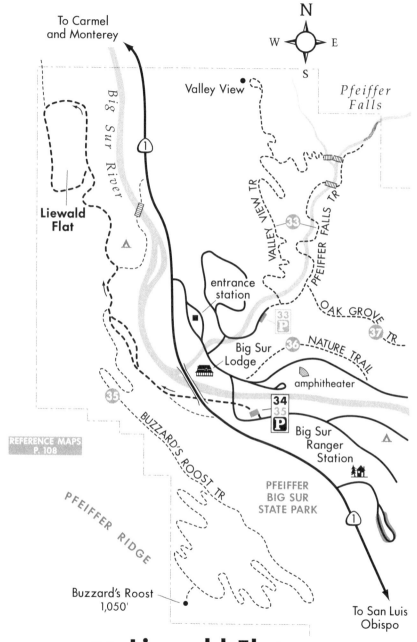

To Carmel
and Monterey

N

W   E

S

Valley View

*Pfeiffer
Falls*

Big Sur River

1

**Liewald
Flat**

VALLEY VIEW TR

33

PFEIFFER FALLS TR

OAK GROVE TR

37

entrance
station

33 P

NATURE TRAIL

36

Big Sur
Lodge

amphitheater

35

34
35
P

Big Sur
Ranger
Station

BUZZARD'S ROOST TR

REFERENCE MAPS
P. 108

PFEIFFER
BIG SUR
STATE PARK

PFEIFFER RIDGE

1

Buzzard's Roost
1,050'

To San Luis
Obispo

34. **Liewald Flat**
PFEIFFER BIG SUR STATE PARK

35. Buzzard's Roost
PFEIFFER BIG SUR STATE PARK

Hiking distance: 2.5 miles round trip
Hiking time: 1.5 hours
Configuration: out-and-back with loop
Elevation gain: 800 feet
Difficulty: easy to slightly moderate
Exposure: forested lowlands and open ridge
Dogs: not allowed
Maps: U.S.G.S. Big Sur and Pfeiffer Point · Pfeiffer Big Sur State Park map
      Big Sur and Ventana Wilderness map

The Buzzard's Roost Trail begins as a streamside stroll along the Big Sur River through groves of bay laurel, oak, and huge old-growth redwoods. Switchbacks wind up the forested hillside slope to Pfeiffer Ridge. The trail forms a 1.7-mile loop along the shrub-lined ridge. From the 1,050-foot Buzzard's Roost are far-reaching views of the Santa Lucia Mountains and the Pacific Ocean.

To the trailhead

From the Big Sur Ranger Station, located 27 miles south of Carmel, drive 0.5 miles north on Highway 1 to the signed Pfeiffer Big Sur State Park entrance. Turn right (inland) past the entrance station to the stop sign at the intersection. Continue straight and turn right after passing the Big Sur Lodge on the right. Drive 0.1 mile, crossing a bridge over the Big Sur River and curving left to the trailhead parking area on the left. An entrance fee is required.

The hike

Take the signed trail, crossing under the bridge that spans the Big Sur River. Follow the river downstream and under Highway 1. Gradually ascend the hillside past redwoods in the shade of the forest. The trail splits and rejoins a short distance ahead. Traverse the hillside to the signed Buzzard's Roost Trail on the left. The main trail leads to the campground and Liewald Flat—Hike 34.

Instead, take the sharp left switchback, and climb up the hillside ledge to a trail split at 0.9 miles. Begin the loop to the left. The path levels out and winds in and out of ravines along the contours of the mountain. Head up more switchbacks to Pfeiffer

Ridge, overlooking the Big Sur Valley, Mount Manuel, and the Pacific Ocean. Steps lead up the eroded ridge to Buzzard's Roost. A short side path on the left (by the large antenna) detours to the 1,050-foot overlook. Return to the main trail, and descend the ridge into the forest. Continue weaving down the mountain, completing the loop. Bear left and retrace your steps to the trailhead. ▪

To Carmel and Monterey

Big Sur River

Liewald Flat

34

entrance station

VALLEY VIEW

33

PFEIFFER FALLS TR

OAK GROVE TR

37

N
W — E
S

Big Sur Lodge

NATURE TRAIL

36

amphitheater

BUZZARD'S ROOST TR

34
35
P

Big Sur Ranger Station

PFEIFFER BIG SUR STATE PARK

1

REFERENCE MAPS P. 108

PFEIFFER RIDGE

Buzzard's Roost
1,050'

To San Luis Obispo

35. **Buzzard's Roost**
PFEIFFER BIG SUR STATE PARK

36. Nature Trail
PFEIFFER BIG SUR STATE PARK

Hiking distance: 0.6 miles round trip
Hiking time: 30 minutes
Configuration: out and back
Elevation gain: level
Difficulty: very easy
Exposure: mostly shaded
Dogs: not allowed
Maps: U.S.G.S. Big Sur · Pfeiffer Big Sur State Park map
Big Sur and Ventana Wilderness map

The Nature Trail in Pfeiffer Big Sur State Park is a short, self-guiding trail that meanders through a variety of plant life native to the Big Sur area. The trail is just across the road from the Big Sur Lodge. The pastoral path parallels the park road and the Big Sur River through an oak woodland. The trail ends in a beautiful redwood grove. Interpretive leaflets available at the trailhead describe the surrounding trees, their effects, and uses.

To the trailhead

From the Big Sur Ranger Station, located 27 miles south of Carmel, drive 0.5 miles north on Highway 1 to the signed Pfeiffer Big Sur State Park entrance. Turn right (inland) past the entrance station to the stop sign at the intersection. Continue straight, passing Big Sur Lodge on the right, for 0.3 miles to the picnic and parking area on the right. An entrance fee is required.

The walk may also be started at the west end from the Big Sur Lodge.

The hike

From the grassy picnic area on the banks of the Big Sur River, cross the park road to the signed Nature Trail. Pick up the interpretive guide, and enter the forest of live oaks and sycamores. The level path continues into a lush redwood grove. Wind through the shady grove, and climb a short flight of wooden steps, reaching the park road across from Big Sur Lodge. Return along the same path or make a loop along the park road.

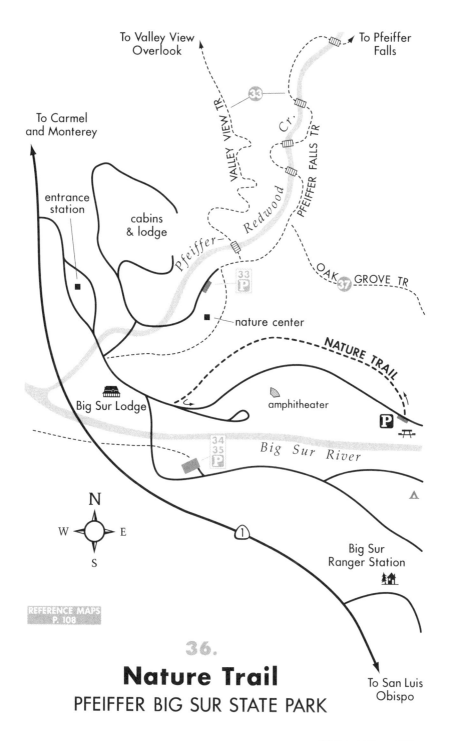

To Valley View Overlook

To Pfeiffer Falls

33

To Carmel and Monterey

VALLEY VIEW TR.

Redwood Cr.

PFEIFFER FALLS TR

entrance station

cabins & lodge

Pfeiffer

33 P

OAK GROVE TR

37

nature center

NATURE TRAIL

Big Sur Lodge

amphitheater

P

Big Sur River

34 35 P

N

W E

S

1

Big Sur Ranger Station

To San Luis Obispo

36.

Nature Trail
PFEIFFER BIG SUR STATE PARK

37. Oak Grove Trail
PFEIFFER BIG SUR STATE PARK

Hiking distance: 2.8-mile loop
Hiking time: 1.5 hours
Configuration: loop (with park road)
Elevation gain: 350 feet
Difficulty: easy
Exposure: both shaded and open forest
Dogs: not allowed
Maps: U.S.G.S. Big Sur and Pfeiffer Point · Pfeiffer Big Sur State Park map
Big Sur and Ventana Wilderness map

The Oak Grove Trail traverses a beautiful, forested hillside through several natural ecosystems in Pfeiffer Big Sur State Park. The plant communities range from dry chaparral to hardwood forests with a mix of oaks and shady redwood groves. The path weaves in and out of numerous gullies, connecting the Pfeiffer Falls Trail (Hike 33) with the Gorge Trail.

To the trailhead

From the Big Sur Ranger Station, located 27 miles south of Carmel, drive 0.5 miles north on Highway 1 to the signed Pfeiffer Big Sur State Park entrance. Turn right (inland) past the entrance station to the stop sign at the intersection. Continue straight, passing Big Sur Lodge on the right. Quickly bear left, following the signs towards the picnic area. At 0.7 miles is the signed trailhead parking area on the left. An entrance fee is required.

The hike

Take the gated road past the trail sign into the shade of the old oak forest. At 0.1 mile is a junction at John Pfeiffer's homestead cabin on the left, built in 1884. The right fork follows the Big Sur River along the Gorge Trail to creekside cascades (Hike 38). Take the left fork on the Oak Grove Trail to the homestead cabin and a trail fork. Keep to the left (straight ahead) through the open coastal oak grove. Switchback up the hillside, alternating between shady oak woodlands to exposed scrub and chaparral. At 0.7 miles, the path levels out on a 560-foot saddle by a signed junction with the Mount Manuel Trail (Hike 39). Stay on the Oak Grove Trail to the left, curving down the oak-covered hillside. Descend into a small ravine, and cross the drainage on a wooden footbridge, reaching the west end of the trail at a T-junction with the Pfeiffer Falls Trail at 1.7 miles. Bear left through a grove of large redwoods, and parallel Pfeiffer-Redwood Creek to the paved park road. Follow the park road downhill and bear left at the lodge. Take the forested road 0.6 miles back to the parking lot. En route is a short nature trail to the left that parallels the road. ▨

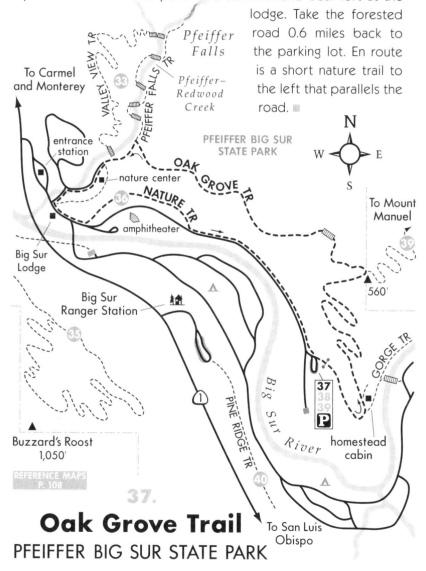

Oak Grove Trail
PFEIFFER BIG SUR STATE PARK

38. Gorge Trail
PFEIFFER BIG SUR STATE PARK

Hiking distance: 1.4 miles round trip
Hiking time: 45 minutes
Configuration: out and back
Elevation gain: 150 feet
Difficulty: easy
Exposure: mostly shaded
Dogs: not allowed
Maps: U.S.G.S. Big Sur · Pfeiffer Big Sur State Park map
      Big Sur and Ventana Wilderness map

The Gorge Trail leads into a narrow gorge to cascades and several swimming holes along the Big Sur River. The trail follows two short, unmaintained paths bordering the rocky east and west banks of the river. Both root-strewn paths scramble through an undeveloped area adjacent to the cascading whitewater. The headwall of the steep gorge is lush with ferns and moss-covered rocks.

To the trailhead

From the Big Sur Ranger Station, located 27 miles south of Carmel, drive 0.5 miles north on Highway 1 to the signed Pfeiffer Big Sur State Park entrance. Turn right (inland) past the entrance station to the stop sign at the intersection. Continue straight, passing Big Sur Lodge on the right. Quickly bear left, following the signs towards the picnic area. At 0.7 miles is the signed trailhead parking area on the left. An entrance fee is required.

The hike

Take the gated road past the trail sign into the shade of the old oak forest. At 0.1 mile is a junction at John Pfeiffer's homestead cabin on the left, a historic log cabin built in 1884. The Oak Grove Trail (Hike 37) bears left. Take the right fork, staying on the Gorge Trail. Follow the west side of the Big Sur River to the bridge spanning the river. Before crossing the bridge, an unsigned footpath veers left along the northwest bank of the river. This path ends where the river meets the sheer rock canyon walls.

Return to the bridge, and cross it into the campground. Follow the campground road left, parallel to the river. As the road curves away from the river, take the well-defined footpath left past redwood trees, staying close to the river. Head up the narrow canyon, maneuvering over and around many boulders and large tree roots. The trail ends at the steep rock cliffs by a series of pools, small waterfalls, and cascades. Return along the same trail. ▨

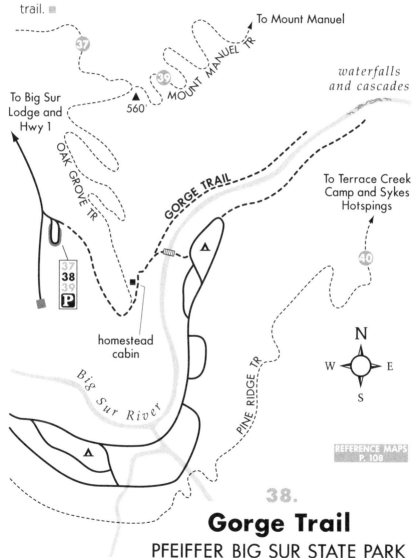

38.
Gorge Trail
PFEIFFER BIG SUR STATE PARK

39. Mount Manuel Trail
PFEIFFER BIG SUR STATE PARK

Hiking distance: 10.4 miles round trip
Hiking time: 5.5 hours
Configuration: out-and-back
Elevation gain: 3,200 feet
Difficulty: very strenuous
Exposure: mostly exposed hillside
Dogs: not allowed
Maps: U.S.G.S. Big Sur and Pfeiffer Point · Pfeiffer Big Sur State Park map
       Big Sur and Ventana Wilderness map

Mount Manuel is the towering mountain that dominates Pfeiffer Big Sur State Park. This hike climbs to a vista point near the 3,379-foot summit. The sweeping 360-degree panoramic views extend

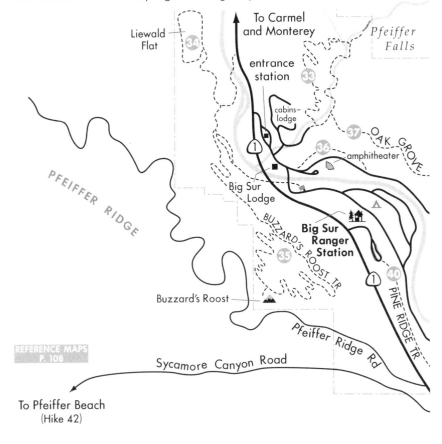

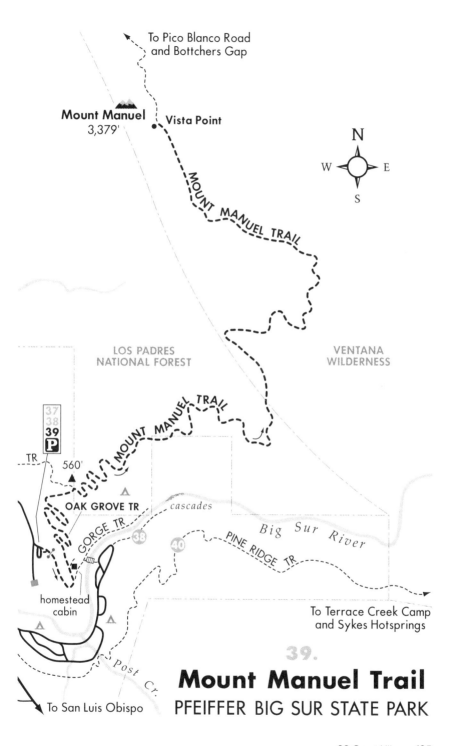

To Pico Blanco Road
and Bottchers Gap

Mount Manuel
3,379'

Vista Point

N
W   E
S

MOUNT MANUEL TRAIL

LOS PADRES
NATIONAL FOREST

VENTANA
WILDERNESS

MOUNT MANUEL TRAIL

37
38
39
P

TR
560'

OAK GROVE TR

cascades

Big Sur River

GORGE TR

38

40

PINE RIDGE TR

homestead
cabin

To Terrace Creek Camp
and Sykes Hotsprings

Post Cr.

39.

To San Luis Obispo

Mount Manuel Trail
PFEIFFER BIG SUR STATE PARK

across the entire Big Sur area, from the Santa Lucia Mountains to the expansive crenelated coastline and the sheer cliffs. The trail begins from the Oak Grove Trail and climbs up to the vista point on exposed, chaparral-covered hillsides that offer little shade.

To the trailhead

From the Big Sur Ranger Station, located 27 miles south of Carmel, drive 0.5 miles north on Highway 1 to the signed Pfeiffer Big Sur State Park entrance. Turn right (inland) past the entrance station to the stop sign at the intersection. Continue straight, passing Big Sur Lodge on the right. Quickly bear left, following the signs towards the picnic area. At 0.7 miles is the signed trailhead parking area on the left. An entrance fee is required.

The hike

Take the gated road past the trail sign into the shade of the old oak forest. At 0.1 mile is a junction at John Pfeiffer's homestead cabin, built in 1884. The right fork follows the Big Sur River along the Gorge Trail to creekside cascades. Take the left fork to the homestead cabin and a trail fork. Keep to the left (straight ahead) through the open coastal oak grove. Switchback up the hillside, alternating between shady oak woodlands and exposed chaparral. At 0.7 miles, the path levels out on a 560-foot saddle by a signed junction with the Mount Manuel Trail.

Bear right up the steps, leaving the oak canopy. Begin zigzagging up the south flank of Mount Manuel above the Big Sur River Valley. Cross the arid, exposed mountainside amid low-growing scrub and forested gullies to a ridge. At 3 miles, the trail curves north and follows the ridge in the Ventana Wilderness, dipping in and out of more gullies. Views expand across Pfeiffer Ridge to the ocean. Cross a forested saddle to a reflector. A short distance ahead is the rocky summit and vista point at 3,379 feet above sea level. After enjoying the expansive views, return along the same trail.

The Mount Manuel Trail continues north to the Little Sur River drainage, connecting to Pico Blanco Road at Bottcher's Gap (Hike 21). ▦

40. Pine Ridge Trail to Terrace Creek
PFEIFFER BIG SUR STATE PARK to VENTANA WILDERNESS

Hiking distance: 10.6 miles round trip
(or optional 12.5-mile loop with Hike 41)
Hiking time: 5.5 hours
Configuration: out-and-back (or optional loop)
Elevation gain: 1,000 feet
Difficulty: strenuous
Exposure: shaded forest and open hillside
Dogs: allowed
Maps: U.S.G.S. Pfeiffer Point, Partington Ridge, Ventana Cross
Pfeiffer Big Sur State Park map
Big Sur and Ventana Wilderness map

**map
page 128**

The Pine Ridge Trail is a key access route to numerous camps and trails throughout the expansive Ventana Wilderness. The trailhead begins at the Big Sur Ranger Station in Pfeiffer Big Sur State Park. The most popular destination from the Pine Ridge Trail is the ten-mile overnight hike to the hot springs at Sykes Camp. This hike takes in the first 5.3 miles of the trail to Terrace Creek Camp, traveling along the Big Sur River Valley 600—800 feet above the river.

The hike can be made into a longer 12.5-mile loop by returning on the Terrace Creek Trail and the Coast Ridge Road—Hike 41. This route involves additional elevation gain and walking along Highway 1 back to the trailhead.

To the trailhead

The trail begins at the Big Sur Ranger Station in Pfeiffer Big Sur State Park. The turnoff is located 27 miles south of Carmel. Turn inland and drive 0.2 miles to the far end of the parking area.

The hike

Take the signed trail at the far end of the parking lot into the shaded forest. Cross the hillside above the Big Sur River through tanbark oak and redwood groves, skirting the edge of the Big Sur Campground to an unsigned trail split. The left fork descends into the campground. Stay to the right and cross a water-carved ravine along Pfeiffer Creek. Zigzag downhill and cross Post Creek. Climb out of the narrow canyon to vistas of the Big Sur River Valley.

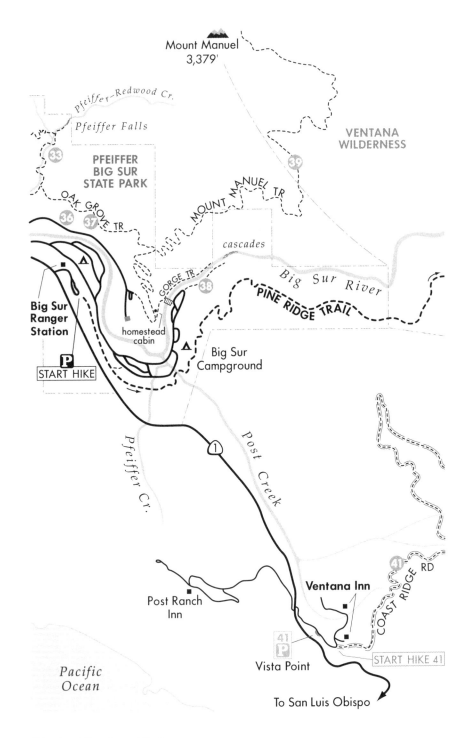

Mount Manuel
3,379'

VENTANA
WILDERNESS

Pfeiffer-Redwood Cr.

Pfeiffer Falls

PFEIFFER
BIG SUR
STATE PARK

OAK GROVE TR.

MOUNT MANUEL TR.

cascades

Big Sur River

PINE RIDGE TRAIL

Big Sur
Ranger
Station

homestead
cabin

GORGE TR.

Big Sur
Campground

START HIKE

Pfeiffer Cr.

Post Creek

1

COAST RIDGE RD

Ventana Inn

Post Ranch
Inn

Pacific
Ocean

Vista Point

START HIKE 41

To San Luis Obispo

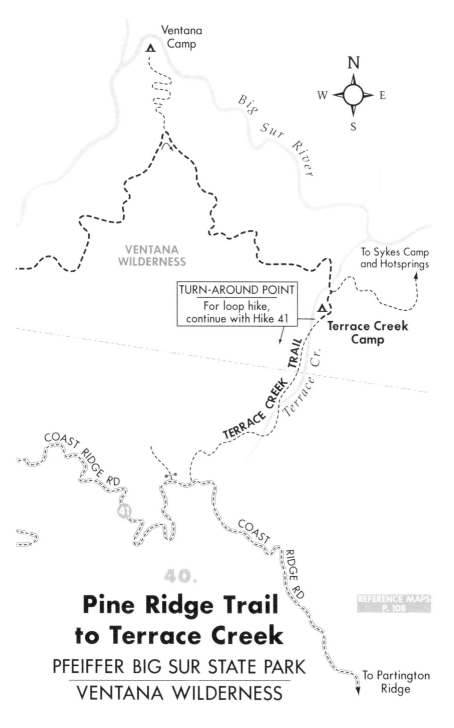

Ventana
Camp

N
W   E
S

Big Sur River

VENTANA
WILDERNESS

To Sykes Camp
and Hotsprings

TURN-AROUND POINT
For loop hike,
continue with Hike 41

Terrace Creek
Camp

TERRACE CREEK TRAIL

Terrace Cr.

COAST RIDGE RD

41

COAST RIDGE RD

40.
Pine Ridge Trail
to Terrace Creek
PFEIFFER BIG SUR STATE PARK
VENTANA WILDERNESS

REFERENCE MAPS
P. 108

To Partington
Ridge

Steadily gain elevation, traversing the cliffs above the valley. The path alternates from exposed chaparral to shady draws. The Mount Manuel Trail (Hike 39) is visible across the canyon.

At 2.5 miles, the trail leaves the state park and enters the Ventana Wilderness by a boundary sign. Continue up the river valley to a junction with the trail to Ventana Camp at 4 miles. The left fork descends 1.2 miles to the camp, situated in a horseshoe bend along the Big Sur River. Continue east on the Pine Ridge Trail for 1.2 miles to Terrace Creek and a signed junction with the Terrace Creek Trail. Terrace Creek Camp sits above and to the right, straddling the creek in a beautiful grove of redwoods. This is the turn-around spot. Retrace your steps along the same trail.

For the 12.5-mile loop, take the Terrace Creek Trail through the lush canyon for 1.6 miles to the Coast Ridge Road. Referencing the hiking directions of Hike 41, follow the Coast Ridge Road southwest to the Vista Point parking area. Return 1.7 miles along Highway 1 back to the Big Sur Ranger Station. ▩

41. Coast Ridge Road to Terrace Creek Trail

Hiking distance: 8 miles round trip
(or optional 12.5-mile loop with Hike 40)
Hiking time: 4 hours
Configuration: out and back (or optional loop)
Elevation gain: 1,600 feet
Difficulty: strenuous
Exposure: forested canyon and open hillside
Dogs: allowed
Maps: U.S.G.S. Pfeiffer Point and Partington Ridge
Big Sur and Ventana Wilderness map

**map
page 132**

The Coast Ridge Road is a private, unpaved road with a public right-of-way for hikers. The road switchbacks to the top of the coastal ridge, then follows the ridge for 30 miles. Starting from the north end of the road, this hike follows the first four miles to the Terrace Creek Trail. The trail offers spectacular views deep into the precipitous Ventana Wilderness, extending across the Big Sur Valley to the Pacific Ocean.

The hike may be combined with the Pine Ridge Trail (Hike 40) for a 12.5-mile loop, returning to the Big Sur Ranger Station. From the ranger station, the loop heads back to the trailhead along Highway 1.

To the trailhead

From the Big Sur Ranger Station, located 27 miles south of Carmel, drive 1.7 miles south on Highway 1 to the signed Ventana Inn turn-off on the left. Turn left (inland) and drive 0.2 miles—staying to the right—to the signed Vista Point parking area on the right.

The hike

Walk 0.1 mile up the paved road past Vista Point to the gated road on the right, where the paved road forks left. Pass the gate and take the unpaved Coast Ridge Road around Ventana Inn. The wooded road winds through the shaded oak, bay, and redwood forest. At one mile, curve sharply left, crossing the trickling head-waters of Post Creek. Pass a narrow 30-foot waterfall cascading off a vertical rock wall on the right. Emerge from the forest, overlooking the canyon filled with redwoods. Steadily climb the open hillside trail while enjoying the commanding coastal views. The road winds slowly upward, following the mountain contours to the ridge and a hairpin right bend just before 2 miles. The serpentine road continues a steady but gentle uphill grade, crossing a saddle with views into the Ventana Wilderness. Cross several shady gullies and rolling grassy hills. At 4 miles, on a saddle just beyond a gated side road, is a signed junction with the Terrace Creek Trail on the left. This is the turn-around spot.

For a 12.5-mile loop, take the Terrace Creek Trail through the lush, wooded canyon. Continue 1.6 miles to Terrace Creek Camp in a redwood grove by a junction with the Pine Ridge Trail—Hike 40. Bear left and return via the Pine Ridge Trail, referencing the hiking directions for Hike 40. At the Big Sur Ranger Station, walk 1.7 miles southbound along Highway 1 back to the Ventana Inn turnoff. ▪

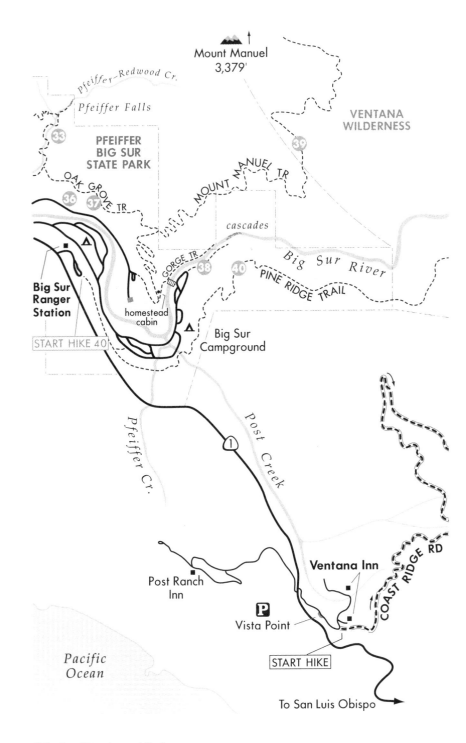

Mount Manuel
3,379'

Pfeiffer-Redwood Cr.

Pfeiffer Falls

VENTANA
WILDERNESS

33

PFEIFFER
BIG SUR
STATE PARK

39

OAK GROVE TR

36 37

MOUNT MANUEL TR

cascades

Big Sur River

GORGE TR

Big Sur
Ranger
Station

38 40

PINE RIDGE TRAIL

homestead
cabin

START HIKE 40

Big Sur
Campground

Pfeiffer Cr.

Post Creek

1

COAST RIDGE RD

Post Ranch
Inn

Ventana Inn

P
Vista Point

START HIKE

Pacific
Ocean

To San Luis Obispo

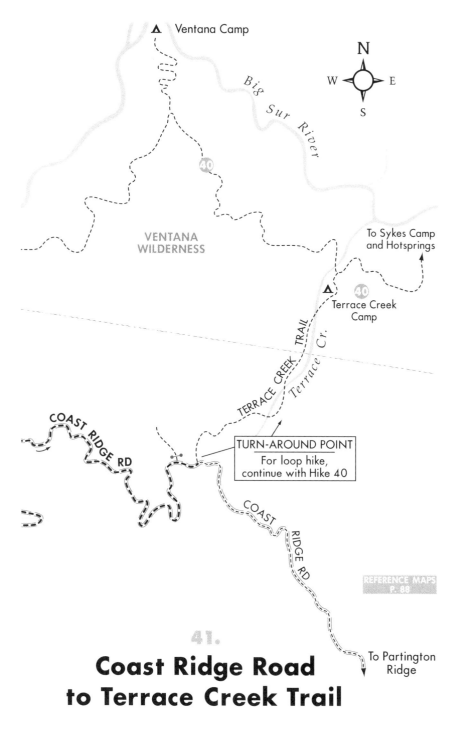

Ventana Camp

Big Sur River

N
W E
S

VENTANA
WILDERNESS

To Sykes Camp
and Hotsprings

Terrace Creek
Camp

TERRACE CREEK TRAIL

Terrace Cr.

COAST RIDGE RD

TURN-AROUND POINT
For loop hike,
continue with Hike 40

COAST RIDGE RD

REFERENCE MAPS
P. 88

41.

Coast Ridge Road
to Terrace Creek Trail

To Partington
Ridge

42. Pfeiffer Beach at Pfeiffer Point

Hiking distance: 1 mile round trip
Hiking time: 30 minutes
Configuration: out and back
Elevation gain: level
Difficulty: easy
Exposure: shaded pockets but mostly open coast
Dogs: allowed
Maps: U.S.G.S. Pfeiffer Point · Big Sur and Ventana Wilderness map

Pfeiffer Beach is a white sand beach surrounded by towering headland cliffs within the Los Padres National Forest. Pfeiffer Point extends outward at the south end of the beach. Dramatic offshore sea stacks have been sculpted by the wind and pounding surf, creating sea caves, eroded natural arches, and blowholes. On the secluded beach, Sycamore Creek forms a small lagoon as it empties into the Pacific. This is a beach-combing walk along the shoreline. Leashed dogs are allowed.

To the trailhead

From the Big Sur Ranger Station, located 27 miles south of Carmel, drive 0.5 miles south on Highway 1 to the unsigned Sycamore Canyon Road. Turn right and drive 2.2 miles down the narrow, winding road through Sycamore Canyon to the parking lot. A parking fee is required.

From the signed Julia Pfeiffer Burns State Park entrance, Sycamore Canyon Road is 9.8 miles north.

The hike

From the west end of the parking area, take the signed trail through a canopy of cypress trees along Sycamore Creek to the wide, sandy beach. The creek divides the beach, which forms a small lagoon. Straight ahead are giant sandstone rock formations with natural arches and sea caves. A short distance to the south are the steep cliffs of Pfeiffer Point. Beachcomb along the shore from the point to the cliffs at the far north end of the beach. An unmaintained trail heads up the cliffs to the north and follows the bluffs. Choose your own turn-around point. ▪

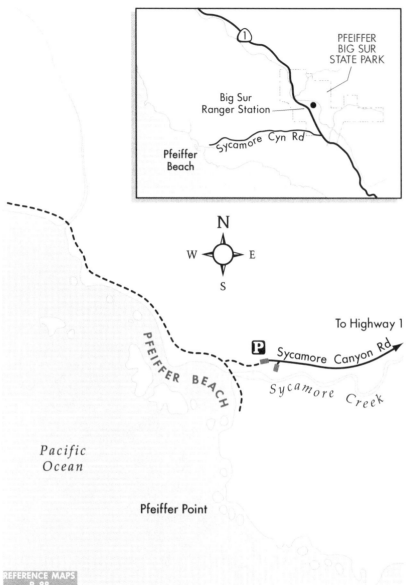

PFEIFFER
BIG SUR
STATE PARK

Big Sur
Ranger Station

Sycamore Cyn Rd

Pfeiffer
Beach

N
W • E
S

To Highway 1

P Sycamore Canyon Rd

PFEIFFER BEACH

Sycamore Creek

Pacific
Ocean

Pfeiffer Point

REFERENCE MAPS
P. 88

42.
Pfeiffer Beach
at Pfeiffer Point

Pfeiffer Rock

43. Boronda Trail
to Coast Ridge Road

Hiking distance: 5 miles round trip
Hiking time: 3.5 hours
Configuration: out-and-back
Elevation gain: 2,525 feet
Difficulty: very strenuous
Exposure: exposed hillside and ridge
Dogs: allowed
Maps: U.S.G.S. Partington Ridge · Big Sur and Ventana Wilderness map
Ventana Wilderness Los Padres National Forest map

The Boronda Trail is a very steep trail that climbs from Highway 1, on the cliff above the coastline, to Timber Top Camp, along the Coast Ridge Road. The primitive camp, which sits on a flat atop the ridge, has a stove, picnic benches, an old water tank, and a corral. The trail (an old ranch road) zigzags up the oceanfront cliffs to the camp and the narrow, grassy road that follows the ridgeline. En route, the trail crosses open hillsides and live-oak forests while offering magnificent, sweeping coastal vistas.

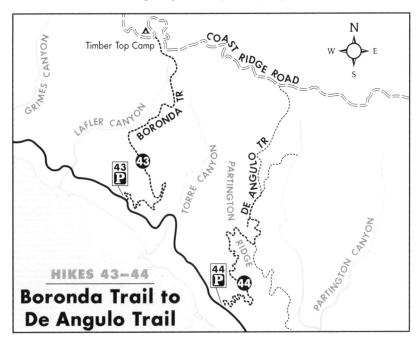

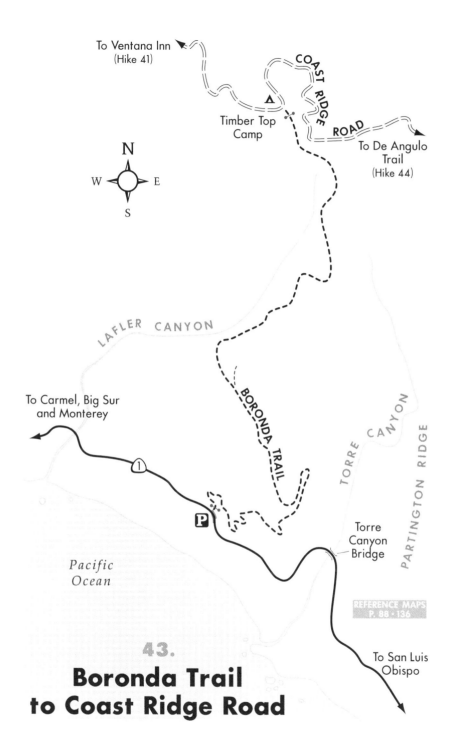

To Ventana Inn
(Hike 41)

COAST RIDGE ROAD

Timber Top
Camp

To De Angulo
Trail
(Hike 44)

N
W · E
S

LAFLER CANYON

BORONDA TRAIL

TORRE CANYON

PARTINGTON RIDGE

To Carmel, Big Sur
and Monterey

1

P

Torre
Canyon
Bridge

Pacific
Ocean

REFERENCE MAPS
P. 88 - 136

To San Luis
Obispo

43.
Boronda Trail
to Coast Ridge Road

To the trailhead

From the Big Sur Ranger Station, located 27 miles south of Carmel, drive 5.3 miles south on Highway 1 to the trailhead on the left (inland) by a cattle gate and an old wooden cattle chute. (The trailhead is located 0.5 miles past the Coast Gallery.) Park in the pullouts on either side of the road.

The hike

From the inland side of Highway 1, pass through the trail gate by the old cattle-loading chute. Begin the climb up the oceanfront slope. The spectacular coastal vistas expand with every step up the mountain. Zig and zag up the narrow dirt road with a few short but steep sections. Traverse the steep west wall of forested Torres Canyon while overlooking Highway 1, snaking down the coastline. At a Y-fork, veer left and continue uphill. Follow the exposed grassy ridge to an overlook on a flat at 1.3 miles.

After taking a breather, continue climbing the upper canyon wall. Follow the ridge, where the near-vertical mountain drops into the sea. Leave Torres Canyon to the upper reaches of Lafler Canyon. Bend to the right and follow the east ridge of the canyon. By a huge gnarled oak, a path curves left into the canyon. Pass the oak to the right, staying atop the ridge. Skirt an eroded rock wall on the right by a steep canyon dropoff on the left. Wind up the curvature of the mountain. The vistas include the endless ridges and canyons of the mountains and down the coastline as far as the eye can see. Return to the exposed, rolling ridge. Steadily climb to an old wood gate near the summit. Walk around the gate to the Coast Ridge Road, a narrow, grassy road. Cross the road into Timber Top, a primitive camp on a knoll atop the mountain. The camp is set amongst pine trees, with picnic benches, a metal grill, a dilapidated corral, an old watering trough, and superb ocean vistas.

To extend the hike, continue along the Coast Ridge Road. To the northwest (left), the road heads approximately 4 miles to the Ventana Inn (Hike 41). To the right, the trail leads 1.8 miles to a junction with the De Angulo Trail (Hike 44). ▨

44. De Angulo Trail to Partington Ridge

Hiking distance: 5 miles round trip
Hiking time: 3 hours
Configuration: out and back
Elevation gain: 1,500 feet
Difficulty: strenuous
Exposure: shaded forest and open ridge
Dogs: allowed
Maps: U.S.G.S. Partington Ridge · Big Sur and Ventana Wilderness map

map
page 141

The De Angulo Trail is a steep, unpaved, narrow road through the Wild Oak Ranch property. The serpentine road climbs up the mountain along the ocean side of Partington Ridge and leads to the Coast Ridge Road at 3.8 miles. This hike heads up the first 2.5 miles to a knoll on Partington Ridge, where there are far-reaching views up and down the Pacific coastline and across the interior mountains. Disregard the "No Trespassing" signs at the trailhead, as the road is a public right-of-way for hikers.

To the trailhead

From the Big Sur Ranger Station, located 27 miles south of Carmel, drive 7.3 miles south on Highway 1 to parking pullouts on both sides of the highway, located by a gated road on the inland side of the highway. The gated road is 0.8 miles south of the large concrete Torre Canyon Bridge and 3 miles north of the signed Julia Pfeiffer Burns State Park entrance.

The hike

Walk past the unsigned trail gate, and begin climbing steep switchbacks through a pine and eucalyptus forest. The narrow road quickly reaches beautiful coastal panoramas and passes a few isolated homes. At the top of the switchbacks, traverse the hillside to the north past a rolling grassy meadow. Continue through shady groves of bay and oak trees to a T-junction at 1.1 mile. The right fork leads to a home. Take the left fork, enjoying additional coastal views. Disregard the numerous side roads that lead to residences.

Soon the road reaches a junction near a home in a redwood grove. Take the middle fork, straight ahead, following the trail sign. Switchbacks lead up to a ridge and curve right past a horse corral. A short distance ahead is a junction with the Partington Ridge Road by a ranch on the left. Straight ahead, the road begins a descent towards Partington Canyon. Bear sharply to the left and follow the fenceline, skirting the ranch to a grassy knoll on the left. After savoring the views, return along the same path.

To extend the hike, continue up the road a short distance to a signed junction. The left fork continues up Partington Ridge to the Coast Ridge Road. To the left (northwest), the grassy road leads 1.8 miles to Timber Top Camp and the Boronda Trail into the next canyon drainage (Hike 43). To the right, the trail heads to Anderson Peak. ■

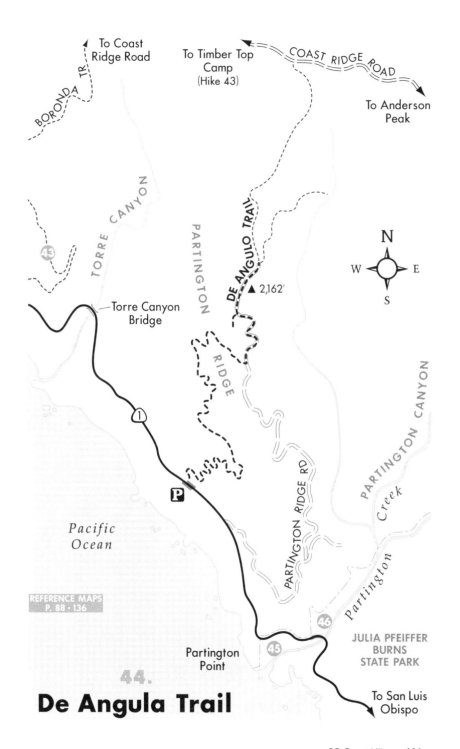

To Coast
Ridge Road

BORONDA TR.

To Timber Top
Camp
(Hike 43)

COAST RIDGE ROAD

To Anderson
Peak

TORRE CANYON

43

Torre Canyon
Bridge

PARTINGTON

DE ANGULO TRAIL

▲ 2,162'

N
W   E
S

RIDGE

1

P

Pacific
Ocean

PARTINGTON RIDGE RD

PARTINGTON CANYON

Creek

Partington

REFERENCE MAPS
P. 88 · 136

46

45

JULIA PFEIFFER
BURNS
STATE PARK

Partington
Point

To San Luis
Obispo

44.
De Angula Trail

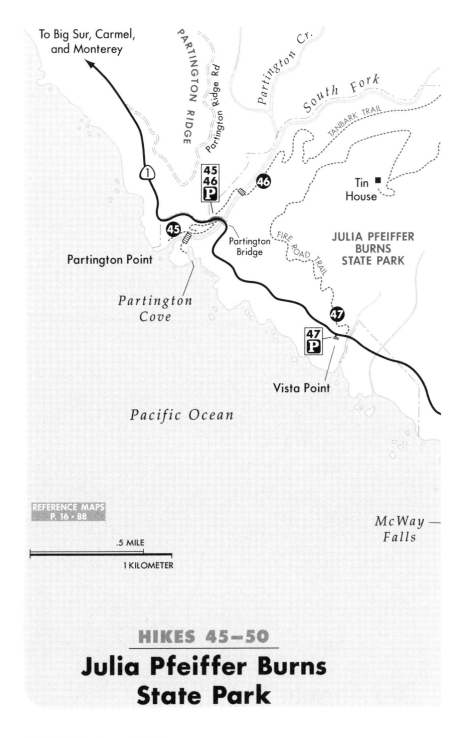

To Big Sur, Carmel,
and Monterey

PARTINGTON RIDGE

Partington Ridge Rd

Partington Cr.

South Fork

TANBARK TRAIL

1

45
46
P

46

Tin
House ■

Partington Point

45

Partington
Bridge

FIRE ROAD TRAIL

**JULIA PFEIFFER
BURNS
STATE PARK**

*Partington
Cove*

47

47
P

Vista Point

Pacific Ocean

REFERENCE MAPS
P. 16 · 88

*McWay
Falls*

.5 MILE

1 KILOMETER

HIKES 45–50
Julia Pfeiffer Burns
State Park

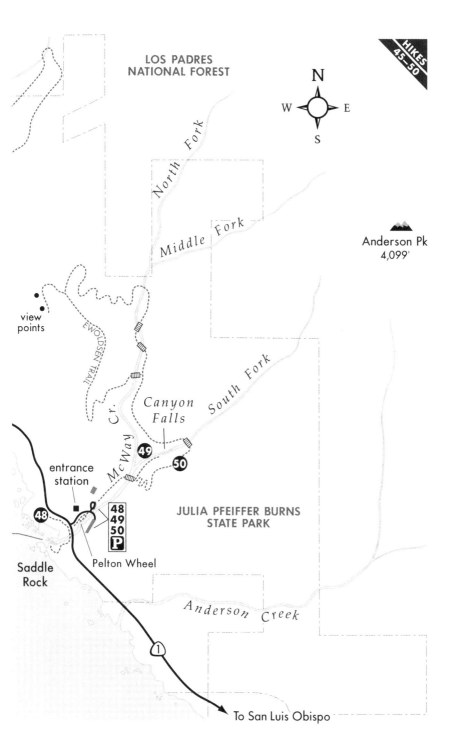

LOS PADRES
NATIONAL FOREST

N

W   E

S

North Fork

Middle Fork

Anderson Pk
4,099'

view
points

EWOLDSEN TRAIL

Cr.

South Fork

Canyon
Falls

McWay

49

50

entrance
station

48

48
49
50
P

JULIA PFEIFFER BURNS
STATE PARK

Saddle
Rock

Pelton Wheel

Anderson Creek

1

To San Luis Obispo

45. Partington Cove
JULIA PFEIFFER BURNS STATE PARK

Hiking distance: 1 mile round trip
Hiking time: 1 hour
Configuration: out-and-back
Elevation gain: 280 feet
Difficulty: easy
Exposure: open canyon wall; enclosed tunnel
Dogs: not allowed
Maps: U.S.G.S. Partington Ridge · Julia Pfeiffer Burns State Park map
Big Sur and Ventana Wilderness map

Partington Cove sits at the northern boundary of Julia Pfeiffer Burns State Park along a pristine and rugged section of the Big Sur coastline. The trail to the enclosed cove descends down Partington Canyon on an old wagon route. The creek, which carved the canyon, empties into the ocean at the rocky west cove. A 120-foot manmade tunnel was cut through the cliffs over 100 years ago, leading to the east cove (an isolated, sheltered cove) and Partington Landing. The tunnel was a transit route to haul tanbark to the ships moored in Partington Cove. The historical landing was used as a shipping dock in the 1880s by homesteader John Partington.

To the trailhead

From the Big Sur Ranger Station, located 27 miles south of Carmel, drive 8.5 miles south on Highway 1 to the wide parking pullouts on both sides of the highway by Partington Bridge, where the road curves across Partington Creek and the canyon.

Heading north along Highway 1, the pullouts are 1.9 miles north of the signed entrance for Julia Pfeiffer Burns State Park.

The hike

Head west on the ocean side of Highway 1 past the trailhead gate. Descend on the eroded granite road along the north canyon wall, high above Partington Creek. The old road weaves downhill to the creek and a junction with an interpretive sign. The left fork follows Partington Creek upstream under a dense forest canopy.

Take the right fork 50 yards to a second junction. The left route crosses a footbridge over Partington Creek and leads to the historic tunnel carved through the granite wall. The tunnel emerges at the east cove, where remnants of Partington Landing remain.

Return to the junction by the bridge, and take the path that is now on the left. Follow the north bank of Partington Creek to an enclosed beach cove surrounded by the steep cliffs of Partington Point. Return along the same trail. ■

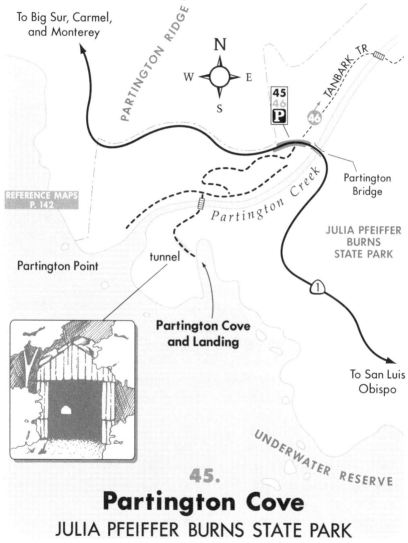

45.
Partington Cove
JULIA PFEIFFER BURNS STATE PARK

46. Tanbark Trail to Tin House
JULIA PFEIFFER BURNS STATE PARK

Hiking distance: 6.4 miles round trip (also 6.4 miles as a loop)
Hiking time: 4 hours
Configuration: out-and-back (or loop with Hike 47)
Elevation gain: 1,900 feet
Difficulty: strenuous
Exposure: shaded forest
Dogs: not allowed
Maps: U.S.G.S. Partington Ridge · Julia Pfeiffer Burns State Park map
Big Sur and Ventana Wilderness map

The 3,762-acre Julia Pfeiffer Burns State Park lies along ten miles of beautiful Big Sur coast backed by 3,000-foot ridges. The Tanbark Trail is a steep climb up Partington Canyon to a grassy meadow with spectacular coastal views from the abandoned Tin House. The house was built during World War II on a 1,950-foot ridge. The path parallels Partington Creek through a dense forest of huge redwoods, tanbark oaks, and a lush understory of ferns. Switchbacks lead up the canyon wall to the ridge separating Partington and McWay Canyons in the heart of the park. The hike can be combined with the Fire Road Trail—Hike 47—for a 6.4-mile loop.

To the trailhead

From the Big Sur Ranger Station, located 27 miles south of Carmel, drive 8.5 miles south on Highway 1 to the wide parking pullouts on both sides of the highway by Partington Bridge, where the road curves across Partington Creek and the canyon.

Heading north along Highway 1, the pullouts are 1.9 miles north of the signed entrance for Julia Pfeiffer Burns State Park.

The hike

From the inland side of the road, take the path on the northwest (left) side of the bridge. Enter the forested canyon. Within a couple hundred yards, cross the wood footbridge over Partington Creek. Continue upstream on the Tanbark Trail along the east side of the creek, passing huge rock formations, redwood groves,

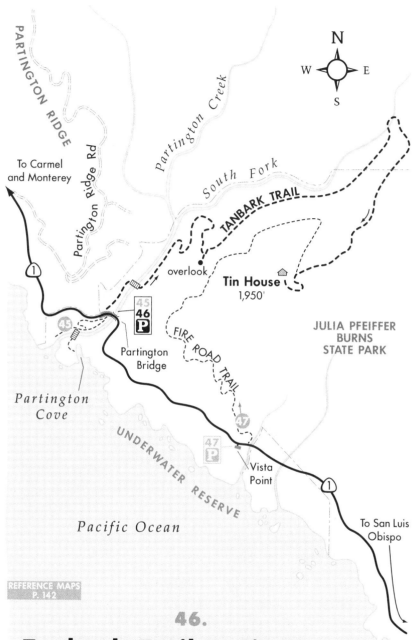

46.

Tanbark Trail to Tin House
JULIA PFEIFFER BURNS STATE PARK

pools, cascades, waterfalls, ferns, and mossy boulders. Cross a tributary stream by McLaughlin Grove, and head up the canyon wall on a few switchbacks, leaving the creek and canyon floor. Weave up the mountain to a sharp left switchback. A short detour to the right leads to a ridge overlooking Partington Point.

Return to the trail and traverse the canyon wall through tanbark oaks and redwoods. Cross planks over the South Fork of Partington Creek. Sharply switchback to the right, and recross the creek by a bench in a redwood grove. Continue uphill towards the south, reaching the high point of the hike at a trail sign. Descend to a T-junction with the Fire Road Trail (Hike 48). Bear left on the unpaved road, and descend a short distance, curving to the right to the abandoned Tin House, perched on a ridge. Below the rusty ruins is a grassy meadow with inspiring views of the Big Sur Coast.

Retrace your steps along the same trail, or return along the Fire Road Trail—Hike 47—for a 6.4-mile loop. The loop requires walking 0.9 miles along Highway 1 back to the trailhead. ■

47. Fire Road Trail to Tin House
JULIA PFEIFFER BURNS STATE PARK

Hiking distance: 4.6 miles round trip (or 6.4 miles as a loop)
Hiking time: 2.5 hours
Configuration: out-and-back (or loop with Hike 46)
Elevation gain: 1,600 feet
Difficulty: moderate to strenuous
Exposure: shaded forest
Dogs: not allowed
Maps: U.S.G.S. Partington Ridge · Julia Pfeiffer Burns State Park map
      Big Sur and Ventana Wilderness map

The Fire Road Trail climbs up a coastal ridge to the Tin House, where there are panoramic views of the ocean and Julia Pfeiffer Burns State Park from an elevation of 1,950 feet. This trail is a shorter and slightly easier route up to the Tin House than the Tanbark Trail (Hike 46). The wide trail begins on the coastal cliffs

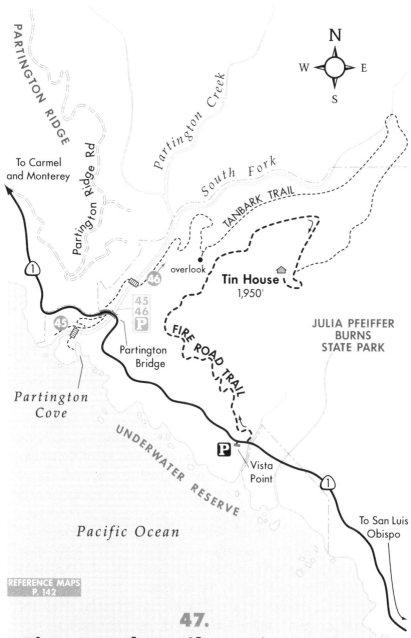

N

W ✦ E

S

PARTINGTON RIDGE

To Carmel
and Monterey

Partington Ridge Rd

Partington Creek

South Fork

TANBARK TRAIL

46

overlook

Tin House
1,950'

45
46
P

45

Partington
Bridge

FIRE ROAD TRAIL

JULIA PFEIFFER
BURNS
STATE PARK

Partington
Cove

UNDERWATER

RESERVE

P

Vista
Point

1

To San Luis
Obispo

Pacific Ocean

REFERENCE MAPS
P. 142

47.
Fire Road Trail to Tin House
JULIA PFEIFFER BURNS STATE PARK

across from Vista Point and heads inland, weaving in and out of gullies to Partington Canyon. The path contours the east wall of the canyon, rich with coastal redwoods, tanbark oaks, and shade-loving plants. The trail ends at the Tin House, a boarded up tin building on the high ridge separating Partington and McWay Canyons. Below the building is a grassy meadow with great coastal vistas. This hike can be combined with the Tanbark Trail—Hike 46—for a 6.4-mile loop.

To the trailhead

From the Big Sur Ranger Station, located 27 miles south of Carmel, drive 9.3 miles south on Highway 1 to the signed Vista Point parking pullout on the right (coastal) side.

Heading north along Highway 1, the pullout is 1.1 miles north of the signed entrance for Julia Pfeiffer Burns State Park.

The hike

Head 75 yards southbound on Highway 1 to the gated Fire Road on the inland side of the highway. Walk around the trail gate into a shady redwood grove, paralleling a trickling stream on the right. Curve left, emerging from the trees, and climb to an overlook of the coast and offshore rocks. The trail follows the coastal cliffs along the oceanfront mountains. As you near Partington Canyon, a thousand feet above Partington Cove, curve right and enter the canyon. The views extend across the canyon to homes on the south-facing cliffs. Curve along the contours of the mountain, winding uphill on the serpentine path through redwoods and tanbark oaks. A few switchbacks aid in the climb through the shady forest. The road tops out at a signed junction with the Tanbark Trail on the left. Continue straight ahead and gently descend for a short distance, looping to the right. The trail ends at the abandoned Tin House, perched on a ridge, and the grassy meadow overlook just below the building.

From the landmark structure, retrace your steps along the same trail, or return on the Tanbark Trail (Hike 46) for a 6.4-mile loop. The loop requires walking 0.9 miles along Highway 1 back to the Vista Point pullout. ▪

48. McWay Falls and Saddle Rock
JULIA PFEIFFER BURNS STATE PARK

Hiking distance: 0.7 miles round trip
Hiking time: 30 minutes
Configuration: out-and-back
Elevation gain: 50 feet
Difficulty: very easy
Exposure: a mix of shaded forest and open hillside
Dogs: not allowed
Maps: U.S.G.S. Partington Ridge · Julia Pfeiffer Burns State Park map
     Big Sur and Ventana Wilderness map

**map
page 152**

McWay Falls pours 80 feet onto a sandy pocket beach along the edge of the Pacific at the mouth of McWay Canyon (cover photo). The incredibly scenic waterfall drops off the granite bluff in a wooded beach cove lined with offshore rocks. A handicap-accessible trail leads to a viewing area of McWay Cove and the cataract on the 100-foot-high bluffs. The pristine beach itself is not accessible. On the south side of the bay is a footpath to a scenic overlook at a cypress-shaded picnic area adjacent to Saddle Rock.

To the trailhead

From the Big Sur Ranger Station, located 27 miles south of Carmel, drive 10.4 miles south on Highway 1 to the signed Julia Pfeiffer Burns State Park. Turn left (inland) and park in the day-use parking lot.

The hike

Descend the steps across the road from the restrooms. At the base of the steps, bear right and head southwest on the signed Waterfall Trail. Follow the north canyon wall above the creek, and walk through the tunnel under Highway 1 to a T-junction. The left fork leads to the Saddle Rock Overlook. For now, take the right fork along the cliffs. Cross a wooden footbridge, with great views of McWay Falls pouring onto the sand. Beyond the bridge is an observation deck that offers expansive coastal views.

 After enjoying the sights, return to the junction and take the footpath towards the south end of the bay. Walk through a canopy of old-growth eucalyptus trees high above the falls. Descend to the trail's end at the 206-foot Saddle Rock Overlook in a cypress grove by a picnic area. ■

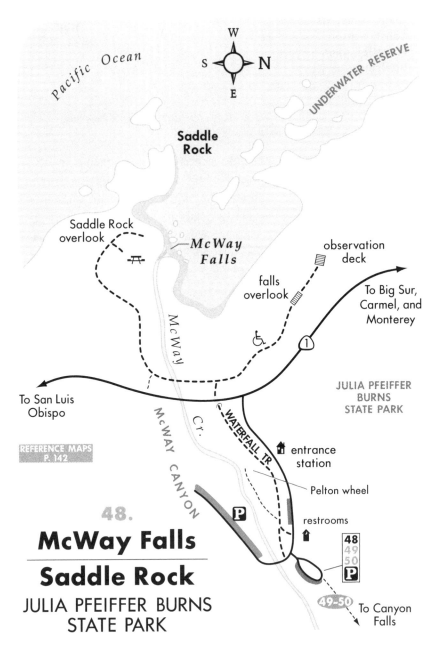

49. McWay Canyon to Canyon Falls
JULIA PFEIFFER BURNS STATE PARK

Hiking distance: 0.7 miles round trip
Hiking time: 30 minutes
Configuration: out and back
Elevation gain: 200 feet
Difficulty: very easy
Exposure: shaded forest
Dogs: not allowed
Maps: U.S.G.S. Partington Ridge · Julia Pfeiffer Burns State Park map
Big Sur and Ventana Wilderness map

**map
page 154**

This easy hike begins from the main entrance of Julia Pfeiffer Burns State Park and meanders up McWay Canyon through a rich, atmospheric coastal redwood forest. The shaded path parallels McWay Creek up the canyon and ends at Canyon Falls, a long, narrow, two-tiered waterfall on the South Fork of McWay Creek. The 30-foot cataract cascades off fern-covered rock cliffs in a lush grotto at the back of the serene canyon. The trail begins on the Ewoldsen Trail, which continues up to a ridgetop overlook for a longer hiking option (Hike 50).

To the trailhead

From the Big Sur Ranger Station, located 27 miles south of Carmel, drive 10.4 miles south on Highway 1 to the signed Julia Pfeiffer Burns State Park. Turn left (inland) and park in the day-use parking lot.

The hike

Take the signed Canyon and Ewoldsen Trails from the upper end of the parking lot. Follow the watercourse of McWay Creek upstream, passing the picnic area shaded by redwoods. Continue along the west bank of the creek through the dense coastal redwood forest and communities of ferns and redwood sorrel. Cross a wooden footbridge over the creek to the east bank, just below the confluence of the South Fork and Main Fork of McWay Creek. A short distance upstream is a posted junction. The right fork continues up the canyon wall on the Ewoldsen Trail

(Hike 50). Take the left fork, staying close to the creek on the Canyon Trail. The narrow, cliffside path ends at the base of the waterfall. Return along the same path. ▨

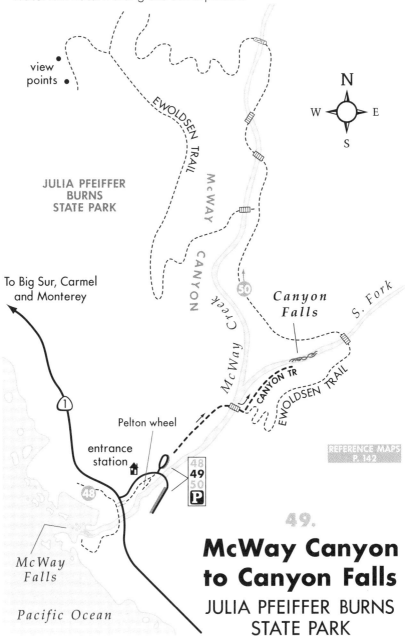

49.
McWay Canyon to Canyon Falls
JULIA PFEIFFER BURNS STATE PARK

50. Ewoldsen Trail
to Canyon Falls and Overlook
JULIA PFEIFFER BURNS STATE PARK

Hiking distance: 4.5 miles round trip
Hiking time: 3 hours
Configuration: out-and-back with large loop
Elevation gain: 1,600 feet
Difficulty: moderate to strenuous
Exposure: shaded forest
Dogs: not allowed
Maps: U.S.G.S. Partington Ridge · Julia Pfeiffer Burns State Park map
      Big Sur and Ventana Wilderness map

map
page 157

The Ewoldsen Trail in Julia Pfeiffer Burns State Park leads through a dense coastal redwood forest in McWay Canyon. The trail crosses several bridges as it heads up to the steep ridge separating McWay and Partington Canyons. From the grassy coastal cliffs are amazing overlooks perched on the edge of the cliffs. The views extend across the park and far beyond, showcasing the jagged coastline and endless mountain ridges and valleys. En route to the ridgetop overlooks is Canyon Falls, a long, narrow, two-tiered waterfall on the South Fork of McWay Creek (Hike 49). The 30-foot cataract cascades off fern-covered rock cliffs in a lush grotto at the back of a serene canyon.

To the trailhead

From the Big Sur Ranger Station, located 27 miles south of Carmel, drive 10.4 miles south on Highway 1 to the signed Julia Pfeiffer Burns State Park. Turn left (inland) and park in the day-use parking lot.

The hike

From the upper end of the parking area, take the signed Canyon and Ewoldsen Trails into a dark redwood forest. Follow McWay Creek upstream past the picnic area. Cross a wooden footbridge over the creek to the east bank, just below the confluence of the South Fork and Main Fork of McWay Creek. A short distance upstream is a posted junction. To see the falls, take the left fork on the Canyon Trail, staying close to the creek. The narrow, cliffside path ends at the base of Canyon Falls.

Return back to the junction, and continue on the Ewoldsen Trail up the switchbacks, leaving the canyon floor and creek. Zigzag up the south wall of the canyon, and cross another footbridge over the South Fork. Traverse the hillside up the mountain contours, and rejoin the main fork of McWay Creek, where views extend down canyon to the sea. Follow the watercourse above the creek to a signed junction at one mile, beginning the loop. Take the right fork along the east bank of the creek. Cross two bridges over the creek, passing cascades, small waterfalls, pools, outcroppings, and moss-covered boulders. Cross a log bridge over the creek, and ascend the west canyon wall. Enter an oak woodland and follow the hillside path to a signed junction. Detour to the right a quarter mile to the view points on the 1,800-foot oceanfront cliffs. Take a break atop the ridge and enjoy the vistas.

Return to the junction and continue on the loop. The winding path descends along the oceanfront ridge, then curves left into the forested canyon. Complete the loop at the bridge over McWay Creek, and retrace your steps back to the right. ▩

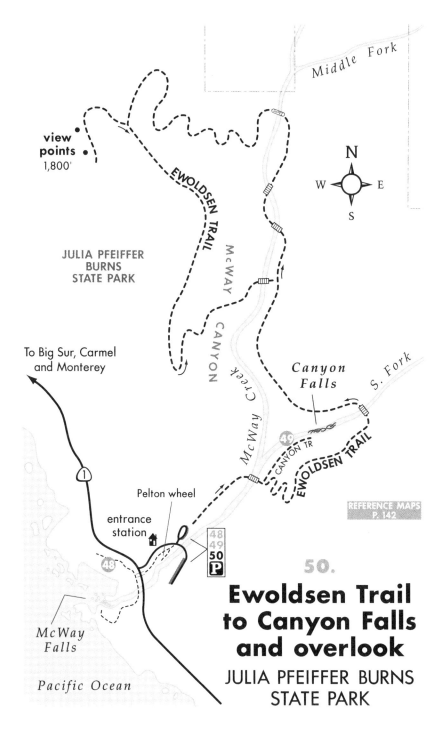

view
points •
1,800'

Middle Fork

N
W   E
S

EWOLDSEN TRAIL

JULIA PFEIFFER
BURNS
STATE PARK

M_cWAY

CANYON

To Big Sur, Carmel
and Monterey

*Canyon
Falls*

S. Fork

M_cWAY   *Creek*

49
CANYON TR

EWOLDSEN TRAIL

1

Pelton wheel

entrance
station

48

48
49
50
P

REFERENCE MAPS
P. 142

*McWay
Falls*

Pacific Ocean

50.
**Ewoldsen Trail
to Canyon Falls
and overlook**
JULIA PFEIFFER BURNS
STATE PARK

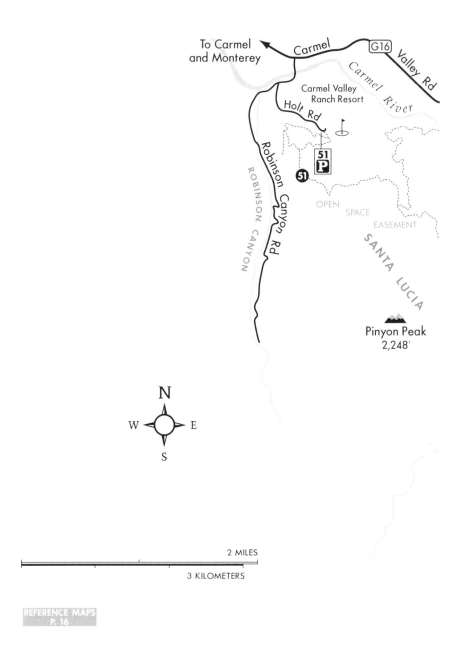

To Carmel and Monterey

Carmel

G16 Valley Rd

Carmel River

Carmel Valley Ranch Resort

Holt Rd

Robinson Canyon Rd

ROBINSON CANYON

51 P

51

OPEN SPACE EASEMENT

SANTA LUCIA

Pinyon Peak
2,248'

N
W E
S

2 MILES
3 KILOMETERS

REFERENCE MAPS
P. 16

HIKES 51-62

Garland Ranch Regional Park

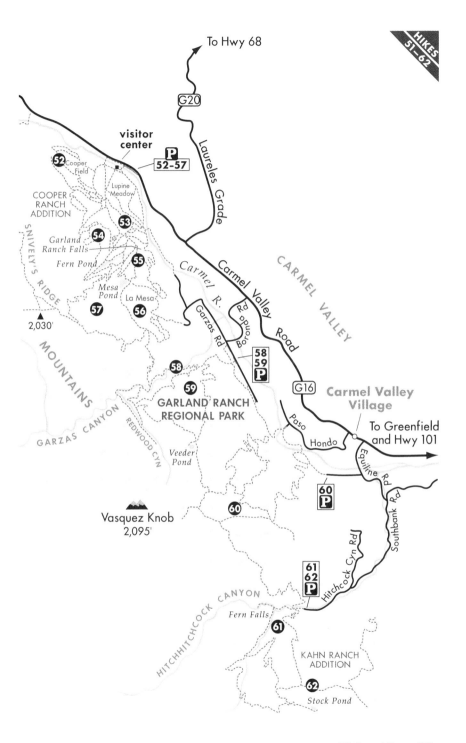

To Hwy 68

G20

Laureles Grade

visitor center

P
52-57

52 Cooper Field

COOPER RANCH ADDITION

Lupine Meadow

53

54

Garland Ranch Falls

Fern Pond

55

Carmel R.

Carmel Valley Road

CARMEL VALLEY

CARMEL VALLEY

Mesa Pond

La Mesa

57

56

SNIVELY'S RIDGE

2,030'

Garzas Rd

Boronda Rd

Rd

58
59
P

G16

Carmel Valley Village

58

59

GARLAND RANCH REGIONAL PARK

MOUNTAINS

GARZAS CANYON

REDWOOD CYN

Veeder Pond

Paso

Hondo

To Greenfield and Hwy 101

Equiline Rd

Vasquez Knob
2,095'

60

60
P

Southbank Rd

Hitchcock Cyn Rd

61
62
P

HITCHHITCHCOCK CANYON

Fern Falls

61

KAHN RANCH ADDITION

62

Stock Pond

51. Snively's Ridge Trail
GARLAND RANCH REGIONAL PARK

Hiking distance: 5.6 miles round trip
Hiking time: 3 hours
Configuration: out-and-back
Elevation gain: 1,730 feet
Difficulty: moderate to somewhat strenuous
Exposure: exposed hillsides and forested pockets
Dogs: allowed
Maps: U.S.G.S. Seaside and Mount Carmel
　　　　 Garland Ranch Regional Park map

Garland Ranch Regional Park stretches from the willow-lined Carmel River to the crest of the Santa Lucia Range. The 3,464-acre park lies along the northern tip of the range. Over 50 miles of trails offer many options for hiking. The multi-use trails criss-cross through the beautiful area, from the Carmel River valley to the highest point of the park along the 2,000-foot summit of Snively's Ridge.

This hike begins from the northern park entrance off of Holt Road and follows Snively's Ridge, the 1,600-foot mountain crest on the northernmost wall of the Santa Lucia Range. The ridge forms the southwest rim of Carmel Valley and offers breathtaking panoramas across the Ventana Wilderness and Carmel Valley. The views extend all the way to Monterey Bay and the peninsula. Snively's Ridge Trail follows the open grassy ridge along an open space easement at the northwest end of the park. The scenic trail is a steady climb at a moderate grade along the contours of the slope. The trail winds up to overlooks of Garland Ranch and its mosaic of trails.

To the trailhead

From Highway 1 and Carmel Valley Road in Carmel, drive 6.1 miles east on Carmel Valley Road to Robinson Canyon Road on the right (south). Turn right and drive 0.3 miles to Holt Road. Turn left and go 0.6 miles to the end of road at the gate. Park in the pullout on the left.

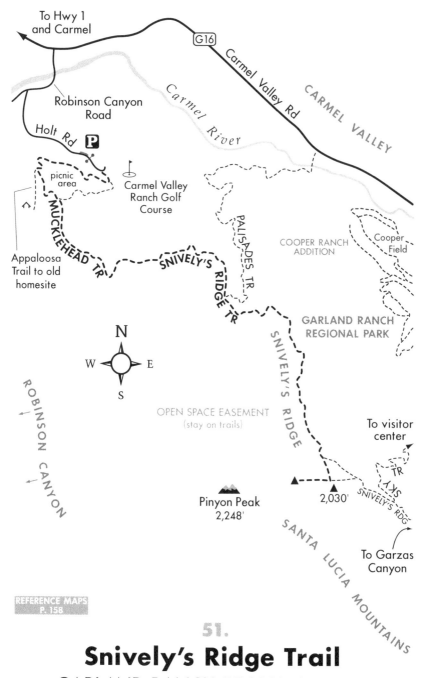

To Hwy 1
and Carmel

G16

Carmel Valley Rd

CARMEL VALLEY

Robinson Canyon
Road

Carmel River

Holt Rd

P

picnic
area

Carmel Valley
Ranch Golf
Course

MUCKLEHEAD TR

Appaloosa
Trail to old
homesite

SNIVELY'S RIDGE TR

PALISADES TR

COOPER RANCH
ADDITION

Cooper
Field

GARLAND RANCH
REGIONAL PARK

N

W   E

S

SNIVELY'S RIDGE

OPEN SPACE EASEMENT
(stay on trails)

ROBINSON CANYON

Pinyon Peak
2,248'

2,030'

To visitor
center

SKY TR

SNIVELY'S RDG

To Garzas
Canyon

SANTA LUCIA MOUNTAINS

REFERENCE MAPS
P. 158

51.
Snively's Ridge Trail
GARLAND RANCH REGIONAL PARK

The hike

Pass through the trail gate, and walk one block down residential Holt Road. At the left bend in Holt Road, bear right onto the trail. Skirt the edge of Carmel Valley Ranch Golf Course to the posted entrance of Garland Ranch Regional Park by a trail fork. Curve right and head up the slope surrounded by lichen-draped oaks and views across Carmel Valley. Steadily walk uphill on an easy grade on the narrow old ranch road to a Y-split. To the right, the Appaloosa Trail leads 200 yards to an old homesite and shed. Stay to the left on the Horseshoe Trail, and continue uphill to a second fork. The left branch leads 50 yards to a picnic area among stately oaks.

Take the signed Mucklehead Trail to the right, and follow the wide path through tall brush. The path quickly opens up and curves left, becoming the Snively's Ridge Trail. Traverse the north-facing slope perched on the mountain cliff. Continue uphill as panoramic views spread out below, from Monterey Bay to Santa Cruz. Just shy of a sweeping left bend is the posted Palisades Trail on the left at 1.5 miles. Continue straight ahead, climbing to vistas that span into the heart of Garland Ranch Regional Park (on the left), the surrounding mountains, and into Robinson Canyon (on the right). Wind through the open ridgetop meadows studded with madrone and oak groves. Follow the ridge, noticing a close-up view of the fire lookout crowning Pinyon Peak. Near the summit is a trail split. Snively's Ridge Trail descends to the left. Stay to the right to the knoll, the high point of the hike at 2,030 feet. To the left, a footpath rejoins Snively's Ridge Trail. To the right, the narrow path follows the ridgeline south to another knoll with oak trees and a bench. This is the turn-around spot. Return by retracing your route.

To extend the hike, the Snively's Ridge Trail continues southeast, connecting with the Sky Trail (Hike 57) in another half mile and Garzas Canyon Trail (Hike 58) in 1.5 miles. ▪

52. Rancho Loop

COOPER RANCH ADDITION
GARLAND RANCH REGIONAL PARK

Hiking distance: 3 mile-loop
Hiking time: 1.5 hours
Configuration: one large loop plus one small loop
Elevation gain: 350 feet
Difficulty: easy to slightly moderate
Exposure: shaded forest and open grassy meadow
Dogs: allowed
Maps: U.S.G.S. Seaside and Mt. Carmel · Garland Ranch Regional Park map

**map
page 165**

The most widely used trailhead for Garland Ranch Regional Park is at the park's northeast end, directly off of Carmel Valley Road. A visitor center, ranger station, and museum are located near the entrance. Hikes 52—57 begin from this trailhead.

The Cooper Ranch addition, at the northwest end of Garland Ranch Park, is one of two sections of the park that are open to mountain biking. (The Kahn Ranch addition, at the south end of the park, is also open to biking.) The ranch is bordered by a forested wildlife habitat reserve and a large eucalyptus grove to the north. The Santa Lucia Mountains lie to the south. The Rancho Loop circles Cooper Field, a large grassy meadow at the base of the towering mountains, then climbs into the forested foothills.

To the trailhead

From Highway 1 and Carmel Valley Road in Carmel, drive 8.6 miles east on Carmel Valley Road to the Garland Ranch Regional Park parking lot on the right.

The hike

Follow the gravel path to the right. Bear left at the bridge, crossing over the Carmel River to a trail junction. The visitor center is to the left. Take the Cooper Trail to the right across the flat grasslands to a posted junction. Begin the loop to the right on the Rancho Loop. Follow the north edge of the meadow to a junction by a eucalyptus grove. The main trail skirts the meadow. The right fork weaves through the towering eucalyptus grove. Both trails rejoin at the west end of Cooper Field. Loop back from the west end along the base of the mountains to a trail fork.

Bear right on the Cooper Trail into the oak–studded forest. Ascend the hillside and take the Acorn Trail to the right (near the ranger cabin). Continue climbing and cross a wooden bridge over a gully to an unsigned trail split. Switchback left through the coastal oak forest to the end of the trail at a junction. The left fork is the return route.

The short, half-mile loop starts here. Take the right fork steadily uphill to a 3-way split at the Live Oak Trail. Begin the small loop path to the right, and climb to the high point of the trail. Panoramic views extend across Carmel Valley. Cross the open slope to a junction. The right fork leads to Maple Canyon (Hike 54). Bear left, staying on the Live Oak Trail, and complete the half-mile upper loop. Return downhill to the main loop at the Acorn Trail junction.

Curve right and head down the shaded hillside to a trail split. Veer left on the posted Orchard Trail, and quickly curve right, heading back to the Live Oak Trail. Bear left and curve left again, staying on the Live Oak Trail. Pass the old homestead barns and outbuildings to the Cooper Trail. Cross the east end of Cooper Field, completing the loop and returning to the Carmel River. ▪

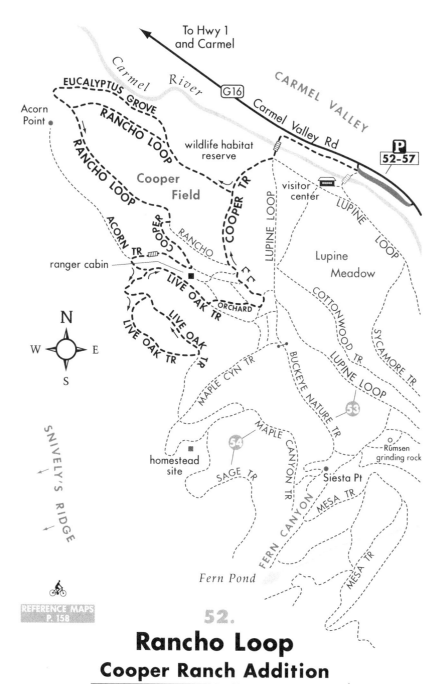

To Hwy 1
and Carmel

Carmel River

G16

CARMEL VALLEY

Carmel Valley Rd

P
52-57

EUCALYPTUS GROVE

Acorn
Point

RANCHO LOOP

RANCHO LOOP

RANCHO LOOP

wildlife habitat
reserve

Cooper
Field

COOPER TR

visitor
center

LUPINE LOOP

LUPINE LOOP

Lupine
Meadow

ACORN TR

COOPER TR

RANCHO

ranger cabin

LIVE OAK TR

ORCHARD

COTTONWOOD TR

SYCAMORE TR

LIVE OAK TR

LIVE OAK TR

N

W   E

S

MAPLE CYN TR

BUCKEYE NATURE TR

LUPINE LOOP

53

Rūmsen
grinding rock

SNIVELY'S RIDGE

MAPLE CANYON TR

54

homestead
site

SAGE TR

Siesta Pt

MESA TR

FERN CANYON

MESA TR

REFERENCE MAPS
P. 158

Fern Pond

52.

Rancho Loop
Cooper Ranch Addition
GARLAND RANCH REGIONAL PARK

53. Buckeye Nature Trail
GARLAND RANCH REGIONAL PARK

Hiking distance: 2 miles round trip
Hiking time: 1 hour
Configuration: out-and-back with large loop
Elevation gain: 250 feet
Difficulty: easy
Exposure: mostly shaded forest
Dogs: allowed
Maps: U.S.G.S. Seaside and Mt. Carmel · Garland Ranch Regional Park map

The Buckeye Nature Trail is an interpretive trail through cool, moist woods lined with ferns, fungi, and poison oak in a forest of buckeye, oak, and bay laurel trees. Information stations describe plants used by Native Americans and settlers, including those used for medicine, food seasonings, fishing, and musical instruments. The trail returns by the Rumsen Grinding Rock, two flat, high boulders with bedrock mortars. The holes were worn into the rock by native people grinding acorns into edible meal.

To the trailhead

From Highway 1 and Carmel Valley Road in Carmel, drive 8.6 miles east on Carmel Valley Road to the Garland Ranch Regional Park parking lot on the right.

The hike

Follow the gravel path to the right. Bear left at the bridge, crossing over the Carmel River to a trail junction. To the left is the visitor center, and to the right is the Cooper Trail. Continue straight ahead along the west edge of the meadow to the Cottonwood Trail on the left. Begin the loop to the right, climbing out of the meadow to a 4-way junction in an oak grove. The Live Oak Trail bears right, and the Lupine Loop continues to the left. Continue straight towards the Buckeye Nature Trail, passing the Maple Canyon Trail on the right. Enter the Buckeye Nature Trail through a fence gate, and wind through the oak grove past interpretive stations to a trail split with the Siesta Trail on the right. A short detour on the Siesta Trail climbs to a rocky perch overlooking Carmel Valley.

Back at the junction, continue on the Buckeye Nature Trail, and head past a large sandstone formation on the right. Descend steps to a T-junction with the Mesa Trail. Bear left 35 yards, and pick up the Buckeye Trail on the right. Take the narrow hillside footpath past fern-covered sandstone cliffs to a large outcropping on the left and the Rumsen Grinding Rock. After the rock, pass through a trail gate to a T-junction. Go to the left 40 yards, returning to the Mesa Trail. Bear right another 40 yards to a junction with the Lupine Loop. Take the right fork, descending through an oak canopy into Lupine Meadow. Follow the Cottonwood Trail along the south edge of the meadow and complete the loop. Return to the right. ■

wildlife
habitat
reserve

COOPER TR

LUPINE LOOP

visitor
center

seasonal

P
52-57

LUPINE LOOP

Lupine
Meadow

G16

N
W — E
S

LIVE OAK TR

COTTONWOOD TR

MAPLE CYN TR

LUPINE LOOP

SYCAMORE TR

Carmel Valley Rd

CARMEL VALLEY

Carmel River

BUCKEYE NATURE TR

MAPLE CANYON TR

MESA TR

Rumsen
grinding rock

WATERFALL TR

RIVER TR

Siesta Pt

CLIFF TR

REFERENCE MAPS
P. 158

53.

Buckeye Nature Trail
GARLAND RANCH REGIONAL PARK

54. Maple Canyon–Fern Canyon Loop
GARLAND RANCH REGIONAL PARK

Hiking distance: 4 miles round trip
Hiking time: 2 hours
Configuration: out-and-back with loop
Elevation gain: 800 feet
Difficulty: easy to somewhat moderate
Exposure: shaded canyon and open meadow
Dogs: allowed
Maps: U.S.G.S. Seaside and Mt. Carmel · Garland Ranch Regional Park map

Garland Ranch Regional Park is home to several different habitats. This hike includes a sampling of several ecosystems. The hike begins at the Carmel River and crosses Lupine Meadow into a shady canyon. The trail then climbs the foothills of the Santa

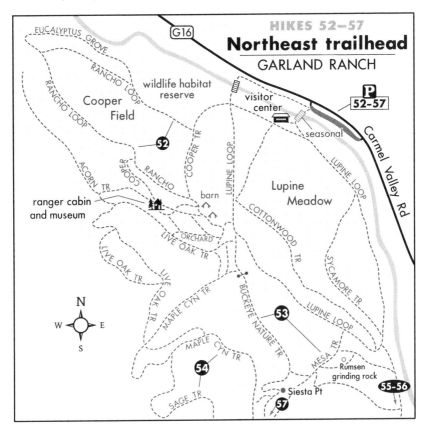

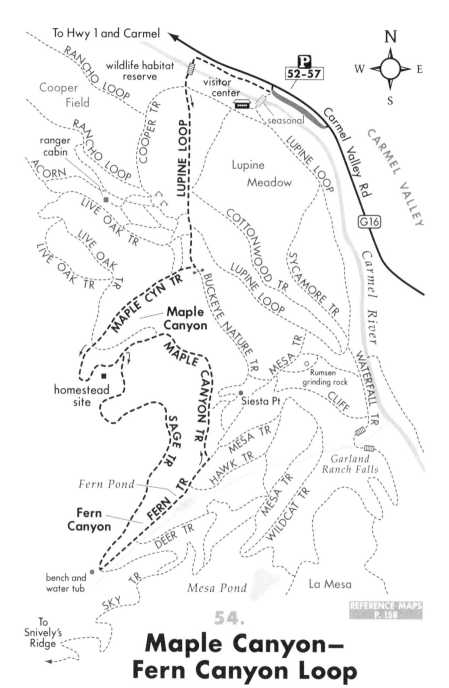

To Hwy 1 and Carmel

wildlife habitat reserve

Cooper Field

RANCHO LOOP

ranger cabin

RANCHO LOOP

ACORN

LIVE OAK TR

LIVE OAK TR

LIVE OAK TR

COOPER TR

LUPINE LOOP

visitor center

seasonal

P
52-57

N
W   E
S

Carmel Valley Rd

G16

CARMEL VALLEY

Lupine Meadow

LUPINE LOOP

COTTONWOOD TR

LUPINE LOOP

SYCAMORE TR

Carmel River

WATERFALL TR

MAPLE CYN TR

Maple Canyon

BUCKEYE NATURE TR

MAPLE CANYON TR

MESA TR

Rumsen grinding rock

homestead site

SAGE TR

Siesta Pt

MESA TR

CLIFF

Garland Ranch Falls

FERN TR

HAWK TR

Fern Pond

Fern Canyon

DEER TR

MESA TR

WILDCAT TR

bench and water tub

SKY TR

Mesa Pond

La Mesa

REFERENCE MAPS
P. 158

To Snively's Ridge

54.

Maple Canyon–
Fern Canyon Loop
GARLAND RANCH REGIONAL PARK

Lucia Mountains through oak groves and open chaparral to an old homestead site. The return route winds through a lush, narrow canyon to Fern Pond, a circular pond rimmed with trees and a variety of ferns.

To the trailhead

From Highway 1 and Carmel Valley Road in Carmel, drive 8.6 miles east on Carmel Valley Road to the Garland Ranch Regional Park parking lot on the right.

The hike

Follow the gravel path to the right. Bear left at the bridge, crossing over the Carmel River to a signed trail split. To the left is the visitor center, and to the right is the Cooper Trail. Continue straight ahead along the west edge of Lupine Meadow towards the mountains. Follow the fenceline, past the Cottonwood and Live Oak Trails, to the signed Maple Canyon and Buckeye Nature Trail junction. Bear right on the Maple Canyon Trail, and steadily climb up the lush, picturesque canyon. Pass the Live Oak Trail, and cross the canyon drainage at a horseshoe bend to the homestead site. The old homestead sits in a small grassy clearing rimmed with trees. A short distance ahead is the Sage Trail junction.

Begin the loop to the right on the Sage Trail, temporarily leaving the lush canyon to the exposed sage and chaparral hillside. Traverse the east-facing hillside, overlooking Fern Canyon and Carmel Valley. Continue to a water trough, bench, and a junction with the Fern Trail. Take the Fern Trail to the left and steeply descend through the narrow, shady canyon. Pass the Deer Trail on the right to Fern Pond, surrounded by aspen, oak, and an abundance of ferns. By the pond is another junction. Take the Maple Canyon Trail to the left, and regain elevation past the Siesta Point Trail, soon after completing the loop. Continue straight ahead— past the homestead site—and retrace your steps. ▪

55. Garland Ranch Falls—Mesa Loop

GARLAND RANCH REGIONAL PARK

Hiking distance: 3.5 miles round trip
Hiking time: 1.5 hours
Configuration: out-and-back with large loop
Elevation gain: 600 feet
Difficulty: easy to slightly moderate
Exposure: shaded canyon and open meadow
Dogs: allowed
Maps: U.S.G.S. Seaside and Mt. Carmel · Garland Ranch Regional Park map

**map
page 172**

This loop hike visits Garland Ranch Falls, a 70-foot cataract off a sandstone cliff in an enclosed, fern-filled canyon. The hike is enjoyable year-round, but to experience the cascade of the ephemeral waterfall, plan your hike after a rain. Beyond the falls, the forested trail continues to La Mesa, a flat river terrace and wildlife habitat pond perched in a saddle above the valley floor.

To the trailhead

From Highway 1 and Carmel Valley Road in Carmel, drive 8.6 miles east on Carmel Valley Road to the Garland Ranch Regional Park parking lot on the right.

The hike

Follow the gravel path to the right. Bear left at the bridge, crossing over the Carmel River to a trail junction. Bear left again, passing the visitor center on the Lupine Loop. Walk southeast through the meadow to a posted junction with the Waterfall Trail. Go to the left on the Waterfall Trail, following the rocky riverbed. Ascend the hillside and enter the tree-shaded slopes, passing the Cliff Trail on the right. Traverse the cliffside up the gulch, and cross a footbridge into the steep-walled box canyon at the base of the transient waterfall. After crossing the tributary, climb steps and cross another footbridge, leaving the canyon and emerging into an oak woodland with a lush understory of ferns and moss. Pass through a trail gate to a junction with the Vaquero Trail on the left. Continue straight ahead, steadily gaining elevation to a large grassy mesa with benches and a 4-way junction at 1.6 miles. The right fork, the Mesa Trail, is the return route.

First, continue 125 yards to La Mesa Pond. After enjoying the pond, return to the junction, and take the Mesa Trail to the north, now on your left. The trail gently winds down the hillside, passing junctions with the Sky Trail, Hawk Trail, and Fern Trail. Cross a trickling stream in the fern-covered drainage to a T-junction with the Lupine Loop above the meadow. Bear right, drop into the meadow, and complete the loop. ▪

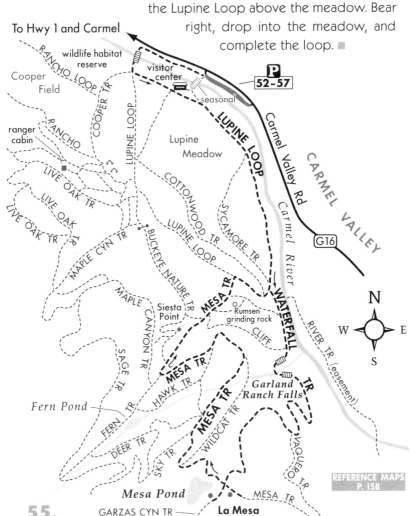

55.

Garland Ranch Falls—Mesa Loop
GARLAND RANCH REGIONAL PARK

56. Lupine Meadow to La Mesa
GARLAND RANCH REGIONAL PARK

Hiking distance: 4.5 miles round trip
Hiking time: 2.5 hours
Configuration: out-and-back with loop
Elevation gain: 800 feet
Difficulty: moderate
Exposure: open meadow and shaded canyon
Dogs: allowed
Maps: U.S.G.S. Seaside and Mt. Carmel · Garland Ranch Regional Park map

**map
page 175**

This hike begins at Lupine Meadow by the Carmel River and climbs to La Mesa, a large grassy terrace with a wildlife habitat pond. En route to La Mesa, the trail passes ephemeral Garland Ranch Falls, then climbs to the Oakview Trail, perched on a mountain cliff overlooking Garzas Canyon. The stream-fed canyon bisects Garland Ranch. The trail follows the hillside 500 feet above Garzas Canyon and returns through a grove of stately oaks.

To the trailhead

From Highway 1 and Carmel Valley Road in Carmel, drive 8.6 miles east on Carmel Valley Road to the Garland Ranch Regional Park parking lot on the right.

The hike

Follow the gravel path to the right. Bear left at the bridge, crossing over the Carmel River to a trail junction. Go left and continue past the visitor center. Head southeast through the flat grassy meadow, passing the Sycamore Trail on the right, to a signed junction with the Waterfall Trail at 0.5 miles. Take the Waterfall Trail to the left, and ascend the hillside in a shady woodland. Head up the ravine, crossing a wooden footbridge into a steep-walled grotto at the base of Garland Ranch Falls, the seasonal waterfall. Cross a second footbridge, leaving the canyon and entering an oak grove. Pass through a trail gate to a signed junction.

To begin the loop, bear left on the Vaquero Trail up the forested path. Near the top, the path widens and views open up of Carmel Valley. The trail ends at a T-junction with the Mesa Trail at the east end of the large, open meadow. Go left on the old ranch road to the Oakview Trail on the right. Take the Oakview Trail, overlooking Garzas Canyon. Pass both junctions with the Oakview Loop, climbing steeply to the ridge. Follow the level ridge to a junction with the Garzas Canyon Trail on the left. Stay right for 30 yards to a junction with Snively's Ridge Trail. Take the Garzas Canyon Trail to the right, gently descending through stately oaks. Emerge from the woodland on the grassy mesa by La Mesa Pond. Past the pond is a 4-way junction. Take the middle fork—the Waterfall Trail—and descend to the Vaquero Trail junction, completing the loop. Return on the Waterfall Trail, following the same route back. ▨

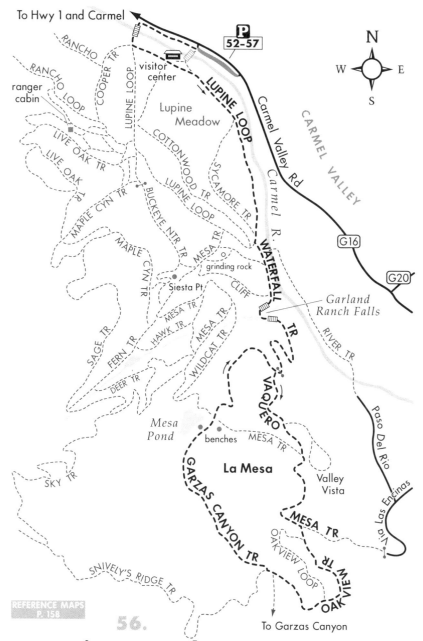

To Hwy 1 and Carmel

P
52-57

visitor center

RANCHO

RANCHO LOOP

ranger cabin

RANCHO COOPER TR

LUPINE LOOP

LUPINE LOOP

LUPINE LOOP

Lupine Meadow

Carmel Valley Rd

Carmel R.

CARMEL VALLEY

N
W — E
S

LIVE OAK TR

LIVE OAK TR

MAPLE CYN TR

COTTONWOOD TR

SYCAMORE TR

BUCKEYE NTR TR

LUPINE LOOP

MAPLE CYN TR

MESA TR

grinding rock

Siesta Pt

SAGE TR

FERN TR

HAWK TR

MESA TR

MESA TR

DEER TR

WILDCAT TR

CLIFF

WATERFALL TR

Garland Ranch Falls

G16

G20

RIVER TR

VAQUERO

Mesa Pond

benches

MESA TR

La Mesa

Valley Vista

Paso Del Rio

GARZAS CANYON TR

SKY TR

MESA TR

SNIVELY'S RIDGE TR

OAK VIEW LOOP

OAK VIEW TR

Via Las Encinas

REFERENCE MAPS
P. 158

56.

To Garzas Canyon

Lupine Meadow to La Mesa
GARLAND RANCH REGIONAL PARK

57. Lupine Meadow to Snively's Ridge
GARLAND RANCH REGIONAL PARK

Hiking distance: 6 miles round trip
Hiking time: 3 hours
Configuration: out-and-back with large loop
Elevation gain: 1,600 feet
Difficulty: moderate to strenuous
Exposure: shaded hillside and exposed ridge
Dogs: allowed
Maps: U.S.G.S. Seaside and Mt. Carmel · Garland Ranch Regional Park map

Garland Park stretches from the willow-lined Carmel River to the crest of the Santa Lucia Range. This hike begins at the river and climbs through oak woodlands to Snively's Ridge at the mountain crest, stretching 1,600 feet above Carmel Valley. From the ridge are sweeping, unobstructed bird's-eye views of Carmel Valley, the Monterey Peninsula, Salinas, and the interior Santa Lucia Mountains. Portions of the Snively's Ridge Trail are tirelessly steep and require frequent rest stops.

To the trailhead

From Highway 1 and Carmel Valley Road in Carmel, drive 8.6 miles east on Carmel Valley Road to the Garland Ranch Regional Park parking lot on the right.

The hike

Follow the gravel path to the right. Bear left at the bridge, crossing over the Carmel River to a signed trail split. Bear left, passing the visitor center on the Lupine Loop. Follow the tree-dotted meadow, passing the Sycamore Trail on the right, to a junction with the Waterfall Trail at 0.5 miles. Stay on the Lupine Loop. Pass the Cottonwood Trail and climb a small rise to a bluff above the meadow. At the signed junction, bear left on the Mesa Trail. Head up the lush drainage and cross a trickling stream. The winding path passes the Buckeye Trail, Siesta Point, Fern Trail, Hawk Trail, and Sky Trail, all on the right.

At Sky Trail, begin the loop to the left, staying on the Mesa Trail. Emerge onto La Mesa, a huge grassy terrace at a 4-way junction.

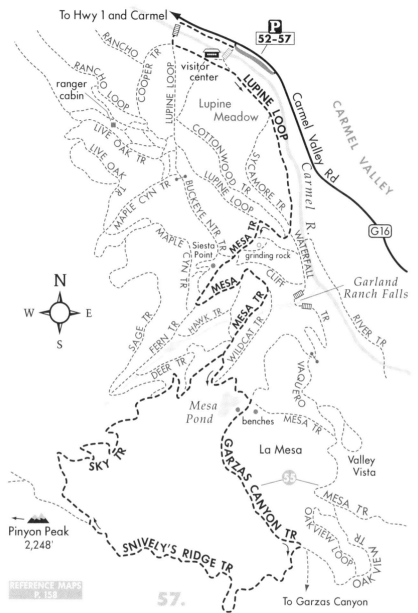

To Hwy 1 and Carmel

RANCHO

RANCHO LOOP

ranger cabin

LIVE OAK TR

LIVE OAK TR

COOPER TR

LUPINE LOOP

visitor center

Lupine Meadow

P
52-57

LUPINE LOOP

Carmel Valley Rd

Carmel R.

CARMEL VALLEY

G16

COTTONWOOD TR

MAPLE CYN TR

BUCKEYE NTR TR

LUPINE LOOP

SYCAMORE TR

MESA TR

WATERFALL TR

Garland Ranch Falls

MAPLE CYN TR

Siesta Point

grinding rock

MESA

CLIFF

N
W E
S

SAGE TR

FERN TR

HAWK TR

DEER TR

MESA TR

WILDCAT TR

RIVER TR

VAQUERO

Mesa Pond

benches

MESA TR

La Mesa

SKY TR

GARZAS CANYON TR

55

Valley Vista

Pinyon Peak
2,248'

SNIVELY'S RIDGE TR

MESA TR

OAKVIEW LOOP

OAKVIEW TR

REFERENCE MAPS
P. 158

57.

To Garzas Canyon

Lupine Meadow
to Snively's Ridge
GARLAND RANCH REGIONAL PARK

Take the Garzas Canyon Trail on the right. Pass La Mesa Pond, a wildlife habitat pond, and continue into the shady grove of stately oaks at the base of the mountain. Curve left and climb the mountain slope to the ridge and a junction with Snively's Ridge Trail. Begin a very steep ascent to the right on Snively's Ridge. Climb through oak groves and small meadows on the east-facing cliffs above Garzas Canyon. The eroded path mercifully levels out at a fenceline by Snively's Corral, a bench, and a junction.

After resting, descend on the winding Sky Trail to an elevated perch overlooking La Mesa Pond and the network of trails below. Stay to the right past the Sage Trail and Deer Trail, completing the loop at the Mesa Trail. Bear left on the Mesa Trail, retracing your steps back to the trailhead. ■

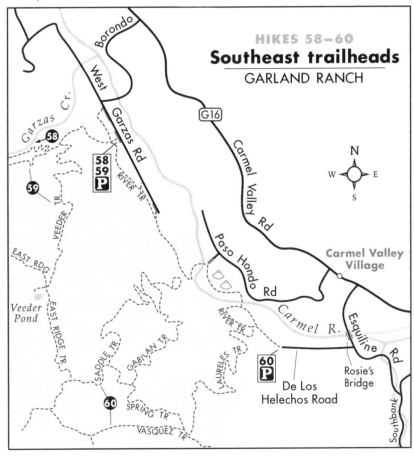

58. Garzas Canyon to Redwood Canyon
GARLAND RANCH REGIONAL PARK

Hiking distance: 3.6-mile loop
Hiking time: 2 hours
Configuration: loop with short spur trail
Elevation gain: 800 feet
Difficulty: easy to moderate
Exposure: mostly shaded canyon
Dogs: allowed
Maps: U.S.G.S. Seaside and Mt. Carmel · Garland Ranch Regional Park map

**map
page 181**

Garzas Canyon is a stream-fed canyon bisecting Garland Ranch Regional Park. The beautiful Garzas Canyon Trail heads up the lush garden-like canyon past rock-lined pools and numerous creek crossings. A short spur trail leads into Redwood Canyon, a remote side canyon with clusters of towering redwoods. The loop hike returns on a cliffside path above Garzas Canyon.

To the trailhead

From Highway 1 and Carmel Valley Road in Carmel, drive 10.3 miles east on Carmel Valley Road to Boronda Road on the right. The turnoff is 1.7 miles past the signed Garland Ranch parking lot. Turn right on Boronda Road and drive 0.6 miles, crossing over the Carmel River to the end of the road. Turn left on East Garzas Road, and continue 0.2 miles to the signed trail on the right. Park alongside the road.

Additional parking, and a signed connector trail into Garzas Canyon, is located a quarter mile ahead at the end of the road.

The hike

Hike into the shady oak grove, passing the River Trail. Head up the forested slope past the Veeder Trail on the left (Hike 59) to the signed junction with the Terrace Trail, the return route.

Begin the loop to the right on the Garzas Canyon Trail. Switchbacks descend to Garzas Creek at the canyon floor. Head up canyon and cross a long wooden footbridge over the creek. The path climbs numerous small rises, then dips back to the floor and a junction. The Garzas Canyon Trail leads up the canyon wall to La Mesa, a huge, grassy terrace to the north. Stay to the left on the creekside path. Cross another footbridge over the creek to a junction with the East Ridge Trail. (For a shorter hike, the East Ridge Trail connects with the Terrace Trail.) Go to the right and pass through a trail gate on the Redwood Canyon Trail. Continue up canyon, crossing the creek four more times. At the fourth crossing, leave Garzas Creek and veer left up Redwood Canyon. Pass clusters of large redwoods in the narrow side canyon. A half mile up the canyon, a bridge crosses the stream at a junction. This is the return route.

First, continue up Redwood Canyon through the forest, rich with ferns and magnificent redwoods. The canyon splits in a wide flat area covered with redwoods. The trail follows the right canyon and soon fades away.

Return to the bridge and cross, heading up the east canyon wall. Pass through a trail gate to a Y-junction with the East Ridge Trail. Take the left fork fifty yards to a signed junction. Bear right on the Terrace Trail. Traverse the narrow cliffside path above Garzas Canyon, following the contours of the mountain. Climb the steps and complete the loop at the Garzas Canyon Trail. Return to the right. ▪

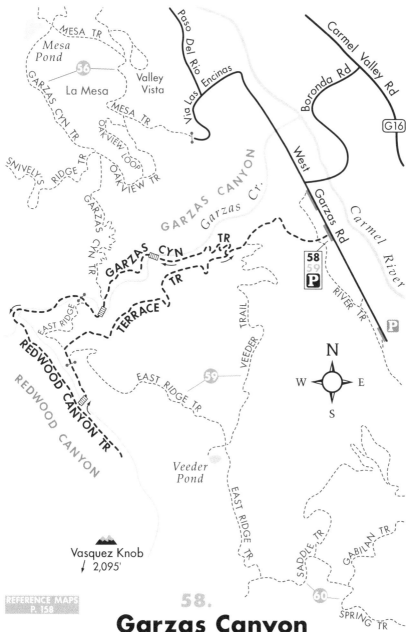

Garzas Canyon
to Redwood Canyon
GARLAND RANCH REGIONAL PARK

59. Veeder—East Ridge—Terrace Loop
GARLAND RANCH REGIONAL PARK

Hiking distance: 3.5-mile loop
Hiking time: 2 hours
Configuration: loop
Elevation gain: 1,300 feet
Difficulty: moderate to somewhat strenuous
Exposure: shaded forest and open meadow
Dogs: allowed
Maps: U.S.G.S. Carmel Valley, Mt. Carmel and Seaside
  Garland Ranch Regional Park map

This loop hike climbs hundreds of feet to an overlook in a mountain meadow. The panoramic views include Garzas Canyon, Redwood Canyon, Snively's Ridge, Carmel Valley, and the ocean at Monterey Bay. The trail winds through oak woodlands and traverses a narrow, cliffside path above Garzas Canyon.

To the trailhead

From Highway 1 and Carmel Valley Road in Carmel, drive 10.3 miles east on Carmel Valley Road to Boronda Road on the right. The turnoff is 1.7 miles past the signed Garland Ranch parking lot. Turn right on Boronda Road and drive 0.6 miles, crossing over the Carmel River to the end of the road. Turn left on East Garzas Road, and continue 0.2 miles to the signed trail on the right. Park alongside the road.

Additional parking, and a signed connector trail into Garzas Canyon, begins a quarter mile ahead at the end of the road.

The hike

Take the signed Garzas Trail through the oak woodland. Cross the River Trail and head up the slope to a signed junction on the left with the Veeder Trail. Bear left on the Veeder Trail—the beginning of the loop—and wind up the oak-studded hill past ferns and poison oak. Steadily climb the east-facing hillside while overlooking Carmel Valley. Curve right up the side canyon to a bench in a clearing with views of Garzas Canyon and Snively's Ridge

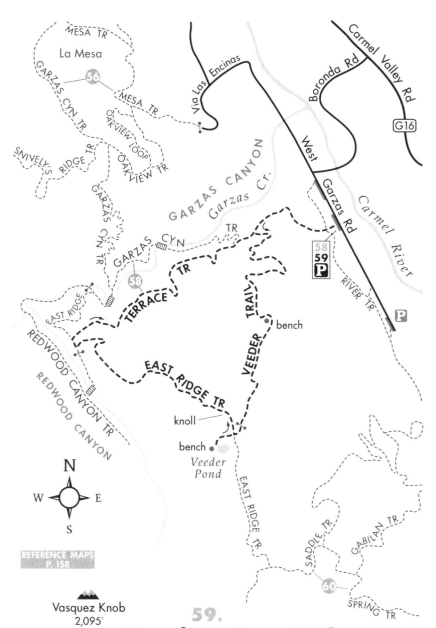

MESA TR

La Mesa

56

GARZAS CYN TR

MESA TR

OAKVIEW LOOP

OAK-VIEW TR

SNIVELY'S RIDGE TR

GARZAS CYN TR

Via Las Encinas

Boronda Rd

Carmel Valley Rd

West Garzas Rd

G16

GARZAS CANYON

Garzas Cr.

Carmel River

GARZAS CYN

TR

58
59
P

RIVER TR

P

58

GARZAS CYN TR

TERRACE TR

VEEDER TRAIL

bench

EAST RIDGE

EAST RIDGE TR

REDWOOD CANYON TR

REDWOOD CANYON

knoll

bench

Veeder Pond

EAST RIDGE TR

SADDLE TR

GABILAN TR

60

SPRING TR

N
W   E
S

REFERENCE MAPS
P. 158

Vasquez Knob
2,095'

59.

Veeder–East Ridge–
Terrace Loop
GARLAND RANCH REGIONAL PARK

to the northwest. Beyond the bench, climb to a ridge, passing through a trail gate to a saddle and a signed junction with the East Ridge Trail. The left branch climbs up to Vasquez Knob. Before taking the right fork (the continuation of the loop), descend into the open meadow to a bench at Veeder Pond, a vernal pool.

Return to the junction and continue west (left) on the loop. Ascend the small hill to a knoll, the highest point on the hike. The 360-degree vistas extend to the ocean and Monterey Bay. Descend to the west, overlooking Redwood Canyon and the towering trees. The path quickly drops down the north wall of Redwood Canyon to a junction. The left fork leads up Redwood Canyon (Hike 58). Take the right fork 50 yards to a junction with the Terrace Trail on the right. Head right, traversing the cliffs on the narrow path above the canyon. Weave in and out of ravines along the contours of the canyon. Climb some steps to a junction with the Garzas Canyon Trail. Bear to the right, completing the loop at the Veeder Trail. Return on the same route. ▨

60. Vasquez Ridge
Laureles—Vasquez—Spring Loop
GARLAND RANCH REGIONAL PARK

Hiking distance: 5.5 miles round trip
Hiking time: 3 hours
Configuration: out-and-back with loop
Elevation gain: 1,700 feet
Difficulty: strenuous
Exposure: shaded canyon and exposed ridge
Dogs: allowed
Maps: U.S.G.S. Carmel Valley and Mt. Carmel
Garland Ranch Regional Park map

map
page 187

This loop hike lies at the southeast end, and lightly hiked area, of Garland Ranch Regional Park. The trail steeply ascends the mountain to Vasquez Ridge at an overlook with a bench and panoramic views. The path follows the ridge, overlooking Hitchcock Canyon and Carmel Valley, then returns through an oak-filled and spring-fed canyon beneath the ridge.

To the trailhead

From Highway 1 and Carmel Valley Road in Carmel, drive 11.9 miles east on Carmel Valley Road to Esquiline Road on the right. The turnoff is just past Carmel Valley Village. Turn right and drive 0.2 miles, crossing Rosie's Bridge over the Carmel River, to De Los Helechos Road. Turn right and park at the end of the street.

The hike

From the end of De Los Helechos Road, walk through the Lazy Oaks right-of-way past a few homes to the Garland Park entrance. Follow the path through oak groves to a posted trail split. Curve left, quickly reaching a second junction. The right fork follows the River Trail. Curve left on the Laureles Trail, and ascend the forested hillside. Climb through the oak woodland to magnificent valley views. Continue climbing through the forest, emerging on the grassy Vasquez Ridge at 1.3 miles. On the ridge is a bench, a junction, and magnificent views. A detour to the left leads 0.2 miles through oak-dotted meadows to the fenced park boundary.

Return to the junction and take the Vasquez Trail 40 yards to a posted trail fork. Begin the loop to the left, staying on the Vasquez Trail. Follow the ridge up the meadow along the south boundary, overlooking Hitchcock Canyon. At the Y-junction, another short detour left leads to the hilltop summit at the park boundary. The right fork heads downhill on the Saddle Trail, crossing the head of Redwood Canyon. Pass a junction on the left with the East Ridge Trail, and skirt around the left side of the knoll. Steadily descend to a Y-fork. Take the Spring Trail to the right, and head downhill into the oak-filled canyon beneath Vasquez Ridge. Pass the narrow Gabilan Trail on the left to a trough, spring, and water tank on the canyon floor. Curve left down canyon, then ascend the hillside, completing the loop on the ridge. Retrace your footsteps on the Laureles Trail. ■

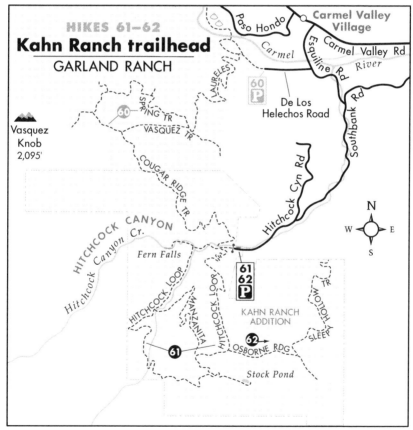

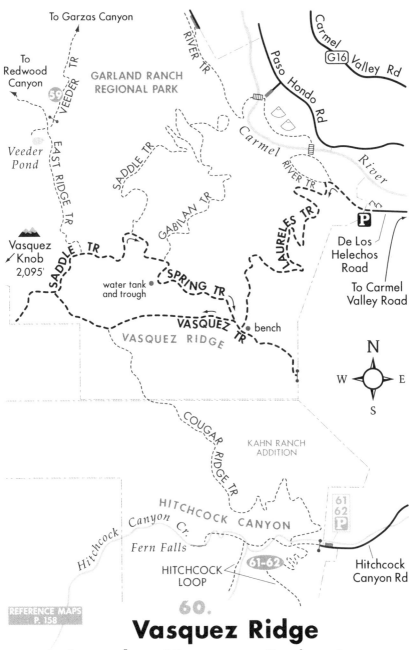

To Garzas Canyon

To Redwood Canyon

GARLAND RANCH REGIONAL PARK

VEEDER TR

59

EAST RIDGE TR

Veeder Pond

SADDLE TR

GABLAN TR

Vasquez Knob 2,095'

SADDLE TR

water tank and trough

SPRING TR

VASQUEZ TR

VASQUEZ RIDGE

bench

Carmel River

Paso Hondo Rd

Carmel Valley Rd

G16

River

RIVER TR

LAURELES TR

P

De Los Helechos Road

To Carmel Valley Road

N
W   E
S

COUGAR RIDGE TR

KAHN RANCH ADDITION

HITCHCOCK CANYON

Hitchcock Canyon Cr.

Fern Falls

HITCHCOCK LOOP

61-62

61 62 P

Hitchcock Canyon Rd

REFERENCE MAPS P. 158

60.

Vasquez Ridge
Laureles–Vasquez–Spring Loop
GARLAND RANCH REGIONAL PARK

61. Hitchcock Loop

KAHN RANCH ADDITION

GARLAND RANCH REGIONAL PARK

An access permit is required on easement to trailhead parking
www.mprpd.org · 831-659-4488, then select option 5

Hiking distance: 4.6-mile loop
Hiking time: 2.5 hours
Configuration: loop
Elevation gain: 1,000 feet
Difficulty: moderate to strenuous
Exposure: shaded forest and exposed slope
Dogs: allowed
Maps: U.S.G.S. Carmel Valley · Garland Ranch Regional Park map

Kahn Ranch, a new addition to Garland Ranch Regional Park, sits at the southern end of the park in the hills above Carmel Valley Village. The ranch covers 1,100 acres and is open to bikes, horses, dogs, and hikers. The Hitchcock Loop climbs up Hitchcock Canyon (a stream-fed drainage), crosses Osborne Ridge, and returns via an open hillside slope with scenic mountain overlooks. En route, the trail visits Fern Falls, a 25-foot waterfall with two pools in a forested, rock-walled box canyon. Another spur trail leads to Stock Pond, a small pond in a ravine.

An access permit from the Monterey Peninsula Regional Park District is required to enter the ranch. Contact information is included above.

To the trailhead

From Highway 1 and Carmel Valley Road in Carmel, drive 11.9 miles east on Carmel Valley Road to Esquiline Road on the right. The turnoff is just past Carmel Valley Village. (Esquiline Road is located 2.2 miles east of Laureles Grade.) Turn right and drive 0.6 miles to Southbank Road. Turn right again and go 0.8 miles up the winding road to Hitchcock Road. Turn left and continue 0.6 miles to the signed Kahn Ranch entrance and parking area on the right.

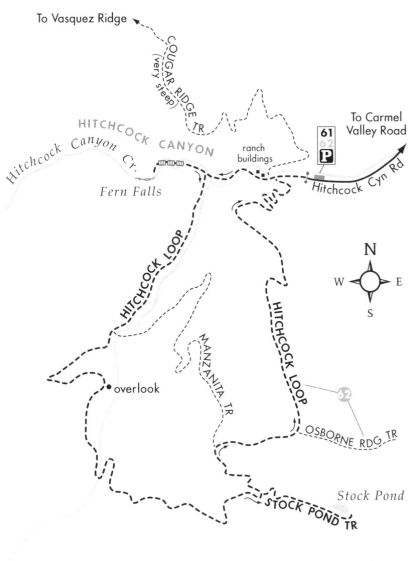

To Vasquez Ridge

COUGAR RIDGE TR (very steep)

HITCHCOCK CANYON

Hitchcock Canyon Cr.

Fern Falls

ranch buildings

To Carmel Valley Road

61
62
P

Hitchcock Cyn Rd

HITCHCOCK LOOP

N
W   E
S

overlook

MANZANITA TR

HITCHCOCK LOOP

62

OSBORNE RDG. TR

Stock Pond

STOCK POND TR

61.

Hitchcock Loop
Kahn Ranch Addition
GARLAND RANCH REGIONAL PARK

The hike

Walk up the narrow, vehicle-restricted dirt road under the shade of oak trees. At 100 yards is a junction with the Hitchcock Loop Trail on the left. Begin the loop straight ahead, passing ranch buildings. Continue up canyon, crossing a seasonal fork of Hitchcock Canyon Creek to a posted junction. To the left is the Hitchcock Loop Trail, the main route.

For a short detour to Fern Falls, go right. Follow the footpath through the narrow, forested drainage alongside the creek to the right. Cross two bridges over the waterway, passing mossy tree trunks and a fern ground cover. Cross a third bridge, where the trail ends in a box canyon by the 25-foot cataract and two pools.

Return to the junction, and continue on the Hitchcock Loop Trail, now on the right. Head south on an easy uphill grade. Stay to the right of the ephemeral stream to a Y-fork. The Manzanita Trail veers left, shortening the loop by a half mile. Stay on the Hitchcock Loop Trail to the right and up to an overlook of the surrounding mountains. Descend back into the oak forest and cross the drainage. Switchback left and steadily climb the mountain at a moderate grade to a signed junction at a U-shaped left bend.

Detour right on the Stock Pond Trail. The 0.3-mile-long path climbs over the hill and drops down to the rock-walled seasonal pond tucked into a ravine.

Back at the main trail, continue uphill on the Hitchcock Loop, with vistas down canyon and of the mountainous backcountry. At the junction with the south end of the Manzanita Trail, go to the right, staying on the Hitchcock Loop Trail. Pass an overlook across Carmel Valley. At the ridge is a sitting bench on the right at another spectacular overlook. A short distance ahead is a posted junction with the Osborne Ridge Trail (Hike 62). Go to the left on the Hitchcock Loop and steeply descend, with alternating views of the forested backcountry and Carmel Valley. Wind down the mountain, completing the loop at the entrance trail. Walk 100 yards to the right, returning to the parking area. ▩

62. Osborne Ridge

KAHN RANCH ADDITION

GARLAND RANCH REGIONAL PARK

An access permit is required on easement to trailhead parking
www.mprpd.org · 831-659-4488, then select option 5

Hiking distance: 6 miles round trip
Hiking time: 3 hours
Configuration: out-and-back
Elevation gain: 1,000 feet
Difficulty: moderate to strenuous
Exposure: shaded forest and exposed slope
Dogs: allowed
Maps: U.S.G.S. Carmel Valley · Garland Ranch Regional Park map

**map
page 193**

Osborne Ridge is a 1,600-foot ridge at the south end of Garland Ranch Regional Park in the Kahn Ranch addition. The ridge stretches over 2 miles between Hitchcock Canyon and the San Clemente Reservoir above Carmel Valley Village. This hike begins in Hitchcock Canyon and climbs up to Osborne Ridge. From the crest, the Sleepy Hollow Trail weaves through the forest to a bench and overlook of Carmel Valley. (Sleepy Hollow is a flat along the Carmel River at the base of the mountain. Unfortunately, access to Sleepy Hollow is off of San Clemente Drive, a private gated road.)

An access permit from the Monterey Peninsula Regional Park District is required to enter the ranch. Contact information is included above.

To the trailhead

From Highway 1 and Carmel Valley Road in Carmel, drive 11.9 miles east on Carmel Valley Road to Esquiline Road on the right. The turnoff is just past Carmel Valley Village. (Esquiline Road is located 2.2 miles east of Laureles Grade.) Turn right and drive 0.6 miles to Southbank Road. Turn right again and go 0.8 miles up the winding road to Hitchcock Road. Turn left and continue 0.6 miles to the signed Kahn Ranch entrance and parking area on the right.

The hike

Walk up the narrow, vehicle-restricted dirt road under the shade of oak trees. At 100 yards is a junction with the Hitchcock Loop Trail on the left. Bear left, leaving the road. Head up the south canyon wall on the Hitchcock Loop Trail. Wind up six switch-backs, climbing at a fairly steep grade. At the sixth bend, views open up into Hitchcock Canyon, Carmel Valley, and the surrounding mountains. Steadily gain elevation to a signed junction atop Osborne Ridge at 1.1 miles. The Hitchcock Loop Trail continues to the right (Hike 61).

Bear left on the Osborne Ridge Trail. Follow the easy rolling ridge south on a wide, grassy path under the shade of oak trees. At 1.5 miles, on a U-shaped left bend, is the old Osborne Loop Trail, now closed to public access. Gently descend on the Sleepy Hollow Trail, temporarily leaving the ridge. Traverse the steep hillside, then stroll along the scenic ridge to a bench and over-look at the end of the trail by the park boundary. Return along the same route. ▦

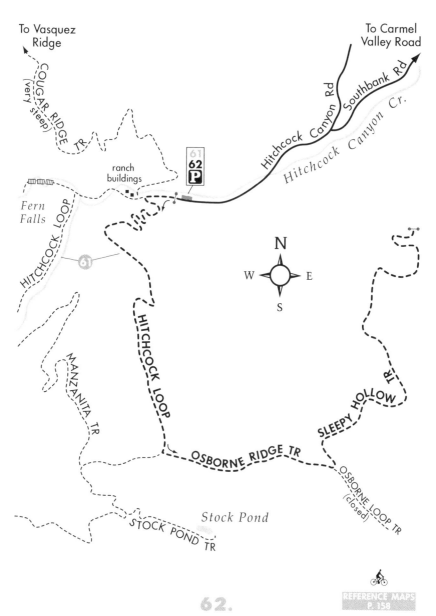

To Vasquez Ridge

COUGAR RIDGE TR (very steep)

To Carmel Valley Road

Hitchcock Canyon Rd
Southbank Rd
Hitchcock Canyon Cr.

ranch buildings

61
62 P

Fern Falls

HITCHCOCK LOOP

61

N
W E
S

HITCHCOCK LOOP

MANZANITA TR

SLEEPY HOLLOW TR

OSBORNE RIDGE TR

OSBORNE LOOP TR (closed)

Stock Pond

STOCK POND TR

REFERENCE MAPS
P. 158

62.

Osborne Ridge
Cooper Ranch Addition
GARLAND RANCH REGIONAL PARK

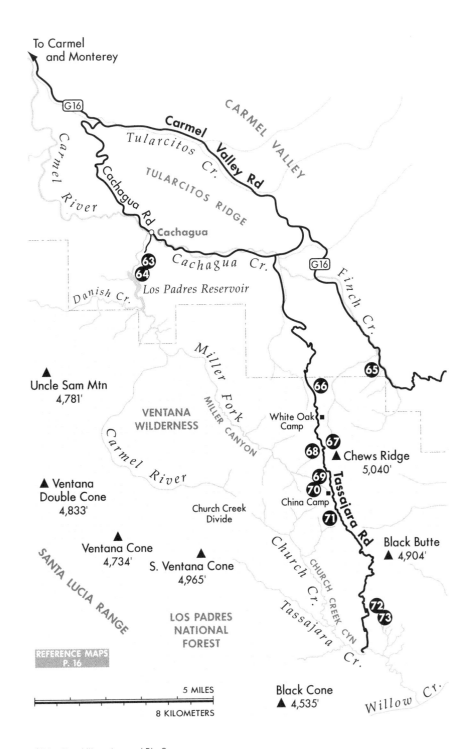

To Carmel
and Monterey

G16

CARMEL VALLEY

Carmel Valley Rd

Tularcitos Cr.

TULARCITOS RIDGE

Cachagua Rd

Carmel River

Cachagua

63
64

Cachagua Cr.

G16

Finch Cr.

Danish Cr.

Los Padres Reservoir

65

Uncle Sam Mtn
4,781'

VENTANA
WILDERNESS

Miller Fork

MILLER CANYON

66

White Oak
Camp

67

68

Chews Ridge
5,040'

Carmel River

Ventana
Double Cone
4,833'

Church Creek
Divide

69

70

China Camp

71

Tassajara Rd

Ventana Cone
4,734'

S. Ventana Cone
4,965'

Church Cr.

CHURCH CREEK CYN

Black Butte
4,904'

SANTA LUCIA RANGE

LOS PADRES
NATIONAL
FOREST

Tassajara Cr.

72
73

REFERENCE MAPS
P. 16

5 MILES

8 KILOMETERS

Black Cone
4,535'

Willow Cr.

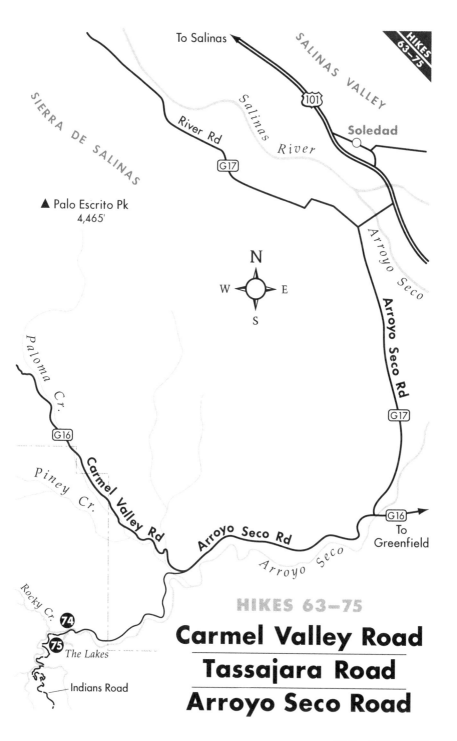

To Salinas

SALINAS VALLEY

101

Soledad

River Rd

G17

Salinas River

SIERRA DE SALINAS

▲ Palo Escrito Pk
4,465'

Arroyo Seco

Arroyo Seco Rd

G17

N

W E

S

Paloma Cr.

G16

Carmel Valley Rd

Piney Cr.

Arroyo Seco Rd

G16
To
Greenfield

Arroyo Seco

Rocky Cr.

74

75

The Lakes

Indians Road

HIKES 63-75

Carmel Valley Road
Tassajara Road
Arroyo Seco Road

63. Carmel River Trail along Los Padres Reservoir

Hiking distance: 5.6 miles round trip
Hiking time: 2.5 hours
Configuration: out-and-back
Elevation gain: 300 feet
Difficulty: easy to moderate
Exposure: mostly shaded forest
Dogs: allowed
Maps: U.S.G.S. Carmel Valley and Ventana Cones
Big Sur and Ventana Wilderness map
Ventana Wilderness Los Padres National Forest map
Los Padres National Forest Northern Section Trail Map

The Los Padres Reservoir is an 1,800-acre dammed lake along the Carmel River. The reservoir, nestled in a gorgeous valley surrounded by the forested mountains, lies adjacent to the Los Padres National Forest. The forested path contours the mountains along the western slope of the long reservoir from one end to the other, gaining little elevation. Be aware of ticks, which are prevalent along the trail during the winter season.

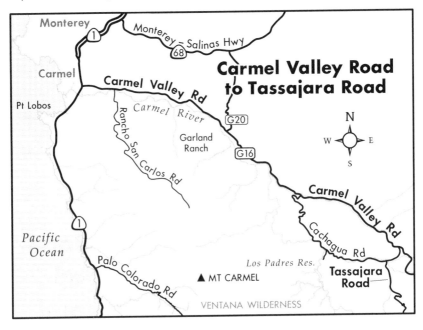

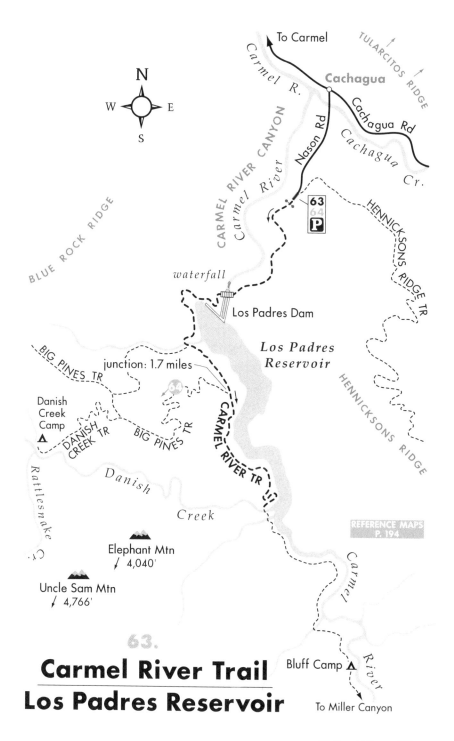

To Carmel

TULARCITOS RIDGE

Carmel R.

Cachagua

Cachagua Rd

Cachagua Cr.

CARMEL RIVER CANYON

Carmel River

Nason Rd

BLUE ROCK RIDGE

63
64
P

HENNICKSONS RIDGE TR

waterfall

Los Padres Dam

Los Padres Reservoir

junction: 1.7 miles

BIG PINES TR

64

Danish Creek Camp ⛺

DANISH CREEK TR

BIG PINES TR

CARMEL RIVER TR

HENNICKSONS RIDGE

Rattlesnake Cr

Danish Creek

REFERENCE MAPS P. 194

Elephant Mtn
↙ 4,040'

Uncle Sam Mtn
↙ 4,766'

Carmel River

63.

Carmel River Trail
Los Padres Reservoir

Bluff Camp ⛺

To Miller Canyon

To the trailhead

From Highway 1 and Carmel Valley Road in Carmel, drive 16 miles east on Carmel Valley Road to the signed Los Padres Dam/Cachagua Road turnoff. Turn right and drive 5.8 miles on the winding road to the posted Nason Road turnoff in the community of Cachagua. Turn right and continue 0.6 miles to the large parking area at the end of the public road.

The hike

Walk through the trailhead gate. Follow the unpaved dam road (Carmel River Trail) up the Carmel River Canyon. Pass stately, twisted oaks to a large open flat with several forking side roads. Stay on the main road to the dam spillway in a granite gorge at a half mile. Cross the gorge on the bridge, and head up the road past the waterfall. Curve right to the Los Padres Dam and an overlook of the reservoir. Walk toward the hills on the west side of the reservoir. Curve sharply south (left) and traverse the hillside above the lake, enjoying a bird's-eye view of the lake and surrounding mountains. Several side paths on the left descend to the reservoir. The wide trail narrows to a single track and reaches a signed junction at 1.7 miles. The Carmel River Trail continues straight along the west side of the reservoir. The right fork is the Big Pines Trail (Hike 64).

Continue straight—on the Carmel River Trail—parallel to the reservoir. The trail alternates from shady forest to open chaparral as it follows the contours of the mountain on the cliff's narrow edge. Near the south end of the lake is an overlook of the snake-shaped reservoir. Gradually descend with the aid of switchbacks to Danish Creek, a tributary of the Carmel River. Follow the creek upstream to a rocky beach at 2.8 miles, the turn-around spot.

To continue, ford the creek and follow the Carmel River Canyon, reaching Bluff Camp at 4 miles. From Bluff Camp, the trail heads into Miller Canyon and up to China Camp off Tassajara Road (Hike 69). ▪

64. Big Pines Trail to Danish Creek Camp
LOS PADRES RESERVOIR

Hiking distance: 7 miles round trip
Hiking time: 3.5 hours
Configuration: out-and-back
Elevation gain: 1,300 feet
Difficulty: moderate to strenuous
Exposure: a mix of shaded forest and open meadow
Dogs: allowed
Maps: U.S.G.S. Carmel Valley · Big Sur and Ventana Wilderness map
Ventana Wilderness Los Padres National Forest map
Los Padres National Forest Northern Section Trail Map

**map
page 201**

The Big Pines Trail lies on the west side of the Los Padres Reservoir in a scenic mountain valley. Hikes 63 and 64 begin on the Carmel River Trail, curving around the dam and spillway along the western slope of the reservoir. While Hike 63 remains mostly level along the side of the reservoir, this hike switchbacks up to a ridge that overlooks the reservoir and surrounding wilderness area. A short spur trail drops into a small canyon at Danish Creek Camp near the confluence of Danish and Rattlesnake Creeks. Be aware of ticks, which are prevalent during the wet season.

To the trailhead

From Highway 1 and Carmel Valley Road in Carmel, drive 16 miles east on Carmel Valley Road to the signed Los Padres Dam/Cachagua Road turnoff. Turn right and drive 5.8 miles on the winding road to the posted Nason Road turnoff in the community of Cachagua. Turn right and continue 0.6 miles to the large parking area at the end of the public road.

The hike

Walk through the trailhead gate. Follow the unpaved dam road (Carmel River Trail) up the Carmel River Canyon. Pass stately, twisted oaks to a large open flat with several forking side roads. Stay on the main road to the dam spillway in a granite gorge at a half mile. Cross the gorge on the bridge, and head up the road past the waterfall. Curve right to the Los Padres Dam and an overlook of the reservoir. Walk toward the hills on the west side of the reservoir. Curve sharply south (left) and traverse the hillside above the lake, enjoying a bird's-eye view of the lake and surrounding mountains. Several side paths on the left descend to the reservoir. The wide trail narrows to a single track and reaches a signed junction at 1.7 miles. The Carmel River Trail continues straight along the west side of the reservoir (Hike 63).

Take the right (west) fork on the Big Pines Trail up the narrow hillside path. Weave up the side canyon, steadily climbing to elevated views of the lake. The trail levels out on a saddle at the head of the canyon. Panoramic views extend west to Blue Rock Ridge, east to Hennicksons Ridge, and south to Elephant Mountain and Uncle Sam Mountain. Follow the ridge to a posted trail split at the high point of the hike at 2,058 feet.

Leave the Big Pines Trail and bear left on the Danish Creek Trail. Zigzag down the steep hillside for 0.7 miles to Danish Creek Camp. The camp is next to the creek on an open flat with a large live oak tree. The trail along Danish Creek is worth exploring. Rattlesnake Creek is a short distance upstream.

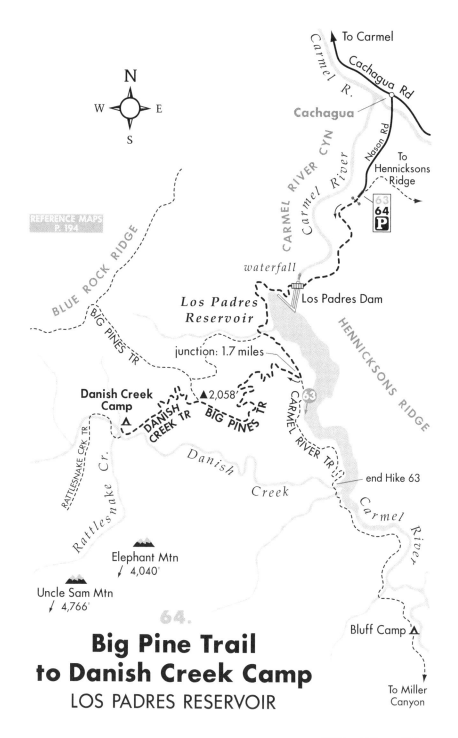

N
W E
S

To Carmel

Cachagua Rd

Carmel R.

Cachagua

Nason Rd

To Hennicksons Ridge

63
64 P

CARMEL RIVER CYN

Carmel River

BLUE ROCK RIDGE

REFERENCE MAPS
P. 194

BIG PINES TR

waterfall

Los Padres Reservoir

Los Padres Dam

HENNICKSONS RIDGE

junction: 1.7 miles

Danish Creek Camp

DANISH CREEK TR

BIG PINES TR

▲ 2,058

CARMEL RIVER TR

63

RATTLESNAKE CRK TR

Danish

Creek

Rattlesnake Cr.

end Hike 63

Carmel River

Elephant Mtn
↙ 4,040'

Uncle Sam Mtn
↙ 4,766'

64.

Bluff Camp ▲

To Miller Canyon

Big Pine Trail
to Danish Creek Camp
LOS PADRES RESERVOIR

65. Anastasia Trail—East Trailhead
Carmel Valley Road to Cahoon Spring

Hiking distance: 7 miles round trip
Hiking time: 4 hours
Configuration: out-and-back
Elevation gain: 600 feet
Difficulty: moderate
Exposure: mostly forested
Dogs: allowed
Maps: U.S.G.S. Chews Ridge · Big Sur and Ventana Wilderness map
Ventana Wilderness Los Padres National Forest map

The Anastasia Trail is a 2.8-mile-long trail connecting Carmel Valley Road with Tassajara Road. This hike follows the remote, stream-fed canyon floor through open valleys and a lush sycamore and black oak forest into Bear Trap Canyon. Cahoon Spring, a natural spring, is located in the canyon. The water flows out of a pipe into a watering trough in the shade of towering black oaks. This is a lightly traveled hiking and equestrian corridor, offering quiet solitude.

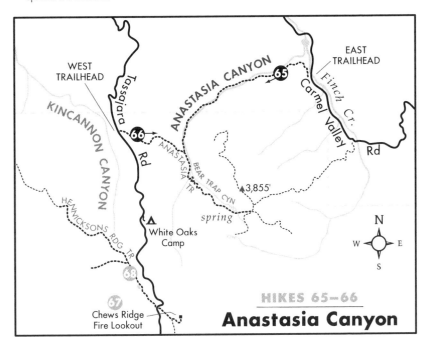

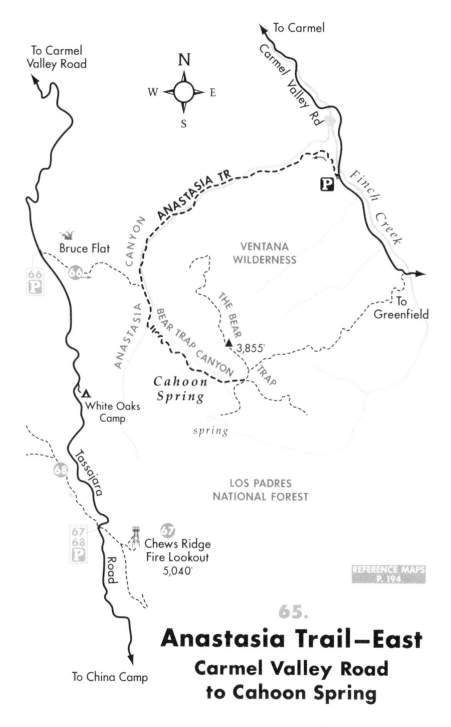

To Carmel

To Carmel Valley Road

Carmel Valley Rd

N
W   E
S

ANASTASIA TR

CANYON

Finch Creek

P

VENTANA
WILDERNESS

Bruce Flat

66
P

66

ANASTASIA

BEAR TRAP CANYON

THE BEAR

3,855'

TRAP

To Greenfield

*Cahoon
Spring*

spring

White Oaks
Camp

Tassajara

68

LOS PADRES
NATIONAL FOREST

67
68
P

67

Road

Chews Ridge
Fire Lookout
5,040'

REFERENCE MAPS
P. 194

To China Camp

65.

Anastasia Trail–East
Carmel Valley Road
to Cahoon Spring

To the trailhead

From Highway 1 and Carmel Valley Road in Carmel, drive 28.4 miles southeast on Carmel Valley Road, (passing through Carmel Valley Village at 11.5 miles) to the trailhead pullout on the right. The turnoff is 5.4 miles past Tassajara Road and 0.3 miles past mile marker 28.5. Park in the large dirt pullout on the right by the trail sign.

The hike

Pass through the gate by the wooden "Anastasia" sign. Follow the narrow dirt road, parallel to Finch Creek on the right. Climb the slope and drop down into the oak-filled, grassy meadows of Anastasia Canyon. Pass a seasonal hunter's cabin on the left, and continue up canyon on the grassy, single-track path. Rock-hop over Anastasia Creek and follow the canyon bottom, passing massive oaks. Hop over the creek two consecutive times, and enter the Los Padres National Forest and Ventana Wilderness. Steadily move up-stream, crossing the creek two more times. Bend to the left, following the curvature of the canyon, to an unsigned (and hard-to-spot) connection with the Anastasia Trail, which climbs up to Tassajara Road (Hike 66). Parallel the stream along the shaded canyon floor. Pass moss-covered tree trunks and rocks. Cross a tributary stream and gently ascend the hillside as the footpath becomes an old jeep road. Cross Anastasia Creek and ascend the east slope of the canyon, weaving up to the ridge.

Leave Anastasia Canyon and descend into Bear Trap Canyon. Curve sharply to the left, crossing a stream-fed draw. Continue downhill to Cahoon Spring in a shady oak grove. The spring flows from a pipe near a clawfoot bathtub used as an animal watering trough. Climb a quarter mile up the canyon to The Bear Trap, an open ridge with panoramic views and an unsigned junction. The left fork leads towards Carmel Valley Road, but the Cahoon Ranch, privately owned land, eliminates public access to the road. This is the turn-around spot. Return by retracing your steps. ▪

66. Anastasia Trail—West Trailhead
Tassajara Road to Cahoon Spring

Hiking distance: 4.8 miles round trip
Hiking time: 2.5 hours
Configuration: out-and-back
Elevation gain: 900 feet
Difficulty: moderate
Exposure: mostly forested
Dogs: allowed
Maps: U.S.G.S. Chews Ridge · Big Sur and Ventana Wilderness map
Ventana Wilderness Los Padres National Forest map

map
page 206

The Anastasia Trail connects Carmel Valley Road with Tassajara Road. This hike begins from Tassajara Road in a large meadow known as Bruce Flat. The trail descends the mountain slope into the bucolic forest to the banks of Anastasia Creek. The path then follows the waterway into Bear Trap Canyon to Cahoon Spring, a natural spring under the shade of towering black oaks. Anastasia Canyon is lightly used, offering deep-forest solitude.

To the trailhead

From Highway 1 and Carmel Valley Road in Carmel, drive 23 miles southeast on Carmel Valley Road (passing through Carmel Valley Village at 11.5 miles) to Tassajara Road. Turn right and drive 1.3 miles to a signed Y-fork with Cachagua Road. Curve left, staying on Tassajara Road, and continue 5.1 miles to a cattle guard at the national forest boundary by barns and corrals on the right (west). Drive 0.2 miles farther to the second gate opening on the left at the south end of Bruce Flat, a flat grassy meadow. Park in the pullouts on either side of the road.

The hike

Pass through the signed trailhead gate, and cross the grassy meadow dotted with oaks, maples, and madrones. Traverse the rolling slope into the forested, east-facing slope of Anastasia Canyon. Descend the hillside, dropping 800 feet in the first 0.8 miles, to an unsigned junction. The junction is near the transient stream in bucolic Anastasia Canyon. The Anastasia Trail continues left to Carmel Valley Road (Hike 65).

For this hike, leave the Anastasia Trail and follow the shaded canyon floor to the right. Parallel Anastasia Creek, passing moss-covered tree trunks and rocks. Cross a tributary stream and gently ascend the hillside as the footpath becomes an old jeep road. Cross Anastasia Creek and ascend the east slope of the canyon, weaving up to the ridge. Leave Anastasia Canyon and descend into Bear Trap Canyon. Curve sharply to the left, crossing a stream-fed draw. Continue downhill to Cahoon Spring in a shady oak grove. The spring flows from a pipe near a clawfoot bathtub used as an animal watering trough. Climb a quarter mile up the canyon to The Bear Trap, an open ridge with panoramic views and an unsigned junction. The left fork leads towards Carmel Valley Road, but the Cahoon Ranch, privately owned land, eliminates access to the road. This is the turn-around spot. Return by retracing your steps. ▪

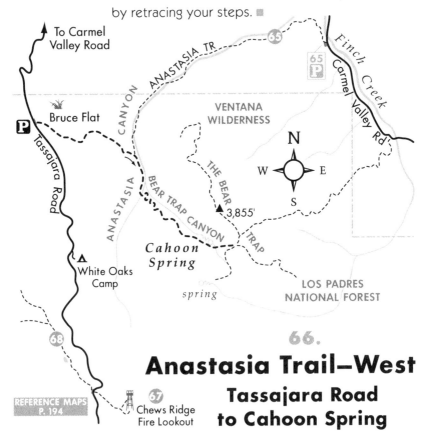

66.
Anastasia Trail–West
Tassajara Road
to Cahoon Spring

67. Chews Ridge Fire Lookout

Hiking distance: 0.7 miles round trip
Hiking time: 30 minutes hours
Configuration: out-and-back
Elevation gain: 160 feet
Difficulty: easy
Exposure: mostly exposed
Dogs: allowed
Maps: U.S.G.S. Chews Ridge · Big Sur and Ventana Wilderness map
       Ventana Wilderness Los Padres National Forest map

**map
page 208**

This trail follows a restricted dirt road to the Chews Ridge Fire Lookout. It is a short and scenic hike with little elevation gain. The abandoned fire lookout sits at an elevation of 5,040 feet and offers 360-degree vistas of the expansive Ventana Wilderness and across the Santa Lucia Range, from Salinas Valley to Monterey Bay. The trail winds through open woodland and chaparral. It is a great location to observe birds, including mountain quail, sparrow, owl, and western tanager.

Opposite the trailhead, going northwest, is the Hennicksons Ridge Trail (Hike 68), which follows Chews Ridge.

To the trailhead

From Highway 1 and Carmel Valley Road in Carmel, drive 23 miles southeast on Carmel Valley Road (passing through Carmel Valley Village at 11.5 miles) to Tassajara Road. Turn right and drive 1.3 miles to a signed Y-fork with Cachagua Road. Curve left, staying on Tassajara Road, and continue 7.7 miles to Chews Ridge. Park in the large dirt pullout on the right.

The hike

Cross Tassajara Road and walk around the left side of the vehicle gate atop 4,881-foot Chews Ridge. Head up the narrow, unpaved road among oaks and Coulter pines with their massive cones. At 0.2 miles is a fork. The right fork heads south towards the pine forest and leads to the MIRA Observatory (Monterey Institute for Research in Astronomy). Stay on the main trail towards the fire lookout, straight ahead. Curve left to the structure at the summit. From the lookout are vistas across the mountain peaks and canyons, spanning from Salinas Valley in the east to the Pacific Ocean in the west.

For a longer hike, take the Hennicksons Ridge Trail, following Chews Ridge to the northwest (Hike 68). ▪

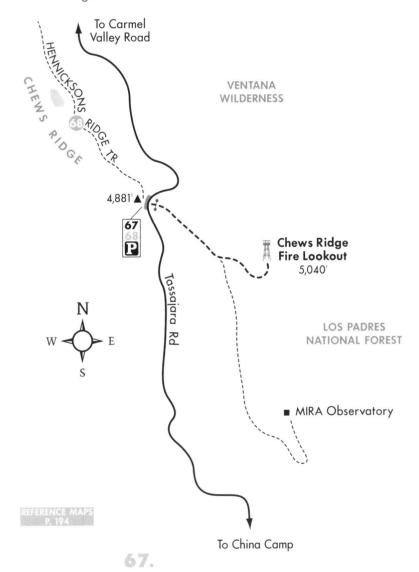

Chews Ridge Fire Lookout

68. Chews Ridge
Hennicksons Ridge Trail from Tassajara Road

Hiking distance: 4 miles round trip
Hiking time: 2 hours
Configuration: out-and-back
Elevation gain: 600 feet
Difficulty: easy to moderate
Exposure: mostly exposed
Dogs: allowed
Maps: U.S.G.S. Chews Ridge · Big Sur and Ventana Wilderness map

**map
page 210**

Chews Ridge is a 4-mile-long spine in the Ventana Wilderness. The ridge sits at an average elevation of 3,500 feet, rising up to 5,000 feet at the fire lookout at its eastern tip. The easiest access to the ridge is from Tassajara Road, which crosses the ridge just west of the Chews Ridge Fire Lookout (Hike 67). The Hennicksons Ridge Trail follows the rolling ridge northwest between Miller Canyon and Kincannon Canyon. The first two miles of trail are maintained by volunteers, passing through open grassland and pockets of large black oak and grey pines. Along the ridge are views across the western ridges of the Ventana Wilderness and into the Carmel River watershed.

To the trailhead

From Highway 1 and Carmel Valley Road in Carmel, drive 23 miles southeast on Carmel Valley Road (passing through Carmel Valley Village at 11.5 miles) to Tassajara Road. Turn right and drive 1.3 miles to a signed Y-fork with Cachagua Road. Curve left, staying on Tassajara Road, and continue 7.7 miles to Chews Ridge. Park in the large dirt pullout on the right.

The hike

Walk around the left side of the vehicle gate and head northeast on an old jeep road. Follow the undulating ridge through groves of grey pines and mature twisted oaks. Pass a small pond on the left while strolling through the rolling landscape. Continue to an unmarked Y-fork. The left fork gently descends a half mile to an overlook into Miller Canyon, with panoramas of the coastal peaks. Beyond the overlook, the trail enters private land.

For this hike, veer right (north) and climb the hill to the ridge overlooking Kincannon Canyon. Curve left along the ridge to panoramas into Miller Canyon as the old dirt road narrows to a footpath. Meander among the oaks to a grassy knoll at two miles, with views across the mountains and across Monterey Bay to Santa Cruz. Beyond this point, the trail has become overgrown with brush and is obscured. This is a good turn-around spot. ▦

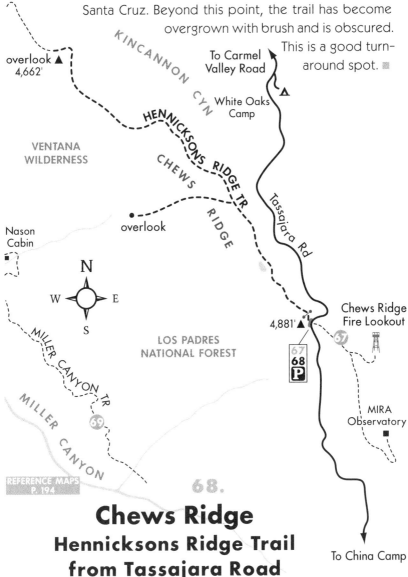

68.

Chews Ridge
Hennicksons Ridge Trail
from Tassajara Road

69. Jeffery Road—Miller Canyon Trail to Nason Cabin Site

Hiking distance: 8 miles round trip
Hiking time: 5 hours
Configuration: out and back
Elevation gain: 1,400 feet
Difficulty: moderate to strenuous
Exposure: forested canyon and exposed hillside
Dogs: allowed
Maps: U.S.G.S. Chews Ridge
    Big Sur and Ventana Wilderness map
    Ventana Wilderness Los Padres National Forest map

**map
page 213**

Jeffery Road is a gated road that begins at China Camp, a public campground along Tassajara Road. The dirt road (Forest Service Road 19S03) follows the Miller Fork of the Carmel River on the northeast side of the canyon. Jeffery Road connects with the Miller Canyon Trail, which leads 14 miles to the Los Padres Reservoir (Hike 63).

This hike takes in the first 4 miles of the trail to the historical Nason Cabin site, tucked into a secluded meadow along a fork of the creek. En route, the trail enters the Ventana Wilderness; passes a pond; descends a minor gorge; and winds through a shaded forest with live oaks, tanbark oaks, Coulter pines, Santa Lucia firs, and madrones.

To the trailhead

From Highway 1 and Carmel Valley Road in Carmel, drive 23 miles southeast on Carmel Valley Road (passing through Carmel Valley Village at 11.5 miles) to Tassajara Road. Turn right and drive 1.3 miles to a signed Y-fork with Cachagua Road. Curve left, staying on Tassajara Road, and continue 9.2 miles (crossing Chews Ridge) to the signed China Camp turnoff on the right. Continue 50 yards past the turnoff to the parking area on the left (east).

The hike

Head fifty yards back up Tassajara Road to the posted China Camp entrance road on the left. Take the road left and walk along the northeast slope of Miller Canyon to a metal gate on the right, located above China Camp on the left. Pass through the gate onto Jeffery Road, a dirt road shaded by an oak and pine forest. Descend along the canyon wall, with far-reaching views of the mountainous Ventana Wilderness. At one mile, the trail reaches the Miller Fork of the Carmel River. Parallel the stream down canyon under a shady forest canopy that includes Coulter pines, sprawling oaks, and madrones. At 1.3 miles, enter the signed private land of the Tanoak Association homes. Stay on the dirt road, part of the Miller Canyon Trail. Pass a grouping of cabins set back on both sides of the road. Cross over a tributary of Miller Creek and to the Tamarack Homes Pond and picnic area on the left, off-limits to the public.

Pass through a metal gate, and enter the Ventana Wilderness at 1.8 miles. Make a sharp right bend and walk 50 yards to a Y-fork by a yellow arrow posted on a tree. The main road—to the right—continues weaving along the contours of the mountains. The Miller Canyon Trail veers left on a gentle downward slope to a Y-fork, forming a small loop with the road. At the far end of the loop is a trail gate at 2 miles. Pass through the gate on the footpath, and drop into a small gorge that runs parallel to Miller Canyon. Weave down the draw, meandering in and out of minor gullies. Walk over an alder-lined creek, then cross a series of three saddles. Descend and cross a seasonal creek to the Nason Cabin site. Return by retracing your steps.

To extend the hike beyond this streamside flat, the trail climbs west, crossing a series of low ridges for two miles to the Hennicksons Ridge Trail. From the Hennicksons Ridge junction, it is another 10 miles to the Los Padres Reservoir. ▨

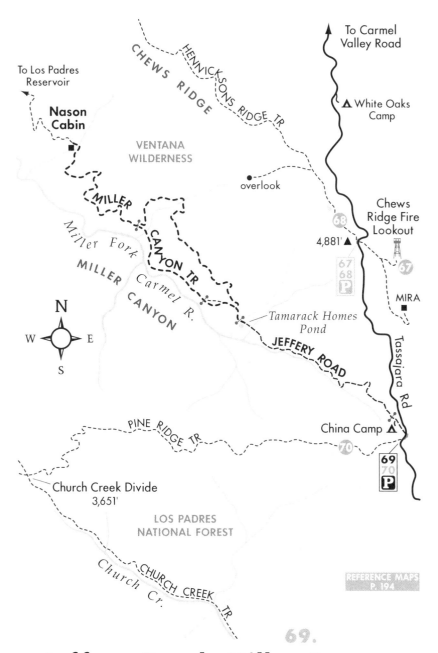

To Carmel
Valley Road

To Los Padres
Reservoir

**Nason
Cabin**

CHEWS RIDGE

HENNICKSONS RIDGE TR.

VENTANA
WILDERNESS

▲ White Oaks
Camp

overlook

MILLER

CANYON TR.

Miller Fork

Carmel R.

MILLER CANYON

Chews
Ridge Fire
Lookout

68

4,881' ▲

67

67
68
P

MIRA

Tamarack Homes
Pond

JEFFERY ROAD

Tassajara Rd.

N
W E
S

PINE RIDGE TR.

China Camp ▲

70

69
70
P

Church Creek Divide
3,651'

LOS PADRES
NATIONAL FOREST

CHURCH CREEK TR.

Church Cr.

REFERENCE MAPS
P. 194

69.

Jeffery Road–Miller Canyon
Trail to Nason Cabin

70. Church Creek Divide
Pine Ridge Trail from Tassajara Road

Hiking distance: 7.2 miles round trip
Hiking time: 3.5 hours
Configuration: out-and-back
Elevation gain: 1,200 feet
Difficulty: moderate to strenuous
Exposure: shaded forest and open grassy slopes
Dogs: allowed
Maps: U.S.G.S. Chews Ridge · Big Sur and Ventana Wilderness map
Ventana Wilderness Los Padres National Forest map

Church Creek Divide is a 1,000-foot-deep cleft below two ridges in the Ventana Wilderness. The 3,651-foot divide sits in a shady tree grove of stately black and tanbark oaks, ponderosa pines, and madrones. It is a major crossroad of wilderness trails.

This hike begins at the northeast end of the Pine Ridge Trail at Tassajara Road. The trailhead sits on a saddle above China

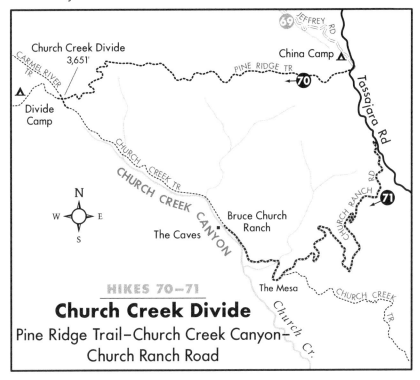

HIKES 70-71

Church Creek Divide
Pine Ridge Trail–Church Creek Canyon–
Church Ranch Road

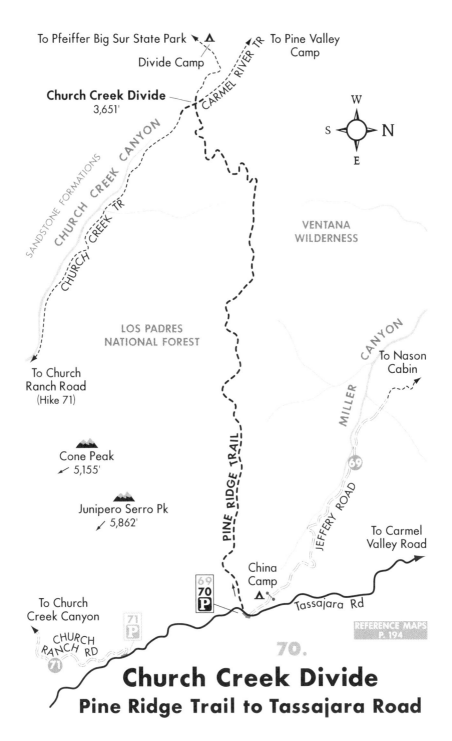

To Pfeiffer Big Sur State Park

Divide Camp

To Pine Valley Camp

CARMEL RIVER TR

Church Creek Divide
3,651'

CHURCH CREEK CANYON

SANDSTONE FORMATIONS

CHURCH CREEK TR

W
N
S
E

VENTANA WILDERNESS

MILLER CANYON

To Nason Cabin

To Church Ranch Road
(Hike 71)

LOS PADRES NATIONAL FOREST

PINE RIDGE TRAIL

Cone Peak
5,155'

Junipero Serro Pk
5,862'

JEFFERY ROAD

69

To Carmel Valley Road

China Camp

69
70
P

To Church Creek Canyon

Tassajara Rd

REFERENCE MAPS
P. 194

71
P

CHURCH RANCH RD

71

70.

Church Creek Divide
Pine Ridge Trail to Tassajara Road

Camp. The path weaves through the remote and rugged wilderness along high ridges with open, grassy slopes. Panoramic views of the mountainous Ventana Wilderness extend to Cone Peak, Junipero Serra Peak, and down the Church Creek Canyon.

To the trailhead

From Highway 1 and Carmel Valley Road in Carmel, drive 23 miles southeast on Carmel Valley Road (passing through Carmel Valley Village at 11.5 miles) to Tassajara Road. Turn right and drive 1.3 miles to a signed Y-fork with Cachagua Road. Curve left, staying on Tassajara Road, and continue 9.2 miles (crossing Chews Ridge) to the signed China Camp turnoff on the right. Continue 50 yards past the turnoff to the parking area on the left (east).

The hike

Cross Tassajara Road to the posted Pine Ridge Trail. Climb the hillside above China Camp through native chaparral and brush. Burned oak and pine stumps remain from the 1977 Marble Cone Fire. After gaining 400 feet to a hilltop ridge, drop back down the hillside, losing the elevation gain on a long saddle in a stand of tanbark oaks. Cross a steep, sloping meadow just below the ridge and high above the Church Creek drainage to the south. Traverse the hillside, overlooking the sandstone formations in Church Creek Canyon to the left. Zigzag down the hillside to the canyon floor at Church Creek Divide. The divide sits in a pastoral forest by a posted 4-way junction. This is the turn-around spot.

To hike farther, the Pine Ridge Trail continues straight ahead to Divide Camp at a half mile and eventually to Pfeiffer Big Sur State Park (Hike 40). To the right (northwest), the Carmel River Trail leads 2 miles to Pine Valley Camp, a flat, grassy meadow lined with pines. To the left (southeast), the Church Creek Trail follows Church Creek, passing massive sandstone formations, to The Caves (2.5 miles ahead), Wildcat Camp (5.7 miles), and Tassajara Road (7 miles). ▪

71. Church Creek Canyon from Church Ranch Road

Hiking distance: 8 miles round trip
Hiking time: 4 hours
Configuration: out-and-back
Elevation gain: 2,100 feet
Difficulty: strenuous
Exposure: mostly exposed
Dogs: allowed
Maps: U.S.G.S. Chews Ridge · Big Sur and Ventana Wilderness map
Ventana Wilderness Los Padres National Forest map

map
page 219

Church Creek Canyon is rich with massive sandstone formations, including caves, rock shelters, arching overhangs, and ancient pictographs from the Esselen people. This hike descends on Church Ranch Road, a gated dirt road overlooking the scenic canyon. The lightly traveled road, branching from Tassajara Road, winds down the brushy slope on an easy grade. The trail offers outstanding vistas but little shade. The road descends to Church Creek, a tributary of the Arroyo Seco that forms at Church Creek Divide. The 4-mile-long creek merges with Tassajara Creek on its journey to the ocean. A trail parallels Church Creek in an open forest of black oaks, Coulter pines, and Santa Lucia firs.

This out-and-back hike is downhill the entire way to Church Creek. Pace yourself accordingly for the strenuous hike back out.

To the trailhead

From Highway 1 and Carmel Valley Road in Carmel, drive 23 miles southeast on Carmel Valley Road (passing through Carmel Valley Village at 11.5 miles) to Tassajara Road. Turn right and drive 1.3 miles to a signed Y-fork with Cachagua Road. Curve left, staying on Tassajara Road, and continue 10.1 miles (crossing Chews Ridge) to the wide pull out on the right by a dirt road, also on the right. (The pullout is located 0.9 miles past the well-marked China Camp.)

The hike

Walk 30 yards up the dirt road and make a U-bend to the left. Pass through a metal vehicle gate and head downhill on Church Ranch Road (Forest Service Road 19S04). Traverse the mountain slope, overlooking Church Creek Canyon. The narrow dirt road, perched on the canyon cliffs, steadily descends while following the contours of the mountain. With every step are changing vistas of the rugged backcountry wilderness and sandstone formations. Near the bottom, pass pockets of oaks and pines. Head towards the base of the mountains on the floor of the canyon.

Pass the Church Creek Trail on the left, which is overgrown and hard to spot. Curve around The Mesa, a flat, unmarked, and nondescript knoll overlooking the canyon. Beyond The Mesa, the road/trail crosses Church Ranch Bridge, a wooden bridge crossing over a major fork of Church Creek. Stroll up canyon on the near-level path among massive sandstone outcrops. Parallel Church Creek from above, eventually reaching the sycamore-lined waterway. At 4 miles, the dirt road enters the private land of Bruce Church Ranch, located directly across the creek from The Caves, dramatic sandstone outcrops which are off-limits to the public. This is a good turn-around spot.

To extend the hike, the trail passes about a half mile along an easement through the private land. The dirt road then narrows to a footpath and leads 2.5 miles to the Pine Ridge Trail and Church Creek Divide (Hike 70). ▨

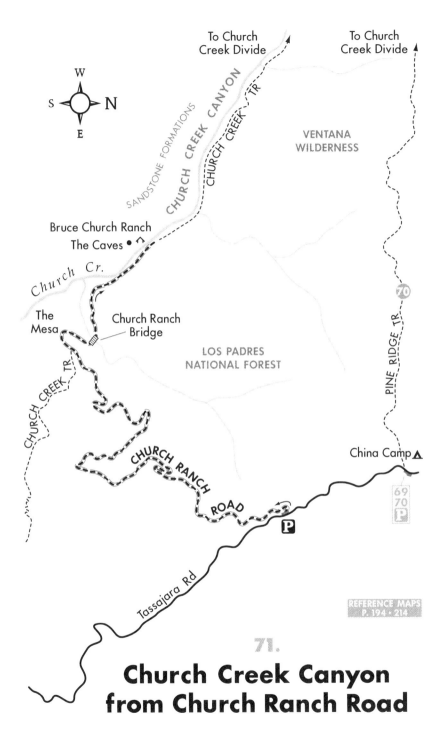

To Church
Creek Divide

To Church
Creek Divide

W
S — N
E

CHURCH CREEK CANYON

CHURCH CREEK TR

SANDSTONE FORMATIONS

VENTANA
WILDERNESS

Bruce Church Ranch
The Caves •

Church Cr.

The
Mesa

Church Ranch
Bridge

LOS PADRES
NATIONAL FOREST

CHURCH CREEK TR

PINE RIDGE TR

70

China Camp ▲

CHURCH RANCH

ROAD

69
70
P

P

Tassajara Rd

REFERENCE MAPS
P. 194 · 214

71.

Church Creek Canyon
from Church Ranch Road

72. Horse Pasture Trail to Horse Pasture Camp

Hiking distance: 2.8 miles round trip
Hiking time: 1.5 hours
Configuration: out-and-back
Elevation gain: 400 feet
Difficulty: easy
Exposure: forested canyon and open grassland
Dogs: allowed
Maps: U.S.G.S. Tassajara Hot Springs · Big Sur and Ventana Wilderness map
　　　　Ventana Wilderness Los Padres National Forest map

Horse Pasture Trail is a lightly traveled trail off the far southern end of Tassajara Road. The trail leads to Willow Creek, linking Tassajara Road with Arroyo Seco. This hike along the first 1.4 miles of the trail leads to Horse Pasture Camp, a quiet, out-of-use campsite on the banks of seasonal Horse Pasture Creek. The camp sits on a beautiful creekside flat inside the Ventana Wilderness boundary.

To the trailhead

From Highway 1 and Carmel Valley Road in Carmel, drive 23 miles southeast on Carmel Valley Road (passing through Carmel Valley Village at 11.5 miles) to Tassajara Road. Turn right and drive 1.3 miles to a signed Y-junction with Cachagua Road. Curve left, staying on Tassajara Road, and continue 14.3 miles to the well-marked trailhead on the left (east) side. Park in the pullouts on either side of the road.

The hike

Take the signed Horse Pasture Trail into the oak forest and head up-hill. Traverse the hillside on a ledge above Tassajara Road. Curving away from the road, cross open grasslands on the narrow path. The gentle grade gains 400 feet in 0.6 miles, reaching a saddle at the wilderness boundary. Descend the east-facing slope under a canopy of oaks and toyon. Switchbacks lead down the hillside into the forested canyon and to seasonal Horse Pasture Creek. Cross the creek and walk downstream a short distance to the abandoned Horse Pasture Camp on a grassy flat. After enjoying the area, return on the same trail. To make a 7-mile loop hike to Tassajara Creek, continue with Hike 73. ■

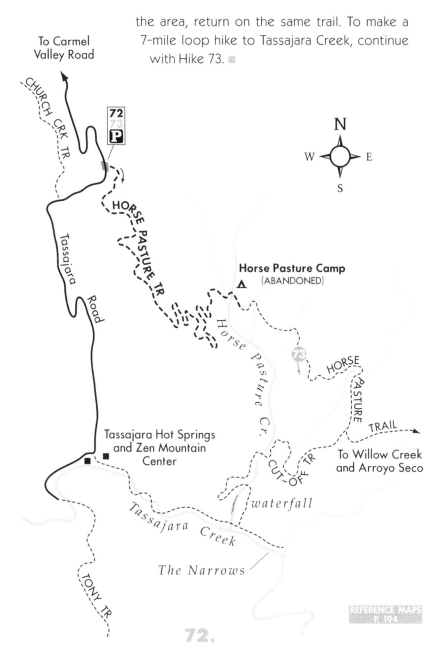

To Carmel Valley Road

CHURCH CRK TR

72
73
P

HORSE PASTURE TR

Tassajara Road

N
W   E
S

Horse Pasture Camp
(ABANDONED)

Horse Pasture Cr.

HORSE PASTURE TRAIL

To Willow Creek and Arroyo Seco

Tassajara Hot Springs and Zen Mountain Center

CUT-OFF TR

Tassajara Creek

waterfall

The Narrows

TONY TR

REFERENCE MAPS P. 194

72.

Horse Pasture Trail to Horse Pasture Camp

73. Horse Pasture Trail to the Narrows at Tassajara Creek

Hiking distance: 7-mile loop
Hiking time: 3.5 hours
Configuration: loop
Elevation gain: 1,200 feet
Difficulty: moderate to strenuous
Exposure: open grasslands and shaded forest
Dogs: allowed
Maps: U.S.G.S. Tassajara Hot Springs · Big Sur and Ventana Wilderness map
Ventana Wilderness Los Padres National Forest map

This scenic trail leads to The Narrows on Tassajara Creek, a series of gorgeous pools and small waterfalls in a narrow canyon. The hike begins on the Horse Pasture Trail and descends down a side canyon, passing a waterfall in a rocky gorge. After exploring the cascades, the trail then loops upstream to Tassajara Hot Springs, located on the monastic Zen Mountain Center grounds at the very end of Tassajara Road.

To the trailhead

From Highway 1 and Carmel Valley Road in Carmel, drive 23 miles southeast on Carmel Valley Road (passing through Carmel Valley Village at 11.5 miles) to Tassajara Road. Turn right and drive 1.3 miles to a signed Y-junction with Cachagua Road. Curve left, staying on Tassajara Road, and continue 14.3 miles to the well-marked trailhead on the left (east) side. Park in the pullouts on either side of the road.

The hike

Take the signed Horse Pasture Trail into the oak forest and head up-hill. Traverse the hillside on a ledge above Tassajara Road. Curving away from the road, cross open grasslands on the narrow path. The gentle grade gains 400 feet in 0.6 miles, reaching a saddle at the wilderness boundary. Descend the east-facing slope under a canopy of oaks and toyon. Switchbacks lead down the hillside into the forested canyon and to seasonal Horse Pasture Creek.

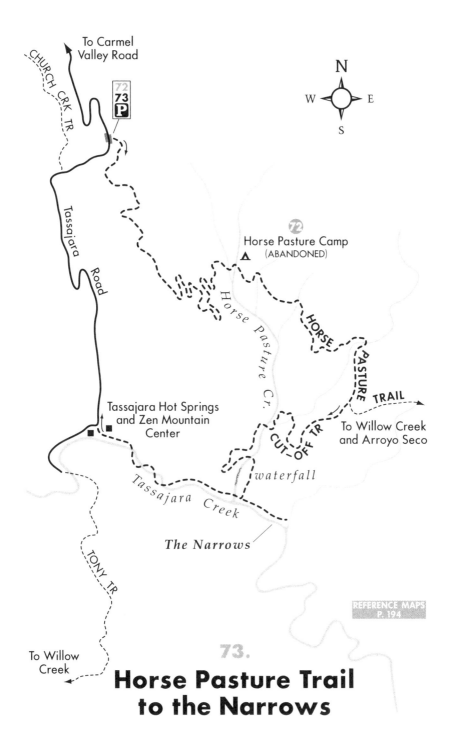

To Carmel
Valley Road

CHURCH CRK TR

72
73
P

N
W E
S

Tassajara Road

Horse Pasture Camp
(ABANDONED)

Horse Pasture Cr.

72

HORSE

PASTURE

TRAIL

CUT-OFF TR

To Willow Creek
and Arroyo Seco

Tassajara Hot Springs
and Zen Mountain
Center

Tassajara Creek

waterfall

The Narrows

TONY TR

To Willow
Creek

REFERENCE MAPS
P. 194

73.

Horse Pasture Trail
to the Narrows

Cross the creek and walk downstream a short distance to the abandoned Horse Pasture Camp on a grassy flat.

Continue on the near-level path through grasslands with oak groves. Cross a shady stream-fed gully lined with ferns. Gradually ascend the hillside, curving right in the seasonal drainage at 2 miles. Continue 0.3 miles to a posted junction. The left fork continues on the Horse Pasture Trail to Willow Creek and Arroyo Seco Road.

Take the right fork on the Tassajara Cut-Off Trail. Descend into the lush draw, winding into the small side canyon. Cross a rocky streambed at 2.8 miles, and parallel the stream. Recross the stream and follow the watercourse along its left bank. Cross Horse Pasture Creek, passing large boulders to an overlook in a rocky gorge at the brink of a waterfall. The narrow, rocky path steeply descends along the canyon wall to a posted T-junction at Tassajara Creek. The left fork follows the creek 100 yards downstream, passing the series of pools and small waterfalls known as The Narrows.

After exploring The Narrows, take the path upstream along the creek past more pools. After several creek crossings, the trail ends at the Tassajara Zen Mountain Center near the south end of Tassajara Road. To make a loop, return along Tassajara Road. ▪

74. Rocky Creek Trail to Rocky Creek Camp

ARROYO SECO

Hiking distance: 4.8 miles round trip
Hiking time: 2.5 hours
Configuration: out and back
Elevation gain: 600 feet
Difficulty: moderate (with several creek crossings)
Exposure: shaded forest and open hillside
Dogs: allowed
Maps: U.S.G.S. Junipero Serra Peak and Tassajara Hot Springs
   Big Sur and Ventana Wilderness map

**map
page 226**

The Arroyo Seco is a major tributary of the Salinas River, emerging from deep within the Ventana Wilderness and traveling on an easterly journey towards the Salinas Valley. From the coast, the river is accessed from the very end of Carmel Valley Road. From the Salinas Valley, the river is accessed from Arroyo Seco Road off of Highway 101.

The Rocky Creek Trail begins at the Arroyo Seco Campground and follows the north canyon wall above the Arroyo Seco to Rocky Creek. The remote path winds up the narrow Rocky Creek drainage through scattered groves of oaks, buckeyes, madrones, maples, manzanitas, and sycamores. After scrambling across several creek crossings, the trail reaches Rocky Creek Camp, which sits on a 6-foot terrace above Rocky Creek and a tributary stream.

To the trailhead

SALINAS/SOLEDAD/HIGHWAY 101. From Salinas, drive 27 miles south on Highway 101 to the Arroyo Seco Road exit in Soledad. Turn right (west) and drive 20.8 miles (passing Carmel Valley Road at 16.2 miles) to the Arroyo Seco Campground entrance. The posted trailhead is on the right (north) side of the entrance kiosk. To park, drive 60 yards ahead, crossing the bridge over the Arroyo Seco. A day use parking lot is located on the right. A parking fee is required.

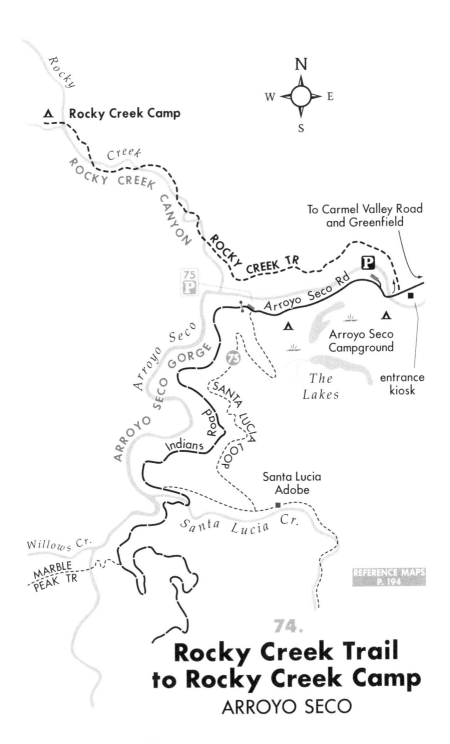

△ **Rocky Creek Camp**

Rocky

Creek

ROCKY CREEK CANYON

ROCKY CREEK TR

To Carmel Valley Road
and Greenfield

75 P

P

Arroyo Seco Rd

Arroyo Seco

ARROYO SECO GORGE

△

Arroyo Seco
Campground

entrance
kiosk

*The
Lakes*

73

SANTA LUCIA LOOP

Road

Indians

Santa Lucia
Adobe

Santa Lucia Cr.

Willows Cr.

MARBLE
PEAK TR

REFERENCE MAPS
P. 194

74.
Rocky Creek Trail
to Rocky Creek Camp
ARROYO SECO

CARMEL. From Highway 1 and Carmel Valley Road in Carmel, drive 40 miles southeast on Carmel Valley Road (passing through Carmel Valley Village at 11.5 miles) to Arroyo Seco Road. Turn right (west) and drive 4.6 miles to the Arroyo Seco Campground entrance. The posted trailhead is on the right (north) side of the entrance kiosk. To park, drive 60 yards ahead, crossing the bridge over the Arroyo Seco. A day use parking lot is located on the right. A parking fee is required.

The hike

Walk back down the road, and cross the bridge over the Arroyo Seco. Bear left on the short, paved driveway by the campground entrance station. The posted footpath heads up the slope and curves west. Traverse the open hillside, overlooking the multi-layered campground and the pools along the Arroyo Seco. At one mile, curve northwest into Rocky Creek Canyon. Follow the east wall of the side canyon past bedrock outcroppings, gradually descending to Rocky Creek. Cross Rocky Creek six times as the tree-shaded canyon narrows. After the sixth crossing, climb up the south-facing hillside, and descend to a grassy flat in an open oak grove. Wind through the flat to Rocky Creek, just above its confluence with a tributary stream. Cross the creek and enter the posted Rocky Creek Camp, bordered by both streams. Return along the same trail. ◼

75. Santa Lucia Loop
ARROYO SECO · SANTA LUCIA CREEK

Hiking distance: 4.5-mile loop
Hiking time: 2.5 hours
Configuration: loop
Elevation gain: 300 feet
Difficulty: easy to slightly moderate
Exposure: mostly shaded forest
Dogs: allowed
Maps: U.S.G.S. Junipero Serra Peak · Big Sur and Ventana Wilderness map

The Arroyo Seco flows eastward from the Santa Lucia Range to-wards the Salinas Valley. The forested headwaters of the creek begin deep in the Ventana Wilderness between Black Cone and Junipero Serra Peak. The Santa Lucia Loop traverses a steep mountain slope high above the scenic Arroyo Seco Gorge. The trail begins at the Arroyo Seco Campground and The Lakes, two small lakes in an open meadow along the Arroyo Seco. The trail leads to the Santa Lucia Adobe, an adobe brick building with a cobblestone foundation built in 1908. The restored adobe (a ranger station until the late 1920s) resides on the banks of Santa Lucia Creek. The return makes a loop back on the unpaved, vehicle-restricted Indians Road that also traverses along the steep slope.

To the trailhead

SALINAS/SOLEDAD/HIGHWAY 101. From Salinas, drive 27 miles south on Highway 101 to the Arroyo Seco Road exit in Soledad. Turn right (west) and drive 20.8 miles (passing Carmel Valley Road at 16.2 miles) to the Arroyo Seco Campground entrance. Enter the campground and drive 0.7 miles to the posted Santa Lucia Trail on the left. Park in the day use lot on the right, across from the trail. A parking fee is required.

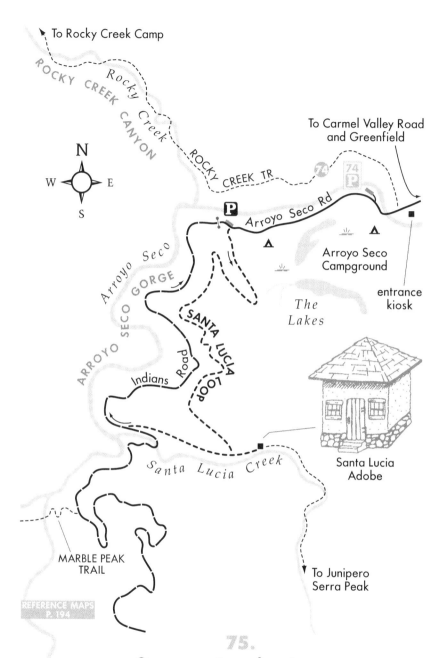

To Rocky Creek Camp

ROCKY CREEK CANYON

Rocky Creek

N
W · E
S

ROCKY CREEK TR

To Carmel Valley Road
and Greenfield

P Arroyo Seco Rd

Arroyo Seco

ARROYO SECO GORGE

SANTA LUCIA LOOP

Indians Road

The Lakes

Arroyo Seco
Campground

entrance
kiosk

Santa Lucia
Adobe

Santa Lucia Creek

MARBLE PEAK
TRAIL

REFERENCE MAPS
P. 194

To Junipero
Serra Peak

75.

Santa Lucia Loop
ARROYO SECO · SANTA LUCIA CREEK

CARMEL. From Highway 1 and Carmel Valley Road in Carmel, drive 40 miles southeast on Carmel Valley Road (passing through Carmel Valley Village at 11.5 miles) to Arroyo Seco Road. Turn right (west) and drive 4.6 miles to the Arroyo Seco Campground entrance. Enter the campground and drive 0.7 miles to the posted Santa Lucia Trail on the left. Park in the day use lot on the right, across from the trail. A parking fee is required.

The hike

Cross the campground road to the posted trail. Ascend the hillside above the upper campground through a forest of oak and buckeye. A short distance up the hill is a view of the north lake. Curve sharply right and climb to the ridge, where there is a view of the south lake. Curve left and follow the narrow, cliffside path overlooking the magnificent Arroyo Seco Gorge and Indians Road, the return route. Traverse the steep slope, contouring along the level hillside path to a saddle by an old wire fence. Descend into an oak-studded meadow to an old, unpaved road above Santa Lucia Creek. Bear left on the road, and head 150 yards downhill to the Santa Lucia Adobe on the banks of the creek. The Santa Lucia Trail continues past the adobe and climbs to the head of Santa Lucia Canyon towards Junipero Serra Peak.

For this hike, return back up the road, passing the Santa Lucia Trail junction, back to the Arroyo Seco and Indians Road. Bear right and follow the serpentine gorge for 2 miles on the narrow, unpaved road. Complete the loop at the parking area. ▪

Limekiln State Park

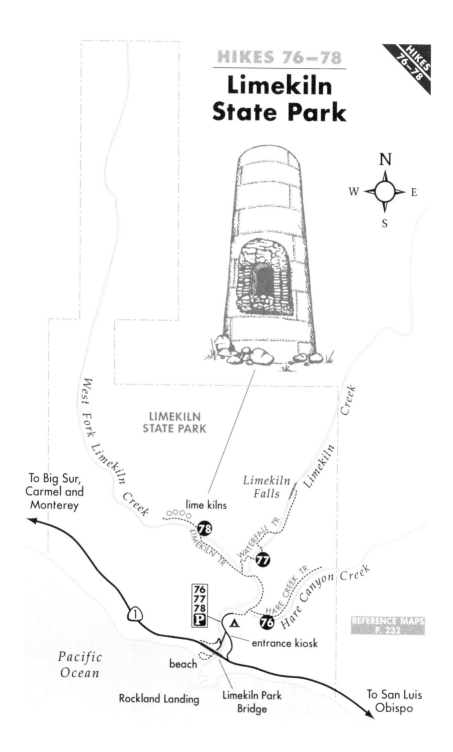

N
W · E
S

West Fork Limekiln Creek

Limekiln Creek

LIMEKILN
STATE PARK

Limekiln
Falls

To Big Sur,
Carmel and
Monterey

lime kilns

WATERFALL TR

LIMEKILN TR

78

77

HARE CREEK TR

Hare Canyon Creek

76

76
77
78
P

entrance kiosk

REFERENCE MAPS
P. 232

Pacific
Ocean

beach

Rockland Landing

Limekiln Park
Bridge

To San Luis
Obispo

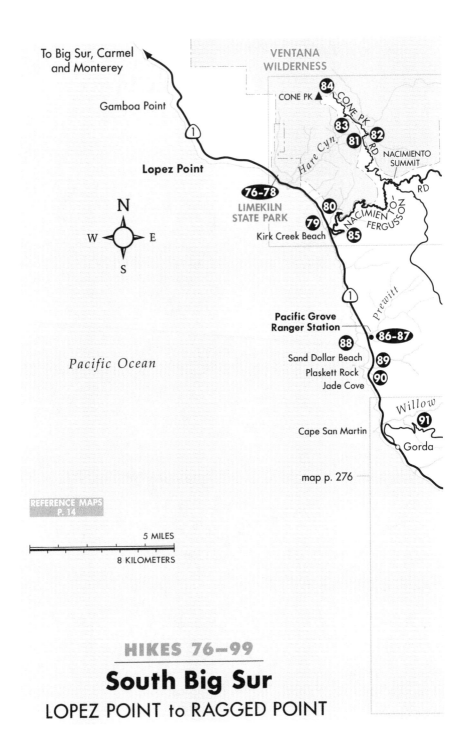

To Big Sur, Carmel and Monterey

VENTANA WILDERNESS

Gamboa Point

CONE PK ▲

84

CONE PK RD

83

Hare Cyn.

82

81

NACIMIENTO SUMMIT

Lopez Point

NACIMIENTO-FERGUSSON RD

76-78

LIMEKILN STATE PARK

80

79

Kirk Creek Beach

85

N
W E
S

Pacific Ocean

1

Prewitt

Pacific Grove Ranger Station

86-87

88

Sand Dollar Beach

89

Plaskett Rock
Jade Cove

90

Willow

91

Cape San Martin

Gorda

map p. 276

REFERENCE MAPS P. 14

5 MILES
8 KILOMETERS

HIKES 76–99

South Big Sur
LOPEZ POINT to RAGGED POINT

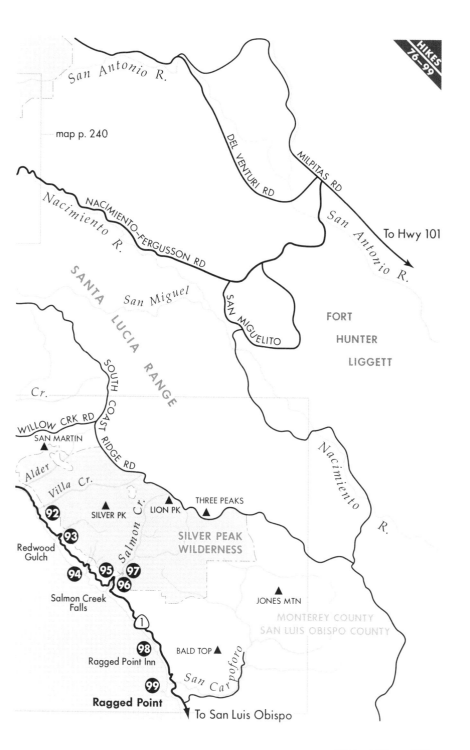

San Antonio R.

map p. 240

DEL VENTURI RD

MILPITAS RD

San Antonio R.

To Hwy 101

NACIMIENTO-FERGUSSON RD

Nacimiento R.

SANTA LUCIA RANGE

San Miguel

SAN MIGUELITO

FORT

HUNTER

LIGGETT

Nacimiento R.

Cr.

SOUTH COAST RIDGE RD

WILLOW CRK RD

SAN MARTIN ▲

Alder

Villa Cr.

92

93

Redwood
Gulch

94

95

97

96

Salmon Creek
Falls

SILVER PK ▲

Salmon Cr.

LION PK ▲

THREE PEAKS ▲

SILVER PEAK
WILDERNESS

JONES MTN ▲

MONTEREY COUNTY
SAN LUIS OBISPO COUNTY

1

98

Ragged Point Inn

BALD TOP ▲

San Carpoforo

99

Ragged Point

To San Luis Obispo

76. Hare Creek Trail and shoreline
LIMEKILN STATE PARK

Hiking distance: 0.9 miles round trip
Hiking time: 30 minutes
Configuration: out and back
Elevation gain: 150 feet
Difficulty: easy
Exposure: shaded forest
Dogs: not allowed
Maps: U.S.G.S. Lopez Point · Limekiln State Park map
Big Sur and Ventana Wilderness map

Limekiln State Park is a magnificent 716-acre park and campground tucked into a narrow valley on the southern end of Big Sur. Three year-round creeks flow through the park under the shade of towering coastal redwoods with a lush mix of sycamores, oaks, and maples. Hare Canyon Creek is a major tributary stream that feeds Limekiln Creek within the dense forest. This gentle trail begins at the mouth of Limekiln Canyon, then parallels Hare Canyon Creek up the narrow canyon past clusters of redwoods, small waterfalls, and cascades. The trail ends at the park boundary, although it once followed Hare Canyon up to Vicente Flat.

To the trailhead

BIG SUR RANGER STATION. From the ranger station, located 27 miles south of Carmel, drive 25.3 miles south on Highway 1 to the signed Limekiln State Park. Turn left (inland) to the entrance kiosk. Park 30 yards ahead in the day use parking area on the right. An entrance fee is required.

RAGGED POINT. From Highway 1 at Ragged Point, located 1.5 miles south of the Monterey County line, drive 22.2 miles north to the state park on the right.

The hike

Walk up the campground road to the road's north end near the confluence of Limekiln Creek and Hare Creek. Cross the footbridge over Hare Creek in a dense redwood forest. At the posted trail fork, the left fork parallels Limekiln Creek to the waterfall and limekilns (Hikes 77 and 78). Take the right fork and head up the shady side canyon along the north bank of the creek. Follow the narrow, rock-walled canyon on a gentle uphill grade, passing continuous cascades and small waterfalls. The trail ends by a beautiful cascade and an 8-foot waterfall.

Return back to the trailhead. To explore the shoreline, walk down the campground road, and cross the campground road bridge over Limekiln Creek. Walk under the Limekiln Park Bridge to the small crescent-shaped beach with offshore rocks. Limekiln Creek flows into the ocean, bisecting the sandy beach cove surrounded by steep rock walls. ■

76.
Hare Creek Trail and shoreline
LIMEKILN STATE PARK

77. Limekiln Falls
LIMEKILN STATE PARK

Hiking distance: 1.3 miles round trip
Hiking time: 30 minutes
Configuration: out and back
Elevation gain: 200 feet
Difficulty: easy (with several creek crossings)
Exposure: shaded forest
Dogs: not allowed
Maps: U.S.G.S. Lopez Point · Limekiln State Park map
      Big Sur and Ventana Wilderness map

Limestone Creek forms on the steep cliffs of Cone Peak and quickly drains into the ocean. En route, Limekiln Falls cascades 100 feet off a mossy, vertical limestone wall, fanning out more than 25 feet. This trail weaves through a stunning redwood forest at the southern end of the coastal redwood range in Limekiln State Park. The trail follows the cascading watercourse of Limekiln Creek to the base of the majestic cataract in a narrow box canyon.

To the trailhead

BIG SUR RANGER STATION. From the ranger station, located 27 miles south of Carmel, drive 25.3 miles south on Highway 1 to the signed Limekiln State Park. Turn left (inland) to the entrance kiosk. Park 30 yards ahead in the day use parking area on the right. An entrance fee is required.

RAGGED POINT. From Highway 1 at Ragged Point, located 1.5 miles south of the Monterey County line, drive 22.2 miles north to the state park on the right.

The hike

Walk up the campground road to the road's north end near the confluence of Limekiln Creek and Hare Canyon Creek. Cross the footbridge over Hare Canyon Creek in a dense redwood forest to a posted trail fork. The right fork parallels Hare Canyon Creek (Hike 76). Take the left fork, following the contours of Limekiln Creek through the shady redwood forest. Cross a second footbridge where Limekiln Creek and the West Fork merge. Seventy yards past the bridge is a posted junction. The left fork continues along the West Fork to the limekilns (Hike 78). Take the right fork down log steps, and boulder hop across the West Fork. Head up the side canyon, and cross Limekiln Creek to its east bank. Pass a magnificent triple-trunk redwood tree, and head upstream past endless cascades, pools, and small waterfalls. After crossing the creek two more times, the path reaches the end of the lush canyon at the base of the waterfall. Return along the same trail. ▪

Limekiln
Falls

lime kilns

West Fork

Limekiln Cr.

LIMEKILN TR

78

WATERFALL TR

N

W ← → E

S

Creek

Limekiln

HARE CREEK TR

76

Hare Canyon Creek

76
77
78
P

To Big Sur,
Carmel and
Monterey

▲

entrance
station

▲

Limekiln Park
Bridge

beach

Rockland
Landing

1

To San Luis
Obispo

77.

Limekiln Falls
LIMEKILN STATE PARK

Pacific
Ocean

78. Limekiln Trail to the limekilns
LIMEKILN STATE PARK

Hiking distance: 1 mile round trip
Hiking time: 30 minutes
Configuration: out and back
Elevation gain: 200 feet
Difficulty: easy
Exposure: shaded forest
Dogs: not allowed
Maps: U.S.G.S. Lopez Point · Limekiln State Park map
    Big Sur and Ventana Wilderness map

Limekiln State Park is named after the on-site stone and steel kilns used to purify quarried limestone into powdered lime in the 1880s. The lime was used as an ingredient in cement. The Limekiln Trail leads to four of the massive kilns. The trail follows the old wagon route used to haul barrels of lime slacked from the furnaces. The hike follows Limekiln Creek and the West Fork up the canyon through dense groves of redwoods, sycamores, oaks, and maples to the giant lime kilns.

To the trailhead

BIG SUR RANGER STATION. From the ranger station, located 27 miles south of Carmel, drive 25.3 miles south on Highway 1 to the signed Limekiln State Park. Turn left (inland) to the entrance kiosk. Park 30 yards ahead in the day use parking area on the right. An entrance fee is required.

RAGGED POINT. From Highway 1 at Ragged Point, located 1.5 miles south of the Monterey County line, drive 22.2 miles north to the state park on the right.

The hike

Walk up the campground road to the road's north end near the confluence of Limekiln Creek and Hare Canyon Creek. Cross the footbridge over Hare Canyon Creek in the dense redwood forest to a posted trail fork. The right fork parallels Hare Canyon Creek (Hike 76). Take the left fork, following the contours of Limekiln Creek through the shady redwood forest. Cross a second footbridge where Limekiln Creek and the West Fork merge.

Follow the west bank of the West Fork, passing the Waterfall Trail on the right (Hike 77). Continue along the creek to a third bridge by cascades and a small waterfall. Head gradually uphill along the east side of the creek, skirting past a large rock outcropping. Thirty yards beyond the rock are the four enormous metal cylinders on the right. On the left are waterfalls and pools. Return along the same trail. ▪

Limekiln Falls

N
W E
S

○ ○ ○ ○ **lime kilns**

West Fork *Limekiln Cr.*

LIMEKILN TR

Creek

WATERFALL TR

77

Limekiln

76

HARE CREEK TR

Hare Canyon Creek

To Big Sur, Carmel and Monterey

76
77
78
P

△

■ entrance station

Limekiln Park Bridge

beach

Rockland Landing

REFERENCE MAPS
P. 231

1

To San Luis Obispo

Pacific Ocean

78.

Limekiln Trail to the limekilns
LIMEKILN STATE PARK

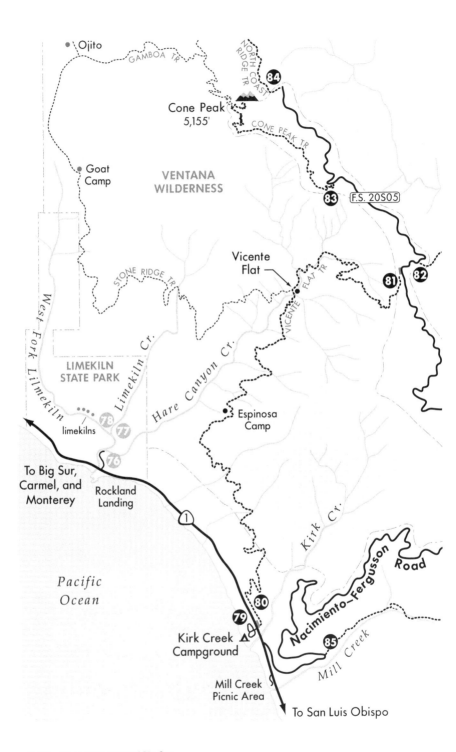

Ojito

GAMBOA TR.

NORTH COAST RIDGE TR.

84

Cone Peak
5,155'

CONE PEAK TR.

83 F.S. 20S05

Goat
Camp

VENTANA
WILDERNESS

82

Vicente
Flat

81

VICENTE FLAT TR.

STONE RIDGE TR.

West Fork Lilmekiln

Lilmekiln Cr.

LIMEKILN
STATE PARK

Hare Canyon Cr.

Espinosa
Camp

limekilns 78

77

76

Kirk Cr.

To Big Sur,
Carmel, and
Monterey

Rockland
Landing

1

Pacific
Ocean

Nacimiento-Fergusson Road

80

79

Kirk Creek
Campground

85

Mill Creek

Mill Creek
Picnic Area

To San Luis Obispo

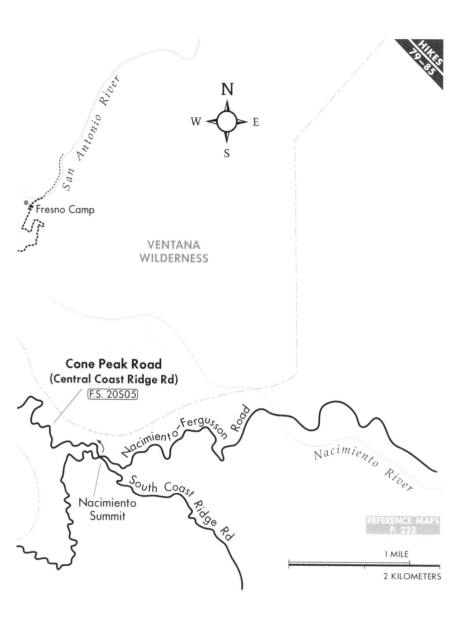

San Antonio River

N
W E
S

Fresno Camp

VENTANA
WILDERNESS

Cone Peak Road
(Central Coast Ridge Rd)
F.S. 20S05

Nacimiento-Fergusson Road

Nacimiento River

South Coast Ridge Rd

Nacimiento
Summit

REFERENCE MAPS
P. 232

1 MILE
2 KILOMETERS

HIKES 79-85

Nacimiento–Fergusson Road
Cone Peak Road

79. Kirk Creek Beach

Hiking distance: 0.5 miles round trip
Hiking time: 30 minutes
Configuration: out and back
Elevation gain: 100 feet
Difficulty: easy
Exposure: open coastal terrace
Dogs: allowed
Maps: U.S.G.S. Cape San Martin
Los Padres National Forest Northern Section Trail Map

Kirk Creek Campground sits atop 100-foot bluffs that overlook the ocean along Highway 1. Below the bluffs lies a beach in a small sandy cove with scattered boulders. The beach is nestled along an otherwise craggy, scalloped shore. The short trail from the campground to the beach crosses the grassy marine terrace, then descends the cliffs to the quiet cove. En route to the edge of the bluffs are views of the dramatic eroded cliffs, coastal rock formations, and expansive vistas north to Lopez Point.

To the trailhead

BIG SUR RANGER STATION. From the ranger station, located 27 miles south of Carmel, drive 27.2 miles south on Highway 1 to the Kirk Creek Campground on the right (ocean) side. Park in the campground day use lot (entrance fee required) or in the pull-outs along the highway (free).

RAGGED POINT. From Highway 1 at Ragged Point, 1.5 miles south of the Monterey County line, drive 20.4 miles north to Kirk Creek Campground on the left (ocean) side. The campground is 4.4 miles north of the Pacific Valley Ranger Station.

The hike

Follow the campground road to the north end of the campground. The signed trail is by campsite 23. Follow the grassy path past the picnic area and through the grove of eucalyptus trees on the bluffs. Descend along the edge of the cliffs. Switchbacks lead down to the small, sandy beach cove. The last 50 feet are a scramble due to erosion. After exploring the cove, return on the same path. ▪

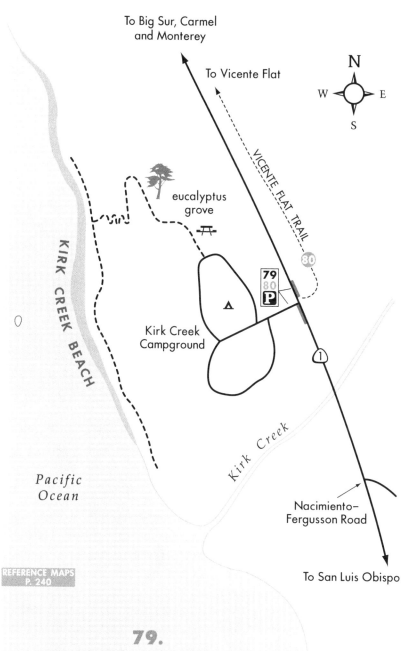

To Big Sur, Carmel
and Monterey

To Vicente Flat

N
W   E
S

KIRK CREEK BEACH

VICENTE FLAT TRAIL

eucalyptus
grove

80

79
80
P

Kirk Creek
Campground

Kirk Creek

1

0

Pacific
Ocean

Nacimiento–
Fergusson Road

To San Luis Obispo

79.
Kirk Creek Beach

80. Vicente Flat
from Kirk Creek Campground

Hiking distance: 10.6 miles round trip (or 7.4-mile shuttle with Hike 81)
Hiking time: 6 hours
Configuration: out and back
Elevation gain: 1,700 feet
Difficulty: strenuous
Exposure: open slopes and shaded forest
Dogs: allowed
Maps: U.S.G.S. Cape San Martin and Cone Peak
Ventana Wilderness Map

Vicente Flat is a large, beautiful camp on the banks of Hare Canyon Creek in the Ventana Wilderness. The camp sits in a grove of majestic old-growth redwoods and a sunny meadow the size of a football field. The Vicente Flat Trail (also known as the Kirk Creek Trail) is one of the most scenic and diverse hikes in the Ventana Wilderness. Along the route are sweeping views from the ocean to Cone Peak as well as deep, forested canyons.

The trail begins at the coast and crosses scrub-covered coastal slopes above Pacific Valley. The trail leads to Hare Canyon, where the path follows the south wall of the canyon into wood-shaded ravines and meadowlands. The trail reaches Hare Canyon Creek under a canopy of towering redwoods.

This hike can be combined with Hike 81 for a 7.4-mile, one-way shuttle hike from Cone Peak Road. (Start from Cone Peak Road to hike downhill.)

To the trailhead

BIG SUR RANGER STATION. From the ranger station, located 27 miles south of Carmel, drive 27.2 miles south on Highway 1 to the Kirk Creek Campground on the right. The posted trail is on the left (inland side), directly across from the campground. Park in a pullout alongside the highway.

RAGGED POINT. From Highway 1 at Ragged Point Inn, 1.5 miles south of the Monterey County line, drive 20.4 miles north to the Kirk Creek Campground and trailhead.

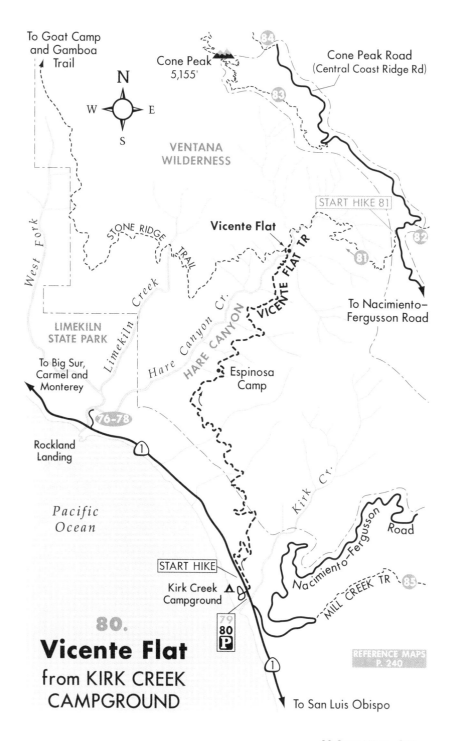

To Goat Camp
and Gamboa
Trail

Cone Peak
5,155'

Cone Peak Road
(Central Coast Ridge Rd)

N
W **E**
S

VENTANA
WILDERNESS

84

83

START HIKE 81

Vicente Flat

VICENTE FLAT TR

STONE RIDGE TRAIL

West Fork

81

82

To Nacimiento–
Fergusson Road

LIMEKILN
STATE PARK

Hare Canyon Cr.

HARE CANYON

Limekiln Creek

Espinosa
Camp

To Big Sur,
Carmel and
Monterey

76-78

1

Rockland
Landing

Kirk Cr.

*Pacific
Ocean*

Nacimiento–Fergusson Road

START HIKE

Kirk Creek
Campground

MILL CREEK TR

85

79

80.
P

80.
Vicente Flat
from KIRK CREEK
CAMPGROUND

1

REFERENCE MAPS
P. 240

To San Luis Obispo

The hike

Climb the exposed, brush-covered coastal slope toward the saddle. The magnificent coastal views from above Pacific Valley improve with every step. Just before reaching the saddle, bear left and cross the sloping grassland to the posted Ventana Wilderness boundary. Cross a gully below the sheer rock cliffs. Curve west to the west tip of the ridge, with sweeping panoramas from north to south. Climb the ridge and curve north. Traverse the upper mountain slope, wending in and out of mature redwood, madrone, and bay groves. Contour around three more sizeable gullies to the south wall of Hare Canyon at 3 miles. The views extend up Limekiln Canyon and Hare Canyon to 5,155-foot Cone Peak to the north. Curve east and follow the level path through redwood groves along the south wall of Hare Canyon. Continue to Espinosa Camp on a small shoulder to the left at 3.4 miles. The camp is 20 yards off the trail on a flat, grassy ridge with an ocean view.

A quarter mile after the camp, cross a redwood-lined stream. Continue through the forest on a moderate grade for 2 miles, then begin a steady descent to Hare Canyon Creek on the canyon floor. Cross the creek to a posted junction with the Stone Ridge Trail on the left. Bear to the right and enter Vicente Flat, the destination. Campsites line the creek among the towering redwoods.

Vicente Flat is also the destination for Hike 81, which leads to the camp from the opposite end of the Vicente Flat Trail. For a one-way shuttle hike along the trail, begin the hike from Cone Peak Road—Hike 81—and continue 7.4 miles down to the Kirk Creek Campground. ▪

81. Vicente Flat
from Cone Peak Road

Hiking distance: 4.5 miles round trip (or 7.4-mile shuttle with Hike 80)
Hiking time: 3 hours
Configuration: out and back
Elevation gain: 1,600 feet
Difficulty: moderate to strenuous
Exposure: shaded forest
Dogs: allowed
Maps: U.S.G.S. Cone Peak · Ventana Wilderness Map

**map
page 249**

Vicente Flat is a spacious camp with a large, verdant meadow along the banks of Hare Canyon Creek. Campsites line the serene streamside glade under a canopy of majestic redwoods. The well-graded Vicente Flat Trail travels from its upper east end at Cone Peak Road and descends 7.4 miles to Kirk Creek Campground along Highway 1. This hike takes in the first 2.3 miles to Vicente Camp. The path drops into wooded Hare Canyon, with exceptional views down the 3,000-foot deep canyon to the sea. The downhill path parallels Hare Canyon Creek beneath the shade of massive redwoods.

This trail may be combined with Hike 80 for a 7.4-mile, one-way downhill shuttle hike.

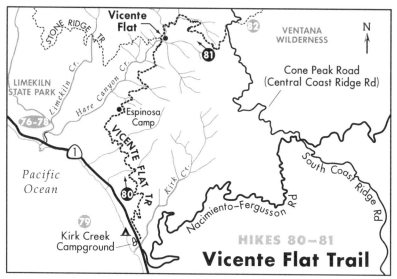

To the trailhead

BIG SUR RANGER STATION. From the ranger station, located 27 miles south of Carmel, drive 27.4 miles south to Nacimiento-Fergusson Road. The road is 0.2 miles south of Kirk Creek Campground. Turn inland and wind up the paved mountain road for 7.1 miles to the South Coast Ridge Road on the right. Turn left on the narrow, unpaved Central Coast Ridge Road (also known as Cone Peak Road), and drive 3.7 miles to the posted trail on the left. Park in the pullout on the left, just past the trailhead. Cone Peak Road is closed from approximately November through May and may be impassable in wet weather.

RAGGED POINT. From Highway 1 at Ragged Point Inn, 1.5 miles south of the Monterey County line, drive 20.2 miles north to Nacimiento-Fergusson Road, located 4.2 miles north of the Pacific Valley Ranger Station. Continue with the directions above.

The hike

Walk up the hill and curve around to the south side of the knoll. Descend from the head of Hare Canyon. At a quarter mile, the path steeply zigzags down the south wall of the canyon and temporarily levels out on a small grassy ridge. Curve to the right and continue down switchbacks to Hare Canyon Creek in the shaded redwood grove. Follow the creek downstream through lush riparian vegetation, climbing over and stooping under a few fallen redwoods while crossing the creek five times. The fifth crossing is at the upper reaches of Vicente Flat, with campsites on each side of the creek. Stroll through the dense grove of redwoods along the west side of the creek to the heart of Vicente Flat by a grassy meadow. A lower path borders the creek to several campsites. Just beyond the meadow is a posted junction, the turn-around spot. The Vicente Flat Trail bears to the left and descends another 5 miles to Highway 1 at Kirk Creek Campground. The Stone Ridge Trail, straight ahead on the right fork, leads to Goat Camp and the Gamboa Trail to the North Coast Ridge Trail.

To hike the 7.4-mile shuttle hike, continue on the Vicente Flat Trail down to the Kirk Creek Campground—Hike 80 in reverse. ∎

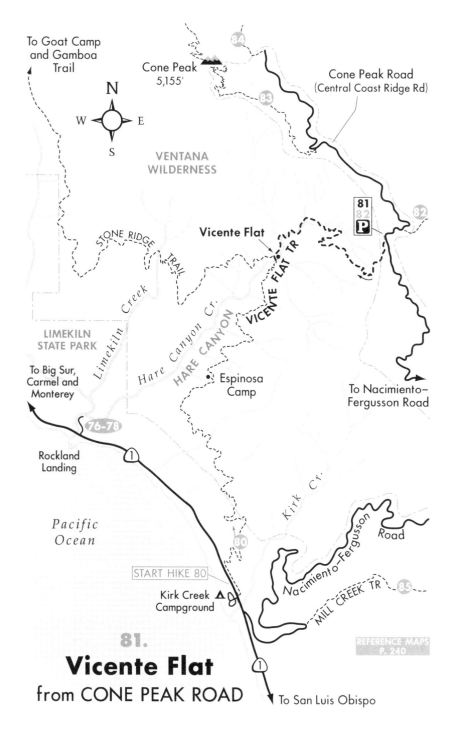

To Goat Camp
and Gamboa
Trail

Cone Peak
5,155'

Cone Peak Road
(Central Coast Ridge Rd)

N
W E
S

VENTANA
WILDERNESS

84

83

81
82
P

82

STONE RIDGE TRAIL

Vicente Flat

VICENTE FLAT TR

Limekiln Creek

LIMEKILN
STATE PARK

Hare Canyon Cr.

HARE CANYON

To Big Sur,
Carmel and
Monterey

Espinosa
Camp

To Nacimiento–
Fergusson Road

76-78

1

Rockland
Landing

Kirk Cr.

Pacific
Ocean

80

Nacimiento-Fergusson Road

START HIKE 80

Kirk Creek ▲
Campground

MILL CREEK TR

85

REFERENCE MAPS
P. 240

81.

Vicente Flat
from CONE PEAK ROAD

1

To San Luis Obispo

82. San Antonio Trail to Fresno Camp

Hiking distance: 3 miles round trip
Hiking time: 2 hours
Configuration: out and back
Elevation gain: 1,000 feet
Difficulty: moderate
Exposure: open hillside and shaded forest
Dogs: allowed
Maps: U.S.G.S. Cone Peak · Ventana Wilderness map

Fresno Camp is a large, picturesque camp on the floor of the San Antonio River canyon in the Ventura Wilderness. The lush camp stretches along the San Antonio River, a major tributary of the Salinas River, in a wide meadow under a broad mix of trees. The trail, which receives minimal use, begins on the dry, brush-covered hillside on Cone Peak Road and descends through groves of oak and bay trees to the verdant, stream-fed camp.

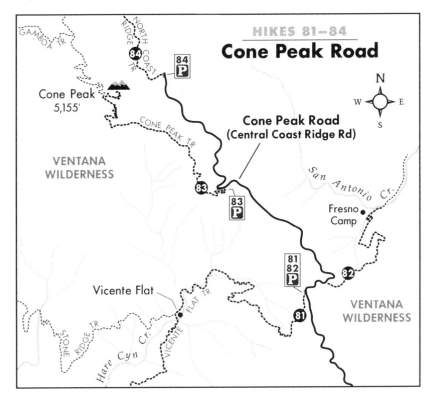

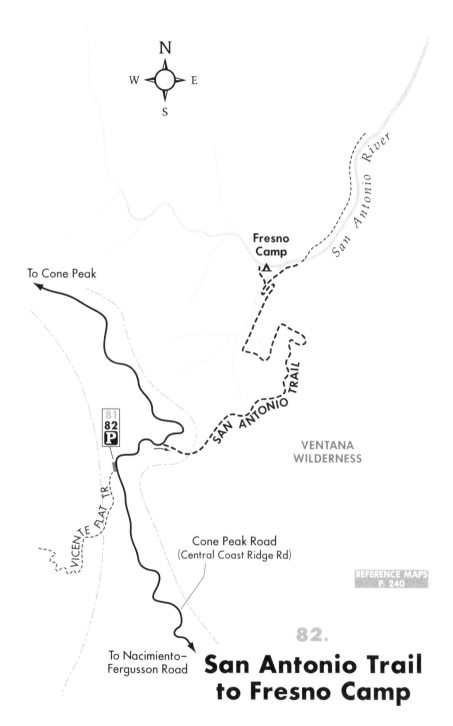

N
W   E
S

To Cone Peak

Fresno
Camp

San Antonio River

SAN ANTONIO TRAIL

81
82 P

VICENTE FLAT TR

VENTANA
WILDERNESS

Cone Peak Road
(Central Coast Ridge Rd)

REFERENCE MAPS
P. 240

To Nacimiento–
Fergusson Road

82.

San Antonio Trail
to Fresno Camp

To the trailhead

Parking is not available directly at the San Antonio Trailhead. Park in the Vicente Flat Trailhead parking pullout:

BIG SUR RANGER STATION. From the ranger station, located 27 miles south of Carmel, drive 27.4 miles south to Nacimiento-Fergusson Road. The road is 0.2 miles south of Kirk Creek Campground. Turn inland and wind up the paved mountain road for 7.1 miles to the South Coast Ridge Road on the right. Turn left on the narrow, unpaved Central Coast Ridge Road (also known as Cone Peak Road), and drive 3.7 miles to the posted trail on the left. Park in the pullout on the left, just past the trailhead. Cone Peak Road is closed from approximately November through May and may be impassable in wet weather.

RAGGED POINT. From Highway 1 at Ragged Point, 1.5 miles south of the Monterey County line, drive 20.2 miles north to Nacimiento-Fergusson Road, located 4.2 miles north of the Pacific Valley Ranger Station.

The hike

Walk up the road 0.15 miles to the brown trail sign on the right. Take the footpath along the north canyon wall, entering the Ventana Wilderness. The narrow path skirts through the brush, reaching a saddle at a quarter mile. Descend from the saddle along the south wall of the San Antonio River drainage under the shadow of Cone Peak, entering groves of oaks, bays, and madrone trees. Follow a gentle downhill grade along the contours of the hillside, with sweeping mountain views to the north and west. Three short switchbacks drop down to the San Antonio River and Fresno Camp in a large grassy flat at 1.5 miles. The large terraced campsite stretches along the river on the canyon floor under sycamores, ponderosa pine, oaks, and maples. The upper camp sits under the shade of maple trees. This is the turn-around spot.

To hike farther, the trail crosses the river at the lower end of the camp and continues to San Antonio Camp, 2 miles ahead. However, the trail becomes hard to follow with fallen trees and heavy brush. ▪

83. Cone Peak

Hiking distance: 4.6 miles round trip
Hiking time: 2.5 hours
Configuration: out and back
Elevation gain: 1,400 feet
Difficulty: moderate to strenuous
Exposure: open ridge with shaded pockets
Dogs: allowed
Maps: U.S.G.S. Cone Peak · Ventana Wilderness map

**map
page 254**

The vistas from atop Cone Peak are some of the most spectacular along the Big Sur coast. The 5,155-foot peak rises nearly a mile from the ocean in just over 3 miles. It is one of the steepest gradients from the ocean to the summit in the United States. From the summit are 360-degree views of the ocean, the surrounding peaks, and the valleys along the Santa Lucia Range. This hike follows the moderate southern slope to a fire lookout atop the peak. The lookout is only occupied during the fire season.

To the trailhead

BIG SUR RANGER STATION. From the ranger station, located 27 miles south of Carmel, drive 27.4 miles south to Nacimiento-Fergusson Road. The road is 0.2 miles south of Kirk Creek Campground. Turn inland and wind up the paved mountain road 7.1 miles to the South Coast Ridge Road on the right. Turn left on the narrow, unpaved Central Coast Ridge Road (also known as Cone Peak Road), and drive 5.3 miles to the posted trail on the left. Park in the pullout on the left, just past the trailhead. Cone Peak Road is closed from approximately November through May and may be impassable in wet weather.

RAGGED POINT. From Highway 1 at Ragged Point, 1.5 miles south of the Monterey County line, drive 20.2 miles north to Nacimiento-Fergusson Road, located 4.2 miles north of the Pacific Valley Ranger Station. Continue with the directions above.

The hike

Walk past the trailhead sign and ascend the hill. Three switchbacks lead a quarter mile to a spectacular view of the ocean, mountains, San Antonio Valley, Nacimiento Valley, and the lookout tower atop Cone Peak. Head north up the ridge through tall brush. Cross a saddle high above Hare Canyon and just below the ridge of Cone Peak. Traverse the mountain slope on the long, ascending grade dotted with Coulter pines, sugar pines, manzanitas, and bays. Several short, steep switchbacks climb the mountain and cross a ridge to a posted junction at 1.8 miles, just below the Cone Peak summit. The left fork drops steeply down the mountain to Trail Spring Camp. Stay to the right (east) and climb a quarter mile on steep switchbacks to the lookout tower. En route are rare Santa Lucia fir, which only grow at these higher elevations. After savoring the views, return along the same route. ■

Trail Spring Camp

NORTH COAST RIDGE TRAIL

Cone Peak
5,155'

lookout tower

Cone Peak Road
(Central Coast Ridge Rd)

CONE PEAK TRAIL

VENTANA WILDERNESS

N
W — E
S

To Nacimiento–Fergusson Road

REFERENCE MAPS
P. 240

HARE CANYON

VICENTE FLAT TR

83.
Cone Peak

Vicente Flat

84. North Coast Ridge Trail to Cook Spring Camp

Hiking distance: 5 miles round trip
Hiking time: 3 hours
Configuration: out and back
Elevation gain: 800 feet
Difficulty: moderate
Exposure: mostly shaded forest
Dogs: allowed
Maps: U.S.G.S. Cone Peak and Lopez Point · Ventana Wilderness map

**map
page 257**

The Coast Ridge Road connects Cone Peak Road to Ventana Inn at Highway 1 (Hike 41). This hike begins from the end of Cone Peak Road on the old road/trail, which is often referred to as the North Coast Ridge Trail at this end. The ridgeline trail begins along the north flank of Cone Peak and follows a craggy ridge with sweeping coastal and mountain views. This hike leads to Cook Spring Camp, a lightly used, multi-level camp with a small spring under a stand of old sugar pines. Just beyond the camp, the trail offers amazing views from a garden of sandstone boulders.

To the trailhead

BIG SUR RANGER STATION. From the ranger station, located 27 miles south of Carmel, drive 27.4 miles south to Nacimiento-Fergusson Road. The road is 0.2 miles south of Kirk Creek Campground. Turn inland and wind up the paved mountain road 7.1 miles to the South Coast Ridge Road on the right. Turn left on the narrow, unpaved Central Coast Ridge Road (also known as Cone Peak Road), and drive 6.6 miles to the parking area at the end of the road. Cone Peak Road is closed from approximately November through May and may be impassable in wet weather.

RAGGED POINT. From Highway 1 at Ragged Point, 1.5 miles south of the Monterey County line, drive 20.2 miles north to Nacimiento-Fergusson Road, located 4.2 miles north of the Pacific Valley Ranger Station. Continue with the directions above.

The hike

Take the old road along the north side of Cone Peak. Wind through craggy metamorphic rock in an open forest of towering pines. Cross a talus slope of fractured rock while overlooking the rugged canyon lands and layered ridges of the Santa Lucia Mountains. At a half mile, the road narrows to a footpath and descends on two short switchbacks. Traverse the steep mountainside through a live oak forest, crossing several more talus slopes. Zigzag up six switchbacks to the head of the canyon, reaching the ridge where the lookout tower atop Cone Peak is in view. Pass a junction with the Gamboa Trail, and continue north along the coastal ridge, passing jagged rock formations to the saddle. Cross the crest to the east-facing slope in an old fire-burned area, where the trail widens. Descend gradually to an unmarked, abandoned road on the right at 2 miles. Take the road, which leads to Cook Spring Camp, and snake steeply downhill to the right, reaching the camp in a grove of huge sugar pines. The spring is to the west of the upper camp.

Return to the North Coast Ridge Trail. Continue north less than a half mile to a garden of rounded sandstone boulders and an overlook at a hairpin left bend. Panoramic 360-degree views extend from the ocean to Salinas Valley. Numerous side paths descend to the boulders. This is the turn-around spot.

To extend the hike, the trail continues to a junction with the Arroyo Seco Trail in just over a half mile, then many miles northwest to Ventana Inn. ▓

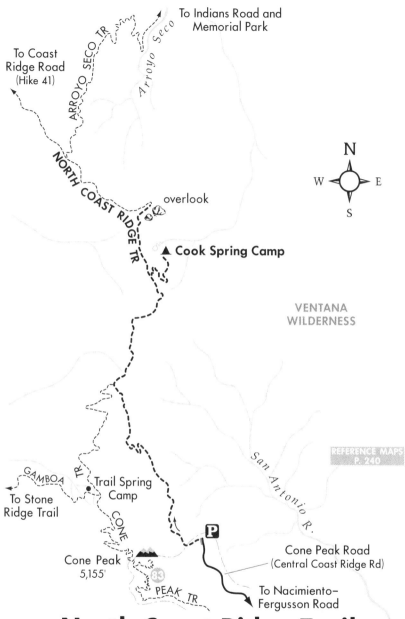

To Indians Road and
Memorial Park

To Coast
Ridge Road
(Hike 41)

ARROYO SECO TR

Arroyo Seco

NORTH COAST RIDGE TR

overlook

▲ Cook Spring Camp

VENTANA
WILDERNESS

N
W — E
S

San Antonio R.

REFERENCE MAPS
P. 240

GAMBOA

TR

• Trail Spring
Camp

To Stone
Ridge Trail

CONE

P

Cone Peak Road
(Central Coast Ridge Rd)

Cone Peak
5,155'

PEAK TR

To Nacimiento-
Fergusson Road

84. North Coast Ridge Trail
to Cook Spring Camp
(COAST RIDGE ROAD)

85. Mill Creek Trail

Hiking distance: 3 miles round trip
Hiking time: 2 hours
Configuration: out and back
Elevation gain: 600 feet
Difficulty: easy to slightly moderate
Exposure: shaded canyon
Dogs: allowed
Maps: U.S.G.S. Cape San Martin · Ventana Wilderness map

The Mill Creek Trail follows the bucolic watershed up beautiful Mill Creek Canyon just south of Nacimiento-Fergusson Road. The canyon was named for an old sawmill that once produced railroad ties. The trail meanders alongside Mill Creek through riparian vegetation under the dark shade of giant redwoods, big leaf maples, and sycamores. The hike ends at a campsite perched above the creek amidst a cluster of redwoods.

To the trailhead

BIG SUR RANGER STATION. From the ranger station, located 27 miles south of Carmel, drive 27.4 miles south on Highway 1 to Nacimiento-Fergusson Road. The road is 0.2 miles south of Kirk Creek Campground. Turn inland and wind up the paved mountain road 0.8 miles to the posted trail on the right, at a distinct left horseshoe bend. Park in the pullout on the right by the trailhead.

RAGGED POINT. From Highway 1 at Ragged Point, 1.5 miles south of the Monterey County line, drive 20.2 miles north to Nacimiento-Fergusson Road, located 4.2 miles north of the Pacific Valley Ranger Station.

The hike

Climb 100 yards up the steep slope to a small saddle. Descend under a canopy of California bay laurel. The undulating path follows the north canyon wall high above Mill Creek. The creek can be heard but not yet seen, as towering redwoods carpet the canyon floor. Gradually drop down the hillside into a wet, lush forest of redwoods, maples, sycamores, bracken and sword ferns, and moss-covered granite rocks at a half mile. Wind through the canyon, following the creek upstream. Rock hop over Lion

Creek to a distinct but unmarked trail fork. Take the left fork and climb up a 15-foot slope. (The right fork ends 30 yards ahead.) Curve right, soon reaching a creek crossing. Rock hop over Mill Creek two consecutive times while passing waterfalls and pools. Scramble over a jumble of boulders at an old landslide, then follow a narrow ledge on the edge of the creek. The main trail curves to a plateau above the creek, where there is a gorgeous campsite surrounded by a cluster of redwoods. This is the turn-around spot and a great place to explore the immediate surroundings. The trail continues up to the South Coast Ridge Road, but it becomes indistinct just beyond the camp. ▪

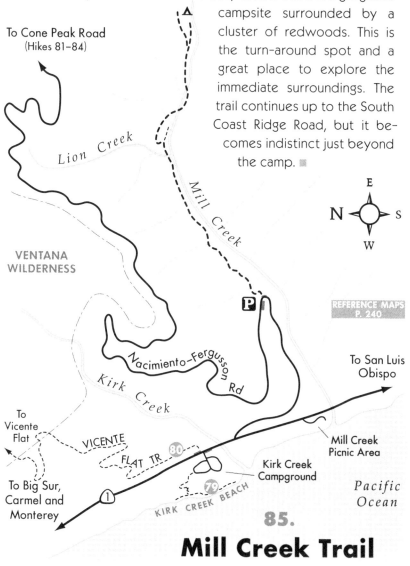

To Cone Peak Road
(Hikes 81–84)

Lion Creek

Mill Creek

VENTANA
WILDERNESS

E
N ✦ S
W

P

REFERENCE MAPS
P. 240

Nacimiento-Fergusson Rd

Kirk Creek

To San Luis
Obispo

To
Vicente
Flat

VICENTE
FLAT TR. 80

To Big Sur,
Carmel and
Monterey

1

79
KIRK CREEK BEACH

Kirk Creek
Campground

Mill Creek
Picnic Area

Pacific
Ocean

85.
Mill Creek Trail

86. Prewitt Loop Trail to Stag Camp
NORTH TRAILHEAD

Hiking distance: 8 miles round trip
Hiking time: 5 hours
Configuration: out and back
Elevation gain: 1,700 feet
Difficulty: moderate to strenuous
Exposure: mix of exposed hillside and forested pockets
Dogs: allowed
Maps: U.S.G.S. Cape San Martin
       Big Sur and Ventana Wilderness map

The Prewitt Loop Trail is a 12.8-mile loop located in the heart of Pacific Valley at the south end of the Big Sur coast. The trail circles the Prewitt Creek watershed through a mix of habitats in the Los Padres National Forest. This hike begins from the north trailhead on the sloping oceanfront grasslands with coastal scrub. The lightly used footpath leads up the canyon through oak, pine, and laurel woodlands; groves of redwoods; and grassy savannas. The trail leads 4 miles up the remote north slope of Prewitt Creek Canyon to Stag Camp, perched in an oak grove on the upper mountain slopes. Although the trail gains 1,700 feet, it is never steep and offers magnificent vistas. The views span across Pacific Valley to the scalloped coastline, including Plaskett Creek, crescent-shaped Sand Dollar Beach, and north to Lopez Point.

To the trailhead

BIG SUR RANGER STATION. From the ranger station, located 27 miles south of Carmel, drive 30.6 miles south on Highway 1 to the signed trailhead on the left (inland). The trailhead is located 3.8 miles south of the Kirk Creek Campground and 0.5 miles north of the Pacific Valley Ranger Station. Park in the pullouts along either side of the road.

RAGGED POINT. From Highway 1 at Ragged Point, located 1.5 miles south of the Monterey County line, drive 16.4 miles north to the trailhead on the right (inland). The trailhead is 0.5 miles north of the Pacific Valley Ranger Station.

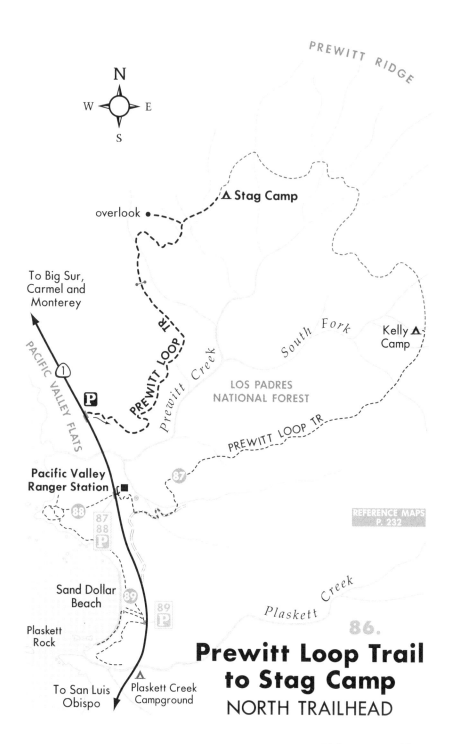

N
W · E
S

PREWITT RIDGE

▲ Stag Camp

overlook ●

To Big Sur,
Carmel and
Monterey

PACIFIC VALLEY FLATS

1

P

PREWITT LOOP TR

Prewitt Creek

South Fork

Kelly ▲
Camp

LOS PADRES
NATIONAL FOREST

PREWITT LOOP TR

87

Pacific Valley
Ranger Station ■

88

87
88
P

REFERENCE MAPS
P. 232

Sand Dollar
Beach

89

Plaskett Creek

Plaskett
Rock

Plaskett Creek

89
P

86.

To San Luis
Obispo

▲
Plaskett Creek
Campground

Prewitt Loop Trail
to Stag Camp
NORTH TRAILHEAD

The hike

Walk through the signed trailhead gate and up the grassy path along the base of the mountains. Traverse the chaparral-clad slope, with a view across Pacific Valley, the scalloped coastline, the circular-shaped Sand Dollar Beach, and the offshore rock formations. Wind up the mountain on an easy grade that offers steady views of the ocean. Weave along the curvature of the mountain through thickets of low-lying coastal scrub. Curve left on the upper northwest wall of forested Prewitt Creek Canyon. The views stretch up the canyon from the ocean to the ridge. The canyon soon forks into two drainages. Veer left, following the west fork. Enter the shade of an oak, pine, bay laurel, and red-wood forest with a lush understory of ferns. Pass through a trail gate and continue gaining altitude. Cross a fork of Prewitt Creek on a horseshoe right bend at 2.7 miles to a distinct spur trail on the left. The side path climbs a short distance to a grassy saddle with views in every direction.

On the main trail, cross a series of gullies and emerge onto the open grassy slopes with exceptional vistas. Pass between two spring-fed water troughs with a view down canyon of Sand Dollar Beach. A quarter mile past the spring, in a small forested flat, is Stag Camp on the right. The primitive camp contains a fire pit and picnic bench. This is the turn-around spot.

Beyond the camp, the trail is not well maintained and obscured by overgrown brush and a lack of use. ▨

87. Prewitt Loop Trail to Kelly Camp
SOUTH TRAILHEAD

Hiking distance: 9.8 miles round trip
Hiking time: 5.5 hours
Configuration: out and back
Elevation gain: 1,600 feet
Difficulty: strenuous
Exposure: a mixed of open chaparral and dense forest
Dogs: allowed
Maps: U.S.G.S. Cape San Martin
Big Sur and Ventana Wilderness map

**map
page 265**

The Prewitt Loop Trail forms a loop in the mountainous back-country adjacent to the coast. The trail, which begins in Pacific Valley, winds up a remote canyon while circling the Prewitt Creek watershed. The path weaves through the arid chaparral on the oceanfront slopes to a dense oak and pine forest with shaded redwood groves. This hike begins from the south trailhead at the Pacific Valley Ranger Station. The trail climbs the south canyon wall to Kelly Camp, a primitive, oak-rimmed camp that sits on a small flat. From the camp are views down the South Fork Prewitt Creek Canyon to the sea. En route, the hike crosses a series of feeder streams and leads to scenic overlooks. Throughout the hike are spectacular coastal views of the expansive marine terrace, jagged coastline, promontories, and the remote backcountry.

To the trailhead

BIG SUR RANGER STATION. From the ranger station, located 27 miles south of Carmel, drive 31 miles south on Highway 1 to the Pacific Valley Ranger Station on the left. The ranger station is located 4.3 miles south of the Kirk Creek Campground. Park in the pullouts on either side of the road. The trailhead is located behind the fire station.

RAGGED POINT. From Highway 1 at Ragged Point, located 1.5 miles south of the Monterey County line, drive 16 miles north to the Pacific Valley Ranger Station.

The hike

The trail starts behind the fire station. From the pullouts along Highway 1, walk up the ranger station road and immediately veer to the right. Pass the fire house on the right to the signed Prewitt Trailhead at the hill. Climb up the grassy footpath with views across the flat marine terrace of Pacific Valley. The footpath passes a water tank on the left and ends at a T-junction with an old dirt road. Bear left on the narrow dirt road, and head east towards the canyon. Climb through the oak, pine, and redwood forest on the road for 0.4 miles to a signed trail on the left. Leave the road and veer left on the footpath. Descend through the bucolic forest that is teeming with redwoods, bracken, and sword ferns. Hop over a creek that flows down the steep, rock-walled canyon. Traverse the north canyon wall to an overlook of Pacific Valley, Sand Dollar Beach, off-shore rocks, and the scalloped coastline.

Head inland and cross over the slope into the South Fork Prewitt Creek Canyon. Crisscross the hillside, alternating between the two canyons. The North Prewitt Trail (Hike 86) can be spotted on the cliffs across the canyon. Head east, straight up the canyon, perched on the canyon wall. Cross a spring trickling out of the mountain. Cross a second stream seeping out of a small rock tunnel under the base of a sprawling oak. Loop around a side canyon, crossing the drainage and returning to the main canyon. Cross another spring by a pair of towering redwoods. The footpath crosses two more springs before reaching Kelly Camp on the left at just under 5 miles. This is the turn-around spot.

The footpath continues across several tributaries of Prewitt Creek, then becomes obscured by a tangle of overgrown brush and a lack of use. ■

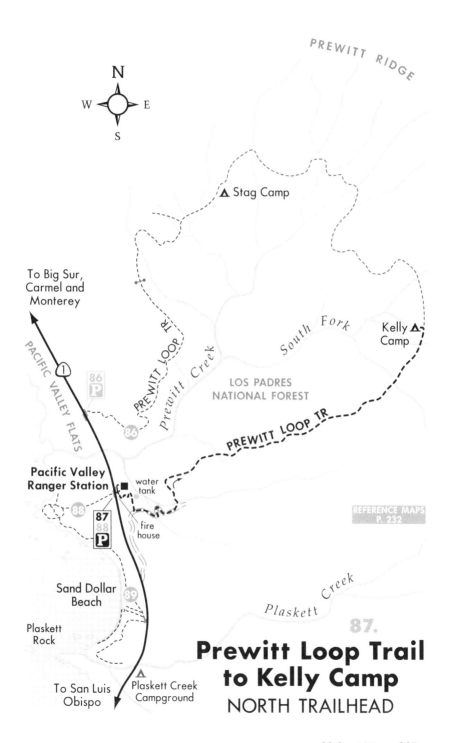

N
W E
S

PREWITT RIDGE

▲ Stag Camp

To Big Sur,
Carmel and
Monterey

PACIFIC VALLEY FLATS

PACIFIC VALLEY

①

86 P

86

PREWITT LOOP TR

Prewitt Creek

South Fork

Kelly ▲ Camp

LOS PADRES
NATIONAL FOREST

PREWITT LOOP TR

Pacific Valley
Ranger Station

water
tank

88

87
88 P

fire
house

REFERENCE MAPS
P. 232

Sand Dollar
Beach

89

Plaskett
Rock

Creek

Plaskett

87.

Prewitt Loop Trail
to Kelly Camp
NORTH TRAILHEAD

To San Luis
Obispo

▲ Plaskett Creek
Campground

88. Pacific Valley Flats

Hiking distance: 2 miles round trip
Hiking time: 1 hour
Configuration: out and back
Elevation gain: 50 feet
Difficulty: easy
Exposure: open marine terrace
Dogs: allowed
Maps: U.S.G.S. Cape San Martin
Los Padres National Forest Northern Section Trail Map

Pacific Valley is a flat, four-mile-long marine terrace along the southern Monterey County coastline. The broad expanse extends west from the steep slopes of the Santa Lucia Mountains to the serrated bluffs above the Pacific Ocean. This hike crosses the grassy coastal terrace to the eroded coastal bluff a hundred feet above the ocean. There are dramatic views of Plaskett Rock, offshore rock formations with natural arches, and the scalloped coastal cliffs. Numerous access points lead to the grassland terrace. This hike begins across from the Pacific Valley Ranger Station.

To the trailhead

BIG SUR RANGER STATION. From the ranger station, located 27 miles south of Carmel, drive 31 miles south on Highway 1 to the Pacific Valley Ranger Station on the left. The ranger station is located 4.3 miles south of the Kirk Creek Campground. Park in the pullouts on either side of the road.

RAGGED POINT. From Highway 1 at Ragged Point, located 1.5 miles south of the Monterey County line, drive 16 miles north to the Pacific Valley Ranger Station.

The hike

The hike begins directly across the road from the ranger station. Step up and over the trail access ladder. Head west across the grassy expanse and past rock outcroppings on the left. Near the point is a rolling sand dune with numerous trails and great overlooks. The main trail stays to the north of the dune, leading to the edge of the cliffs along the jagged coastline high above the pounding surf. At one mile, the trail ends at a fenceline above Prewitt Creek. The trails around the dunes connect with the bluff trail, which leads south for one mile to Sand Dollar Beach (Hike 89). The dune trails circle back to the first junction at the cliff's edge. ■

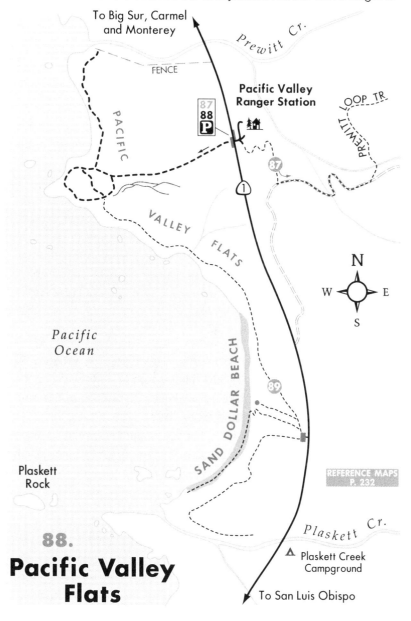

88.
Pacific Valley Flats

89. Sand Dollar Beach

Hiking distance: 3.5 miles round trip
Hiking time: 2 hours
Configuration: out and back
Elevation gain: 150 feet
Difficulty: easy
Exposure: open marine terrace
Dogs: allowed
Maps: U.S.G.S. Cape San Martin
       Los Padres National Forest Northern Section Trail Map

**map
page 270**

Sand Dollar Beach is a protected horseshoe-shaped sand and rock beach between two rocky headlands that jut into the Pacific Ocean. The mile-wide beach cove is backed by Pacific Valley, an expansive marine terrace 100 feet above the sea. The grassy bluff offers sweeping coastal vistas. The trail passes a picnic area lined with Monterey cypress trees to the steep, eroded cliffs and an overlook with interpretive signs. From the overlook is access to the shoreline. There are great coastal views of large offshore rock outcroppings. Plaskett Rock sits off the southern point. Cone Peak can be seen inland along the Santa Lucia Range, steeply rising upward to 5,155 feet.

To the trailhead

BIG SUR RANGER STATION. From the ranger station, located 27 miles south of Carmel, drive 32.4 miles south on Highway 1 to the parking lot on the right (ocean) side. Park in the lot (entrance fee) or in the pullouts along the highway (free).

RAGGED POINT. From Highway 1 at the Ragged Point Inn, located 1.5 miles south of the Monterey County line, drive 15 miles north on Highway 1 to the parking lot on the left (ocean) side, just north of Plaskett Creek Campground.

The hike

Pick up the signed trail at the north end of the parking lot. Walk through the opening in the fence to a Y-fork. The left fork descends down the gully to interpretive panels at an oceanfront overlook perched on the cliffs. From the overlook, zigzag left, then right, and descend steps to the rocky beach at the base of the 100-foot cliffs.

After exploring the crescent-shaped cove and massive sea stacks, return to the junction. Continue on the right fork (now on your left). Walk twenty yards to another unsigned trail split. The left fork leads 100 yards to another coastal overlook atop the bluffs. Returning to the junction, take the grassy path north. Cross the chaparral-clad marine terrace for one mile across Pacific Valley. The trail connects with the headland at the northern end of the Sand Dollar Beach crescent (Hike 88).

Back at the Sand Dollar Beach parking lot, an additional trail heads west across the grassy coastal terrace to a cliffside overlook. The meandering path follows the bluffs less than a half mile south to the deep ravine carved by Plaskett Creek. ▨

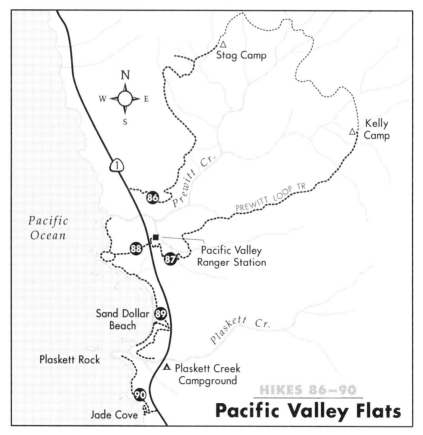

HIKES 86-90
Pacific Valley Flats

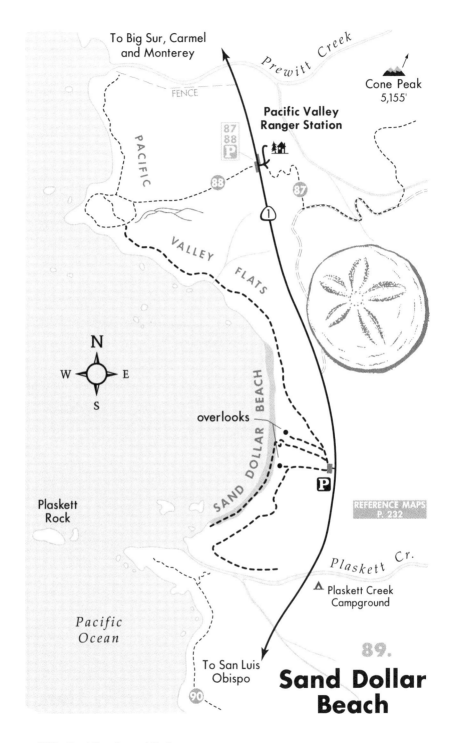

To Big Sur, Carmel
and Monterey

Prewitt Creek

Cone Peak
5,155'

FENCE

PACIFIC

87
88
P

Pacific Valley
Ranger Station

88

87

1

VALLEY

FLATS

N
W   E
S

overlooks

SAND DOLLAR BEACH

Plaskett
Rock

P

REFERENCE MAPS
P. 232

Plaskett Cr.

▲ Plaskett Creek
Campground

*Pacific
Ocean*

To San Luis
Obispo

90

89.
Sand Dollar Beach

90. Jade Cove and Plaskett Rock

Hiking distance: 0.4 to 1.5 miles round trip
Hiking time: 30 to 60 minutes
Configuration: out and back
Elevation gain: 150 feet
Difficulty: easy (with some scrambling required)
Exposure: open marine terrace
Dogs: allowed
Maps: U.S.G.S. Cape San Martin

**map
page 272**

This hike leads to ocean cliffs with classic California coast views. A short trail crosses the grassy marine terrace to the edge of the cliffs, where the coastal vistas are spectacular. A path scrambles down the cliffs to Jade Cove, a small, rocky inlet with smooth, ocean-tumbled stones and nephrite jade. The isolated cove sits at the base of steep 100-foot serpentine cliffs eroded by the rough surf. Plaskett Rock, a dramatic outcropping, sits offshore to the north. Cape San Martin extends out to sea to the south.

To the trailhead

BIG SUR RANGER STATION. From the ranger station, located 27 miles south of Carmel, drive 32.9 miles south on Highway 1 (0.4 miles south of Plaskett Creek Campground) to the Jade Cove Beach trailhead sign. There are pullouts on both sides of the highway.

RAGGED POINT. From Highway 1 at Ragged Point, 1.5 miles south of the Monterey County line, drive 14.6 miles north (3 miles north of Gorda) to the signed trailhead.

The hike

From the ocean side of the highway, head over the access ladder. Continue down the steps, heading west across the wide, grassy terrace to the edge of the bluffs and a junction. To reach Jade Cove, zigzag down the steep, eroded cliffs. The descent is made easier with the help of switchbacks. Near the bottom, some boulder hopping is required to reach the shoreline. The path ends in Jade Cove amid the rounded stones.

Return to the junction atop the bluffs. To extend the hike to Plaskett Rock, take the blufftop path to the north, skirting the edge of the cliffs a half mile to Plaskett Creek. A narrow path drops down the water-carved ravine to the creek. Another path follows the bluffs out on the headland that points toward Plaskett Rock. Return along the same blufftop path. ▪

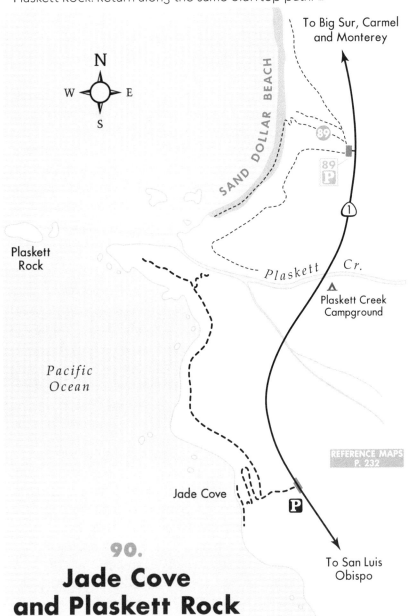

90.

Jade Cove
and Plaskett Rock

91. Willow Creek Trail

Hiking distance: 3.4 miles round trip
Hiking time: 2 hours
Configuration: out and back
Elevation gain: 500 feet
Difficulty: easy
Exposure: shaded canyon
Dogs: allowed
Maps: U.S.G.S. Cape San Martin
  Los Padres National Forest Northern Section Trail Map

**map
page 275**

The Willow Creek Trail is a little gem tucked between the Ventana Wilderness and the Silver Peak Wilderness. The unmarked and seldom hiked trail drops into an isolated stream-fed canyon under shady redwoods, oaks, and maples. At Willow Creek is an old, rickety "Indiana Jones" style suspension bridge that spans 80 yards across the gorge.

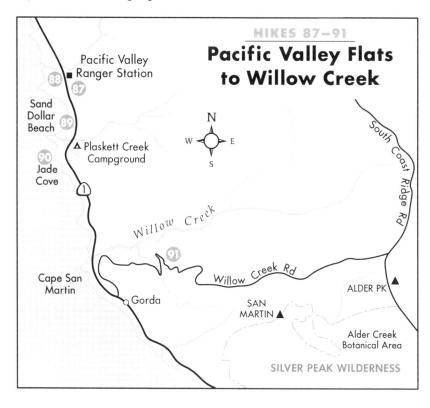

To the trailhead

BIG SUR RANGER STATION. From the ranger station, 27 miles south of Carmel, drive 35 miles south on Highway 1 to Willow Creek Road. It is located 2.5 miles south of Plaskett Creek Campground and just south of the Willow Creek bridge. Turn inland and wind up the narrow, unpaved mountain road 2.4 miles to an unsigned road junction on the left. This road—the Willow Creek Trail—no longer accommodates vehicles. Park in the pullout on the right, 40 yards before the junction.

RAGGED POINT. From Highway 1 at Ragged Point, 1.5 miles south of the Monterey County line, drive 12.5 miles north to Willow Creek Road. The road is one mile north of Gorda.

The hike

Walk 60 yards up Willow Creek Road to the narrow, rutted road. Bear left and descend through the shade of pine and bay trees to an oak grove on a circular flat. Drop deeper into Willow Creek Canyon along the south canyon wall, passing a spur road on the left at 0.6 miles. The main road ends at one mile in a redwood grove, then continues as a footpath.

Descend under the deep shade of the towering redwoods on the fern-lined path. Contour around a rocky, stream-fed gully, and traverse the lush hillside to an unmarked trail split. The left (lower) fork drops down to the creek at the dilapidated and unsafe suspension bridge spanning the gorge. To the left is a series of pools among a jumble of rocks.

Back on the main trail, continue 0.15 miles to another unsigned trail fork. The left fork zigzags a short distance down to a campsite on a grassy flat perched 20 feet above Willow Creek. Back on the main trail, the right fork gradually descends to the creek, passing huge, mossy, fern-covered boulders and fallen redwoods. To the right are two small campsites surrounded by redwoods. Beyond the camp, the trail is overgrown and hard to follow. Return by retracing your steps. ▩

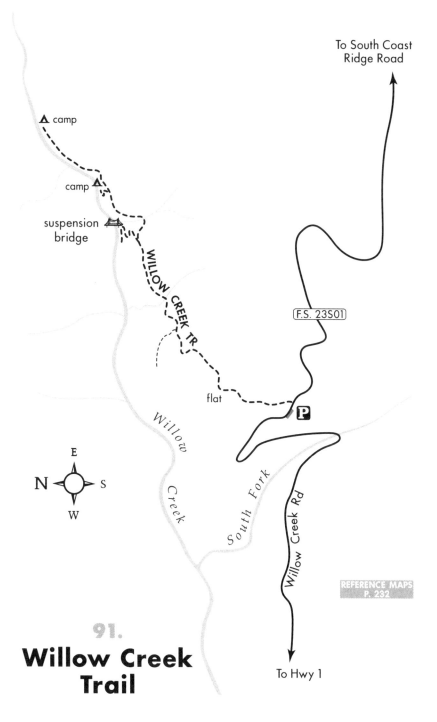

To South Coast
Ridge Road

△ camp

camp △

suspension
bridge

WILLOW CREEK TR

F.S. 23S01

flat

P

Willow

Creek

South Fork

Willow Creek Rd

N E S W

REFERENCE MAPS
P. 232

To Hwy 1

91.
Willow Creek
Trail

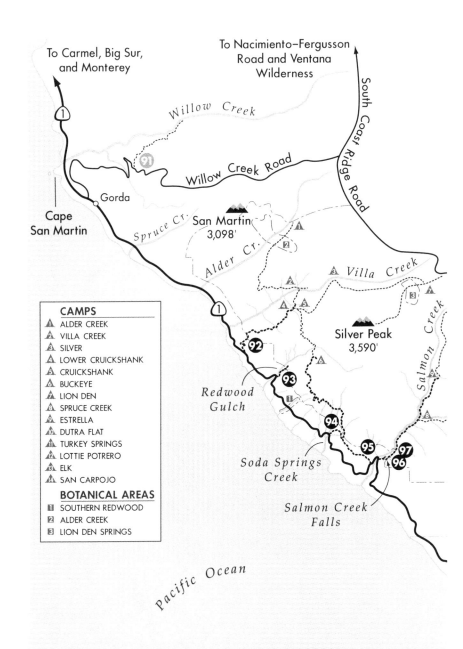

To Carmel, Big Sur, and Monterey

To Nacimiento–Fergusson Road and Ventana Wilderness

Willow Creek

Willow Creek Road

South Coast Ridge Road

91

Gorda

Cape San Martin

Spruce Cr.

San Martin 3,098'

Alder Cr.

Villa Creek

Salmon Creek

1

Silver Peak 3,590'

92

Redwood Gulch

93

Soda Springs Creek

94

95

97
96

Salmon Creek Falls

CAMPS
- ⛺ ALDER CREEK
- ⛺ VILLA CREEK
- ⛺ SILVER
- ⛺ LOWER CRUICKSHANK
- ⛺ CRUICKSHANK
- ⛺ BUCKEYE
- ⛺ LION DEN
- ⛺ SPRUCE CREEK
- ⛺ ESTRELLA
- ⛺ DUTRA FLAT
- ⛺ TURKEY SPRINGS
- ⛺ LOTTIE POTRERO
- ⛺ ELK
- ⛺ SAN CARPOJO

BOTANICAL AREAS
- 1 SOUTHERN REDWOOD
- 2 ALDER CREEK
- 3 LION DEN SPRINGS

Pacific Ocean

HIKES 92–99
Silver Peak Wilderness Area

T he rugged Silver Peak Wilderness, established in 1992, is located in the Santa Lucia Range of the Los Padres National Forest. This remote 14,500-acre wilderness at the southwestern corner of Monterey County is home to California's southernmost coastal redwoods. Three year-round creeks—Villa Creek, Salmon Creek, and San Carpoforo Creek—flow from the upper mountain reaches to the Pacific. Several steep, intersecting trails weave through the wilderness from the ocean to the mountain ridge, gaining nearly 3,600 feet within a couple of miles. The trails wind through open meadows, forest groves, down stream-fed canyons, and across ridgelines with sweeping coastal views.

HIKES 92-99

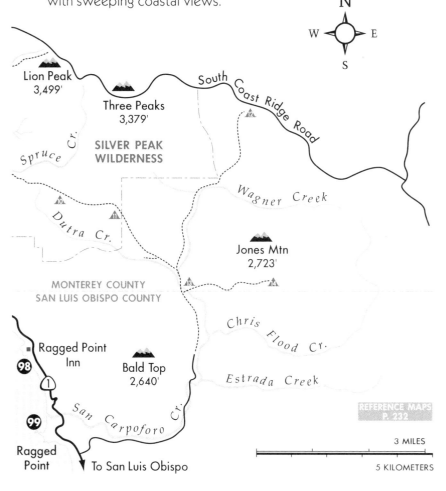

92. Cruickshank Trail to Cruickshank Camp

SILVER PEAK WILDERNESS AREA

Hiking distance: 5 miles round trip
Hiking time: 3 hours
Configuration: out and back
Elevation gain: 1,200 feet
Difficulty: moderate
Exposure: open hillside and shaded canyon
Dogs: allowed
Maps: U.S.G.S. Villa Creek
          Los Padres National Forest Northern Section Trail Map

The Cruickshank Trail in the Silver Peak Wilderness begins from Highway 1 and climbs the exposed oceanfront hillside to magnificent coastal vistas before dropping into Villa Creek Canyon. The lush canyon path winds through giant redwood groves to Cruickshank Camp in an oak-shaded grassland.

To the trailhead

BIG SUR RANGER STATION. From the ranger station, located 27 miles south of Carmel, drive 39.6 miles south on Highway 1 to the grassy parking pullout on the east (inland) side of the road by the signed Cruickshank trailhead.

RAGGED POINT. From Highway 1 at Ragged Point, 1.5 miles south of the Monterey County line, drive 7.9 miles north on Highway 1 to the grassy parking pullout on the east (inland) side of the road by the signed Cruickshank trailhead.

The hike

From the signed trailhead, climb switchbacks up the brushy mountain slope. Wind through the thick coastal scrub overlooking the ocean and offshore rocks. More switchbacks lead up the exposed south-facing slope to a ridge with sweeping coastal vistas at 900 feet. Descend a short distance into Villa Creek Canyon above the coastal redwoods carpeting the canyon floor. Traverse the south canyon slope through lush vegetation under

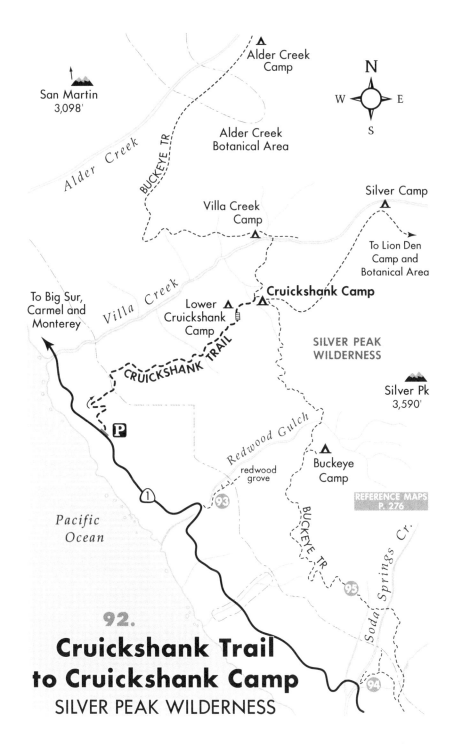

San Martin
3,098'

Alder Creek

Alder Creek
Camp

N
W   E
S

BUCKEYE TR

Alder Creek
Botanical Area

Silver Camp

Villa Creek
Camp

To Lion Den
Camp and
Botanical Area

To Big Sur,
Carmel and
Monterey

Villa Creek

Lower
Cruickshank
Camp

Cruickshank Camp

SILVER PEAK
WILDERNESS

CRUICKSHANK TRAIL

Silver Pk
3,590'

P

Redwood Gulch

redwood
grove

Buckeye
Camp

REFERENCE MAPS
P. 276

1

Pacific
Ocean

93

BUCKEYE TR

95

Soda Springs Cr.

94

92.
Cruickshank Trail
to Cruickshank Camp
SILVER PEAK WILDERNESS

oak and redwood groves. Pass the unexplained "Hjalmur's Loop" sign, and continue through the shade of the redwoods. Emerge from the forest to a picturesque view of the ocean, framed by the V-shaped canyon walls. Reenter the forest, passing a tall stand of narrow eucalyptus trees on the left. Cross a log plank over a seasonal stream to Lower Cruickshank Camp fifty yards ahead, a small camp with room for one tent. A quarter mile farther is the upper Cruickshank Camp in a large oak flat. This is the turn-around spot for a 5-mile round-trip hike.

To extend the hike, two trails depart from the upper camp. To the left (north), the Buckeye Trail crosses a stream by a giant redwood and descends 0.6 miles to Villa Creek Camp in a dense redwood grove at Villa Creek. From Villa Creek Camp, the trail climbs back out of the drainage and up to Alder Creek Botanical Area, then to Alder Creek Camp at the trail's end.

From Cruickshank Camp heading right (east), the combined Cruickshank and Buckeye Trails cross through the camp to an oak-dotted grassland and a posted junction. From here, the Buckeye Trail bears right and heads 1.5 miles south to Buckeye Camp (Hike 95). The Cruickshank Trail climbs 500 feet in one mile to Silver Camp and 1,500 feet in 3 miles to Lion Den Camp. ■

93. Redwood Gulch

NATHANIEL OWINGS MEMORIAL REDWOOD GROVE
SILVER PEAK WILDERNESS AREA

Hiking distance: 0.4 miles round trip
Hiking time: 30 minutes
Configuration: out and back
Elevation gain: 200 feet
Difficulty: very easy
Exposure: shaded forest
Dogs: allowed
Maps: U.S.G.S. Villa Creek
Los Padres National Forest Northern Section Trail Map

**map
page 282**

Redwood Gulch is home to one of California's southernmost groves of coastal redwoods. The gulch is a narrow, eroded gorge with chutes of cascading water, small waterfalls, and a myriad of tub-size pools surrounded by huge boulders. This short trail begins at the creek bottom amidst the lush streamside vegetation and climbs through the dank, damp, atmospheric terrain beneath a magnificent stand of imposing redwoods. The site was named for Nathaniel and Margaret Owings, early conservationists that worked to protect Big Sur's coastline from development.

To the trailhead

BIG SUR RANGER STATION. From the ranger station, located 27 miles south of Carmel, drive 40.5 miles south on Highway 1 to the parking pullout on the east (inland) side of the road at the base of the horseshoe-shaped bend in the road.

RAGGED POINT. From Highway 1 at Ragged Point, 1.5 miles south of the Monterey County line, drive 7 miles north to the trailhead on the right.

The hike

Walk up the wide path along the south side of the creek to the trail sign. Pass a rock fountain and descend to the streambed surrounded by towering redwoods. A short distance ahead is a waterfall that cascades over a jumble of large boulders. At the base of the falls, the water disappears underground. The stream returns above ground west of the highway near the ocean. Continue along the south edge of the waterfall, climbing over fallen redwoods and boulders. Follow the steep path through a wet, dense forest with huge redwoods, boulders, and an understory of ferns. Several side paths on the left lead down to pools and smaller waterfalls. At just under a quarter mile is an old rock fire pit on a small flat. This is a good turn-around area. The undeveloped path continues up canyon, but it is a steep scramble and requires careful footing, especially back down on the descent. ▣

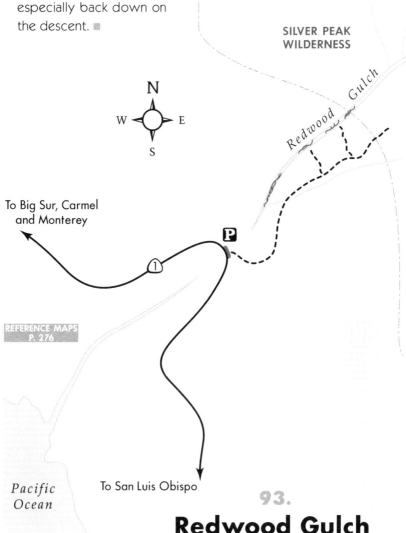

SILVER PEAK
WILDERNESS

N
W ←◇→ E
S

Redwood Gulch

To Big Sur, Carmel
and Monterey

P

To San Luis Obispo

Pacific
Ocean

REFERENCE MAPS
P. 276

93.
Redwood Gulch

94. Soda Springs and Lower Buckeye Trails

Hiking distance: 3 miles round trip
Hiking time: 1.5 hours
Configuration: out and back
Elevation gain: 750 feet
Difficulty: easy to moderate
Exposure: mostly shaded hillside
Dogs: allowed
Maps: U.S.G.S. Burro Mountain
Los Padres National Forest Northern Section Trail Map

map
page 284

The Soda Springs Trail begins along Soda Springs Creek in the lush riparian vegetation of ferns, alders, and California bay laurel along the border of the Silver Peak Wilderness. The trail climbs the forested slope to an overlook with coastal views that extend south to the Point Piedras Blancas lighthouse and Point Buchon, beyond Morro Bay. The path descends to the Salmon Creek drainage, where there are magnificent views of Salmon Creek Falls (Hike 96).

To the trailhead

BIG SUR RANGER STATION. From the ranger station, located 27 miles south of Carmel, drive 42.2 miles south on Highway 1 to the paved parking pullout on the east (inland) side of the road by the signed Soda Springs trailhead.

RAGGED POINT. From Highway 1 at Ragged Point, 1.5 miles south of the Monterey County line, drive 5.3 miles north to the trailhead on the right. It is located 1.6 miles after the signed Salmon Creek trailhead.

The hike

At the trailhead, a left fork drops down to Soda Springs Creek by a waterfall and pool in a rock gorge. The Soda Springs Trail stays to the right and heads up the hill, parallel to the creek, to an unsigned junction. Bear right, away from the creek, and steadily gain elevation. Thread your way through verdant undergrowth on the shaded forest path. Cross a seasonal stream by a huge boulder, reaching a posted junction with the Buckeye Trail at a coastal overlook. The left fork continues to Buckeye Camp (Hike 95).

This hike stays to the right on the lower section of the Buckeye Trail. Cross through the stock gate, and traverse the hillside, parallel to the coastline. The path levels out on a grassy plateau with sweeping oceanfront views. Descend from the ridge on the open slope, noticing the great view of Salmon Creek Falls. Pass a water trough by an underground spring, and cross through two more trail gates. A few short switchbacks quickly descend the hill to the Buckeye Trailhead by the abandoned Salmon Creek Ranger Station. This is the turn-around point.

To extend the hike to Salmon Creek Falls, follow Highway 1 downhill (left) 0.1 mile to the Salmon Creek trailhead on the south side of Salmon Creek. The falls is 0.3 miles up the trail (Hike 95). ■

To Cruickshank Camp (Hike 92)

Buckeye Camp

Soda Springs Cr.

To Big Sur, Carmel and Monterey

SILVER PEAK WILDERNESS

REFERENCE MAPS P. 276

waterfall

P

Salmon Cr.

96 97 P

Salmon Creek Falls

N
W E
S

1

trough

95 P

Salmon Creek Ranger Station (abondoned)

To San Luis Obispo

94.

Soda Springs and Lower Buckeye Trails

95. Buckeye Trail to Buckeye Camp
SILVER PEAK WILDERNESS AREA

Hiking distance: 7 miles round trip
Hiking time: 4 hours
Configuration: out and back
Elevation gain: 1,600 feet
Difficulty: strenuous
Exposure: shaded canyons and open grassy plateaus
Dogs: allowed
Maps: U.S.G.S. Burro Mountain and Villa Creek
      Los Padres National Forest Northern Section Trail Map

**map
page 287**

Buckeye Camp sits in a large meadow rimmed with oaks and pines in the mountainous interior of the Silver Peak Wilderness. The camp has a developed spring, picnic bench, and a rock fire pit under the canopy of an immense bay tree with expansive overhanging branches. The scenic but strenuous trail up to the camp begins from the abandoned Salmon Creek Ranger Station and climbs the exposed coastal slopes to sweeping views of the Pacific Ocean and Salmon Creek Falls. The path weaves in and out of several small canyons with shaded oak groves and passes an ephemeral 30-foot waterfall.

To the trailhead

BIG SUR RANGER STATION. From the ranger station, located 27 miles south of Carmel, drive 43.7 miles south on Highway 1 to the paved parking area on the inland side of the road by the abandoned Salmon Creek Ranger Station.

RAGGED POINT. From Highway 1 at Ragged Point, 1.5 miles south of the Monterey County line, drive 3.8 miles north on Highway 1 to the paved parking area on the inland side of the road by the abandoned Salmon Creek Ranger Station. It is located just after the signed Salmon Creek trailhead.

The hike

Walk through the trailhead gate at the north end of the parking area. Ascend the hillside on a few short switchbacks, passing through a second trail gate. Climb through the chaparral and grasslands, passing a trough and underground spring to a third gate. The path levels out on a grassy plateau that overlooks the ocean and Salmon Creek Falls. Traverse the hillside high above the ocean, and pass through a gate to a posted Y-fork at one mile. The Soda Springs Trail bears left, returning to Highway 1 at Soda Springs Creek (Hike 94).

Take the Buckeye Trail to the right. Cross a stream-fed gully with a seasonal waterfall off a sheer, moss-covered rock wall. Climb out of the gully, following the contours of the mountains in and out of small oak-shaded canyons. Cross Soda Springs Creek at 2 miles to a grassy ridge a half mile ahead. The ridge offers far-reaching vistas of the coastline and across to the peaks and canyons of the Santa Lucia Range. Follow the exposed ridge uphill to an elevated perch in an open pine grove above Redwood Gulch. Curve inland and descend into the rolling mountainous interior, reaching Buckeye Camp at the head of a long valley at 3.5 miles. Return along the same trail.

To extend the hike, the Buckeye Trail continues another 1.5 miles north to the upper Cruickshank Camp (Hike 92). ▦

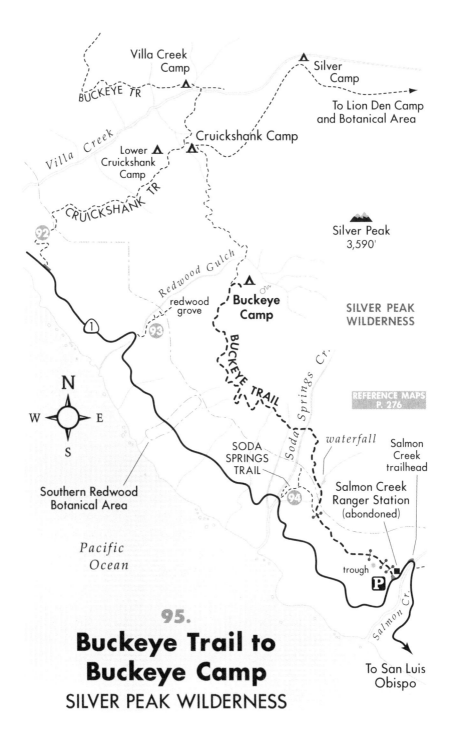

Villa Creek
Camp

Silver
Camp

BUCKEYE TR

To Lion Den Camp
and Botanical Area

Villa Creek

Cruickshank Camp

Lower
Cruickshank
Camp

CRUICKSHANK TR

92

Silver Peak
3,590'

Redwood Gulch

redwood
grove

Buckeye
Camp

SILVER PEAK
WILDERNESS

1

93

BUCKEYE TRAIL

Soda Springs Cr.

REFERENCE MAPS
P. 276

N

W   E

S

SODA
SPRINGS
TRAIL

waterfall

Salmon
Creek
trailhead

Southern Redwood
Botanical Area

94

Salmon Creek
Ranger Station
(abondoned)

Pacific
Ocean

trough

P

Salmon Cr.

95.

Buckeye Trail to
Buckeye Camp
SILVER PEAK WILDERNESS

To San Luis
Obispo

96. Salmon Creek Falls
SILVER PEAK WILDERNESS AREA

Hiking distance: 0.6 miles round trip
Hiking time: 30 minutes
Configuration: out and back
Elevation gain: 150 feet
Difficulty: easy
Exposure: shaded canyon
Dogs: allowed
Maps: U.S.G.S. Burro Mountain
Los Padres National Forest Northern Section Trail Map

The Salmon Creek Trail runs through the deep interior of the Silver Peak Wilderness in the Santa Lucia Mountains. The trail connects the coastline with the 3,000-foot South Coast Ridge Road. This hike follows a short section at the beginning of the trail to the dynamic Salmon Creek Falls, where a tremendous volume of water plunges from three chutes. The beautiful waterfall drops more than 100 feet off the vertical rock face, crashing onto the rocks and pools below. A cool mist sprays over the mossy green streamside vegetation under a shady landscape of sycamores, maples, alders, and bay laurels.

To the trailhead

BIG SUR RANGER STATION. From the ranger station, located 27 miles south of Carmel, drive 43.8 miles south on Highway 1 to the signed Salmon Creek trailhead at a sweeping horseshoe bend in the road. Park in the wide pullout on the left by the guardrail.

RAGGED POINT. From Highway 1 at Ragged Point, 1.5 miles south of the Monterey County line, drive 3.7 miles north on Highway 1 to the signed Salmon Creek trailhead on the right.

The hike

Walk alongside the guardrail to the signed trailhead on the south side of Salmon Creek. Salmon Creek Falls can be seen from the guardrail. Take the Salmon Creek Trail up the gorge into the lush, verdant forest. Pass an old wooden gate, and cross a small tributary stream. Two hundred yards ahead is a signed junction. The right fork continues on the Salmon Creek Trail (Hike 97). Take the left fork towards the falls. Cross another small stream, then descend around huge boulders towards Salmon Creek at the base of the plummeting falls. Head towards the thunderous sound of the waterfall. Climb around the wet, mossy boulders to explore the various caves and overlooks. Return along the same trail. ■

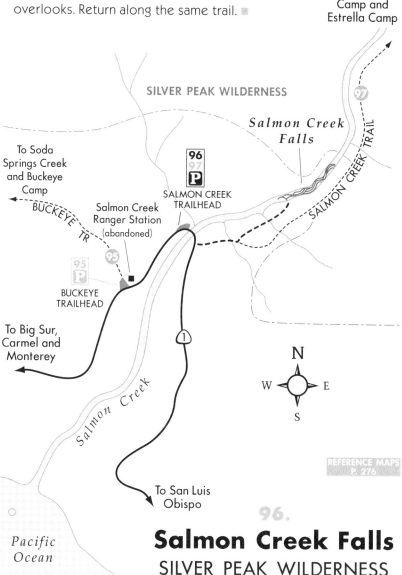

To Spruce Creek
Camp and
Estrella Camp

SILVER PEAK WILDERNESS

*Salmon Creek
Falls*

To Soda
Springs Creek
and Buckeye
Camp

96
97
P
SALMON CREEK
TRAILHEAD

Salmon Creek
Ranger Station
(abandoned)

BUCKEYE TR

95
P
95
BUCKEYE
TRAILHEAD

SALMON CREEK TRAIL

To Big Sur,
Carmel and
Monterey

1

N
W ← ⊕ → E
S

Salmon Creek

REFERENCE MAPS
P. 276

To San Luis
Obispo

*Pacific
Ocean*

96.
Salmon Creek Falls
SILVER PEAK WILDERNESS

97. Salmon Creek Trail
to Spruce Creek Camp and Estrella Camp
SILVER PEAK WILDERNESS AREA

Hiking distance: 6.5 miles round trip
Hiking time: 3.5 hours
Configuration: out and back
Elevation gain: 1,300 feet
Difficulty: strenuous
Exposure: mostly shaded forest
Dogs: allowed
Maps: U.S.G.S. Burro Mountain
　　　　Los Padres National Forest Northern Section Trail Map

The Salmon Creek Trail begins at stunning Salmon Creek Falls and follows the southeast wall of the V-shaped canyon through forests and open slopes. There are far-reaching views up the canyon and down to the ocean. The trail, which cuts across the Silver Peak Wilderness to the South Coast Ridge Road, leads to Spruce Creek Camp and Estrella Camp, midway to the road. After Spruce Creek Camp, the cliffside path parallels Salmon Creek, overlooking endless cascades, small waterfalls, and pools. Estrella Camp sits in a large grassy meadow under the shade of oak, pine, and madrone trees.

To the trailhead

BIG SUR RANGER STATION. From the ranger station, located 27 miles south of Carmel, drive 43.8 miles south on Highway 1 to the signed Salmon Creek trailhead at a sweeping horseshoe bend in the road. Park in the wide pullout on the left by the guardrail.

RAGGED POINT. From Highway 1 at Ragged Point, 1.5 miles south of the Monterey County line, drive 3.7 miles north on Highway 1 to the signed Salmon Creek trailhead on the right.

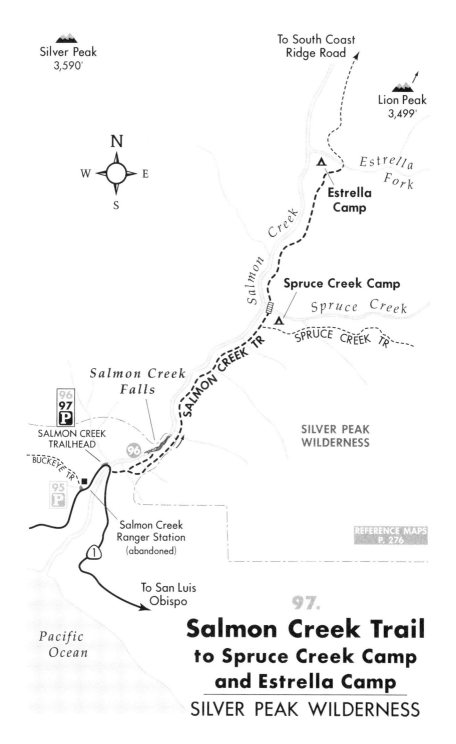

Silver Peak
3,590'

To South Coast
Ridge Road

Lion Peak
3,499'

N
W · E
S

Estrella Fork

Estrella
Camp

Salmon Creek

Spruce Creek Camp

Spruce Creek

SPRUCE CREEK TR

Salmon Creek
Falls

SALMON CREEK TR

96
97
P
SALMON CREEK
TRAILHEAD

BUCKEYE TR

96

SILVER PEAK
WILDERNESS

95
P

Salmon Creek
Ranger Station
(abandoned)

1

To San Luis
Obispo

Pacific
Ocean

REFERENCE MAPS
P. 276

97.
Salmon Creek Trail
to Spruce Creek Camp
and Estrella Camp
SILVER PEAK WILDERNESS

The hike

Walk alongside the guardrail to the signed trailhead on the south side of Salmon Creek. Salmon Creek Falls can be seen from the guardrail. Take the Salmon Creek Trail up the gorge into the lush, verdant forest. Pass an old wooden gate, and cross a small tributary stream. Two hundred yards ahead is a signed junction. The left fork drops down a short distance to Salmon Creek Falls.

After viewing the falls, continue on the main trail. Head up the hillside to an overlook of Highway 1 and the Pacific. The path winds through the fir forest, steadily gaining elevation to a clearing high above Salmon Creek. The sweeping vistas extend up Salmon Creek canyon and back down across the ocean. Follow the contours of the south canyon wall, with small dips and rises, to a posted junction with the Spruce Creek Trail at 1.9 miles. Stay to the left and descend a quarter mile to Spruce Creek Camp on the banks of Spruce Creek.

Cross Spruce Creek on a log bridge just above its confluence with Salmon Creek. Follow Salmon Creek upstream on the southeast canyon slope, overlooking a long series of cascades, pools, and waterfalls. Continually ascend the hillside contours above the creek, crossing an old mudslide. The trail levels out on a grassy flat with scattered oaks, then enters the shady Estrella Camp at 1,500 feet. Descend 50 yards to the Estrella Fork of Salmon Creek, just beyond the camp. This is the turn-around point.

The trail continues past the creek, climbing 1,800 feet in 2.5 miles, where it terminates at the South Coast Ridge Road. ▓

98. Ragged Point Inn

Nature Trail • Cliffside Trail

Hiking distance: 1 mile round trip
Hiking time: 30 minutes
Configuration: out and back
Elevation gain: 300 feet
Difficulty: Nature Trail is easy
           Cliffside Trail is steep and unstable—use caution
Exposure: open bluff and cliffside
Dogs: allowed
Maps: U.S.G.S. Burro Mountain

**map
page 294**

The Ragged Point Inn is the last stop in San Luis Obispo County, just 1.5 miles south of Monterey County. The resort sits upon a rugged cliff where the San Luis Obispo coast turns into the Big Sur coast. (The actual Ragged Point land formation is located 1.8 miles south of the Ragged Point Inn, Hike 99.)

Two short trail options begin atop the cliff. The Ragged Point Cliffside Trail begins at the inn and cuts across the edge of the steep cliff. The tenuous trail ends at the black sand beach and rocky shore at the base of Black Swift Falls, a 300-foot tiered waterfall. Benches are perched on the 400-foot promontory for great views of the sheer coastal mountains plunging into the sea. Staying atop the cliff, the Ragged Point Nature Trail follows the perimeter of the peninsula along the high blufftop terrace. There are several scenic vista points and an overlook of the crashing surf and waterfalls.

To the trailhead

BIG SUR RANGER STATION. From the ranger station, located 27 miles south of Carmel, drive 47.5 miles south on Highway 1 to the Ragged Point Inn and Restaurant on the right (oceanside). Turn right and park in the paved lot.

CAMBRIA. From Cambria, drive 23 miles north on Highway 1 to the Ragged Point Inn and Resort on the left (oceanside).

The hike

Take the gravel path west between the snack bar and gift shop. Walk across the level, grassy terrace towards the point. Fifty yards ahead is a signed junction at an overlook that lies 300 feet above the ocean, with views of the dramatic Big Sur coast. The Nature Trail continues straight ahead, circling the blufftop terrace through windswept pine and cypress trees. At the northwest point is a viewing platform. Waterfalls can be seen cascading off the cliffs on both sides of the promontory.

Back at the junction, the Cliffside Trail can be overgrown, washed out, and potentially dangerous—use caution! The path descends down the steps over the cliff's edge past a bench and across a wooden bridge. Switchbacks cut across the edge of the steep north-facing cliff to the base of Black Swift Falls at the sandy beach. After enjoying the surroundings, head back up the steep path. ▩

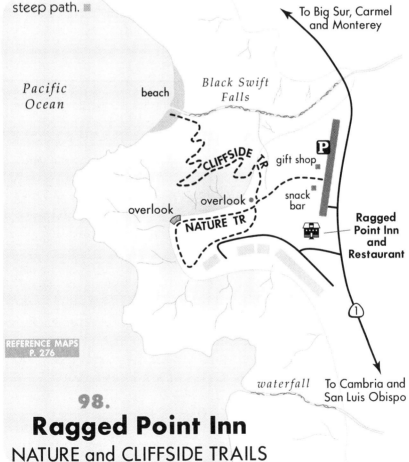

98.
Ragged Point Inn
NATURE and CLIFFSIDE TRAILS

99. Ragged Point

Hiking distance: 0.8 miles round trip
Hiking time: 30 minutes
Configuration: out and back
Elevation gain: 40 feet
Difficulty: easy (with the exception of unstable footing in some areas)
Exposure: open meadow and shaded forest
Dogs: allowed
Maps: U.S.G.S. Burro Mountain

**map
page 296**

This hike crosses a marine terrace to Ragged Point, which is actually located 1.8 miles south of the Ragged Point Inn (Hike 98). From the point are overlooks of the scalloped coastline, a sandy beach cove, offshore rocks pounded by the surf, and Bald Top along the Santa Lucia Mountains. San Carpoforo Creek empties into the ocean north of Ragged Point. The well-defined trail crosses through Hearst Corporation ranchland to the headland. Although there are no public easements, the well-worn trails have been used by surfers, fishermen, and hikers for many years. Portions of the bluff top cliffs are unstable and caution is advised.

To the trailhead

RAGGED POINT INN. From the signed Ragged Point Inn and Restaurant, located 1.5 miles south of the Monterey County line, drive 1.8 miles south on Highway 1 to a large, unsigned dirt turnout on the right. It is located 0.4 miles south of the San Carpoforo Creek bridge.

CAMBRIA. From Cambria, drive 21 miles north on Highway 1 to the large turnoff on the left, located on a right bend in the road. Turning left here is dangerous. Instead, continue 0.4 miles past the turnoff, then turn around after crossing the bridge over San Carpoforo Creek.

The hike

Cross over the fence and follow the wide path west. Walk through a scrub brush meadow backed by the towering Santa Lucia Mountains. Enter a shady canopy of twisted pines on the soft needle-covered path. Emerge from the forest to the edge of the 100-foot bluffs. From the north-facing cliffs of Ragged Point are views below of a crescent-shaped beach with magnificent rock outcroppings. Several paths weave along the bluffs to additional coastal views. A narrow, razor-edged path leads west to the point. If you choose to venture west, exercise caution and good judgement. ▪

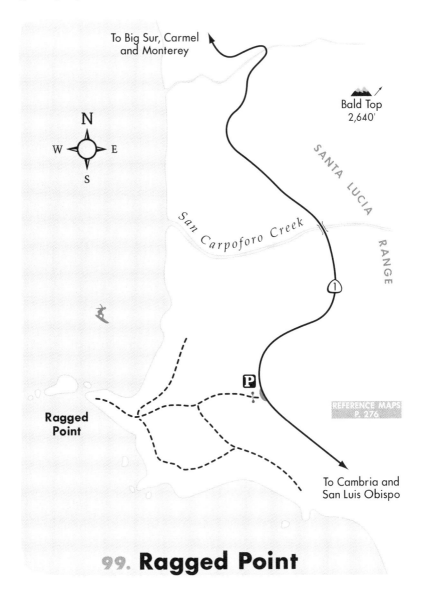

99. Ragged Point

Day Hikes Around Monterey and Carmel

Monterey County in Central California is home to a hundred miles of picture-perfect coastline, from Monterey Bay to the rugged Big Sur oceanfront. Mountains backdrop the coast, separating the coastline from the rich agricultural land. Carmel and other quaint communities dot a landscape that is abundant with green valleys, woodlands, beaches, parks, natural preserves, and calm bays along the scalloped Pacific coast.

This second edition of *Day Hikes Around Monterey and Carmel* has been greatly expanded to include 127 hikes throughout the area. Highlights include waterfalls, canyons, huge stands of redwoods, tidepools, isolated beaches, rugged peninsulas, long-spanning bridges, walking paths through the towns, and incredible views from the coast to the inland valleys.

384 pages • 127 hikes • 2nd Edition 2013 • ISBN 978-1-57342-067-9
BEST BOOK SERIES AWARD: Rocky Mountain Outdoor Writers and Photographers

Day Hikes On the California Central Coast

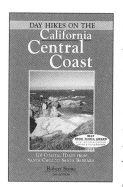

The Central California coast has some of the most spectacular scenery in the state. Rugged coastal terraces are backdropped by mountain ranges that run parallel to the Pacific. Curving highways wind through picturesque communities, valleys, forests, and state preserves while overlooking the coast and white sand beaches. The surf crashes onto weather-sculpted headlands and carved canyons along the Big Sur stretch of coast.

This guide includes 400 miles of coastline between San Francisco and Los Angeles. The hike descriptions include how and where to access the best trails and geographical features from Highway 1, offering many opportunities to explore the beautiful landscape.

320 pages • 120 hikes • 2nd Edition 2009 • ISBN 978-1-57342-058-7
BEST BOOK SERIES AWARD: Rocky Mountain Outdoor Writers and Photographers

DAY HIKE BOOKS

DAY HIKES ON THE
California
Central
Coast

120 COASTAL HIKES FROM
SANTA CRUZ TO SANTA BARBARA
Robert Stone

DAY HIKES ON THE
California
Southern
Coast

100 GREAT HIKES
Robert Stone

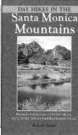
DAY HIKES IN THE
Santa Monica
Mountains

FROM LOS ANGELES TO POINT MUGU
INCLUDING THE ENTIRE BACKBONE TRAIL
Robert Stone

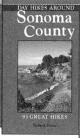
DAY HIKES AROUND
Sonoma
County

95 GREAT HIKES
Robert Stone

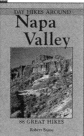
DAY HIKES AROUND
Napa
Valley

88 GREAT HIKES
Robert Stone

DAY HIKES AROUND
Monterey
& Carmel

125 GREAT HIKES
Robert Stone
2nd EDITION

DAY HIKES AROUND
Big Sur

99 GREAT HIKES
Robert Stone
2nd EDITION

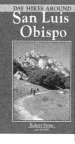
DAY HIKES AROUND
San Luis
Obispo

Robert Stone
2nd EDITION

DAY HIKES AROUND
Santa
Barbara

115 GREAT HIKES
Robert Stone
2nd EDITION

DAY HIKES AROUND
Ventura
County

116 GREAT HIKES
Robert Stone
2nd EDITION

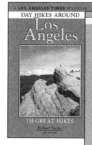
A LOS ANGELES TIMES BESTSELLER
DAY HIKES AROUND
Los
Angeles

135 GREAT HIKES
Robert Stone
2nd EDITION

DAY HIKES AROUND
Orange
County

108 GREAT HIKES
Robert Stone

DAY HIKES IN
Yosemite
NATIONAL PARK

80 GREAT HIKES
Robert Stone
2nd EDITION

DAY HIKES IN
Sequoia
&
Kings Canyon
NATIONAL PARKS

Robert Stone

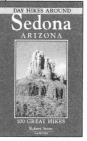
DAY HIKES AROUND
Sedona
ARIZONA

100 GREAT HIKES
Robert Stone
2nd EDITION

DAY HIKES IN
Yellowstone
NATIONAL PARK

82 GREAT HIKES
Robert Stone
4th EDITION

DAY HIKES IN
Grand
Teton
NATIONAL PARK

89 GREAT HIKES
Robert Stone
3rd EDITION

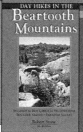
DAY HIKES IN THE
Beartooth
Mountains

INCLUDING RED LODGE to YELLOWSTONE
BOULDER VALLEY • PARADISE VALLEY
Robert Stone

DAY HIKES AROUND
Bozeman
MONTANA

INCLUDING THE GALLATIN
CANYON AND PARADISE VALLEY
Robert Stone

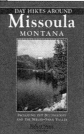
DAY HIKES AROUND
Missoula
MONTANA

INCLUDING THE BITTERROOT
AND THE NINE-MILE • SWAN VALLEY
Robert Stone

INDEX

DEBRA COFFEY

About the Author

Since 1991, Robert Stone has been writer, photographer, and publisher of Day Hike Books. He is a Los Angeles Times Best Selling Author and an award-winning journalist of Rocky Mountain Outdoor Writers and Photographers, the Outdoor Writers Association of California, the Northwest Outdoor Writers Association, the Outdoor Writers Association of America, and the Bay Area Travel Writers.

Robert has hiked every trail in the Day Hike Book series. With 24 hiking guides in the series, many in their fourth and fifth editions, he has hiked thousands of miles of trails throughout the western United States and Hawaii. When Robert is not hiking, he researches, writes, and maps the hikes before returning to the trails. He spends summers in the Rocky Mountains of Montana and winters on the California Central Coast.